THE TIGER AND THE TAXI DRIVER

THE TIGER AND THE TAXI DRIVER

BOOK ONE

ANNA AND THE HEAVENLY HORSE

Nigelle de Visme

Photograph Credits:

*1,2 by a passing photographer; 3: R.A.F. I.D. photograph for travelling to
Singapore; 4: Whipsnade Zoo tourist photographer; 5: Unknown,
photograph given to author 1986; 6, 12, 13, 14, 18, 19, 20, 21, 24, 25,
26, 27, 28, 30, 31, 32, 33, 34, 35, 36, 37 by author. 7: Unknown; 8:
Another passing photographer; 9: Nanette Whitehead; 10: Roger
Beaumont-Wilkins; 11: Michael Holt; 15: Roger Beaumont-Wilkins; 16:
Unknown; 17: Unknown; 22: Darren Sense; 23: a passing N.Z. tourist;
29: Unknown*

*The author photographed the tiger art on the cover from a very old postcard
belonging to a friend. It had no authorship or name on the reverse and
despite hours online looking at Japanese, Chinese and Korean tiger art in an
attempt to find it to acknowledge — its artist remains as elusive as its
depiction. I love it, and thank you, its artist, wherever you are*

Hoopoe — original gouache by author 2012

*Categories: Memoir — Black Madonna — Goddess — Natural Magic —
Adventure — Travel — Indian Metaphysics — Aboriginal Spirituality*

DEDICATION

Mrs Irina Tweedie and Dom Bede Griffiths: you scanned my soul, sheltered me under your wings until I found wings of my own. Paramahansa Satyananda, who told me to write, helped me unweave the words which wove my birthing. And to dear friends near and far who stayed true through all.

ACKNOWLEDGEMENTS

Lauren Raine, *Spiderwoman* ... the threads that weave us ...

Spiderwoman – Weaver of Destiny

You don't know my Name, it doesn't matter. I've had a lot of Names, it doesn't matter what you call me. Call me Tse Che Nako – the Woman Who Makes The World with the stories I tell. Call me Spiderwoman.

You can bring your offerings if you wish; I'll give them to the Bird People and the Mouse People, to Snake and Mallow and Rabbit.

Listen, I'm going to tell you something: you came in with empty hands. At times your spirit was caught and woven into bad things. It's time now to weave a new story.

Walk out into the desert and sit beneath a cholla. Notice the shapes of things. A hawk hunting against the sky, the shapes of the clouds. Old man mountain sleeping; saguaro pointing the way. Notice the shapes of shadows; notice the shapes of your own shadows. There are stories here; they are like threads that are woven into the Land, stories that wrap themselves around old bones and pottery shards; stories running on four legs, or two. Stories written in the rocks about yellow women and the hearts of sleeping mountains, and cracks in the land like a spider's web, full of light.

Once you could see the Web, you could see it as plain as day; songlines, leylines, threads, connections, patterns. Each shining light-woven thread – and now you say you can't see it.

Well take a look around, you don't need to climb a mountain to get the big picture; all of its snaking rivers and twining roots are inside of you. All those threads come right out of your hands and out of your hearts, and all those threads just go on forever into the earth and into each other, into all your stories, into everyone you'll ever know; into all those who came before you and all those who will come after you.

O Mitákuye Oyás'iŋ

INTRODUCTION

Setting the Warp for Anna to Weave

Anna and the Heavenly Horse, the short story that begins at the beginning, was written more than thirty years ago. I was not thirteen when I lived with my Russian aunt, Anastasia; I was thirty-nine, and Russian Anastasia was Russian Mrs Irina Tweedie. *Anna and the Heavenly Horse* is not exactly a children's story; it is about a young girl growing to a spiritual maturity. Meeting Mrs Tweedie began my own never-ending journey to maturity, sorting out the painful tangles of being an unwanted child that bound me.

Mnemosyne is a capricious Muse, memories fall as they will, random and wild and not very chronological. Events carried me beyond my own boundaries of belief, and *Growing* took a very long time, right to this minute. I needed signposts (but not satnavs which I have found to be suspiciously formulaic and untrustworthy) and these I found, like those marvellous yellow scallop shells that made my heart sigh with relief as I came to every fork along the Camino far far in the future, a future where I discovered one could ossify at forty-five while others in their seventies still heard the siren song of the Lorelei.

All is true, but perhaps mutable, for only God can know the whole truth.

CONTENTS

Acknowledgements
Introduction
Illustrations between Chapters 7 and 8

Part One
Anna and the Heavenly Horse

Part Two
Where there's Rosemary, there's Rue...

ANNA AND THE HEAVENLY HORSE

1

In the Very Beginning

In the Beginning, so the ancient Sufi says, He gilded the stars and He put the dust on the tail of the Bird of the Soul:

He made the ocean liquid and the mountaintops He capped with ice and snow:

He makes clusters of roses spring from the face of the Fire; and in His wisdom He caused the spider to spin her web:

He made the ant the companion of Solomon and a gown of shimmering brocade He gave to the peacock.

From the mists of His lakes He created the lotus and on the head of the tulip He placed a red bonnet:

It is God who has spread out the day in whiteness and it is He who has folded up the black night:

To the parrot He gave a collar of gold, and He washed the Earth's face with the waters of the seas:

The depths of the earth and the heights of Heaven worship Him each with their special homage:

He produced the wind, and the earth, and the fire, and the blood and within these He announces His secret.

Because of God the heavens turn, the earth spins, the moon waxes and wanes and the stars hold their place in the firmament:

In winter He scatters the silver snow, in autumn the gold of the falling leaves:

Sometimes He causes the dog to go before the traveller, but the cat He uses to show The Way:

He took a handful of southerly wind and blew His breath over it and created the horse:

The hoopoe with her crest of Truth He made a messenger of the Way.
From the back of the fish to the moon every atom is a witness to His Being ...

Walk carefully, there is a different door and a different way for every heart. My friend! let the quest for Truth bind our journey.

2

The Decision

Anastasia put down the letter which had come with the weekly mail delivery and gazed out of the window to watch the huge peaks of the high Himalayas fade from the deep coral pink glow of the setting sun, the reflection of which caused a roseate halo around her own snow white hair. She absorbed the ephemeral beauty of one more glorious display of colour from the colour box of the Greatest Painter as she placed the letter on the small writing table beside her. She did not need to make a conscious decision on the content of the letter for the answer, she knew, would arise from the heart when the time was right.

She was old. Her work was done. There were no more books in her needing to be written, her retreat high on the Kumaon Hills in the shadow of Nanda Devi was really a preparation for a journey of a very different kind. She didn't feel particularly enamoured with the idea of a young visitor. Particularly a young visitor from the kind of unsettled background as that of her young niece. The connection by marriage was a slender thread remembered by the writer of the letter, echoed as a reason for the strange request. It was an attempt to persuade Anastasia to take a little girl from halfway across the world, where, because the family had no other relatives there, her mother and stepfather wanted "space to settle down" for an indefinite period on their own in the new society they had chosen to begin their new life. That the little girl was called after her great aunt was only a small consideration to family allegiance. Yet persistently the voice of the heart quietly murmured "yes" to all the reasons of convenience the mind proposed for saying "no".

There was time before she needed to reply and Anastasia patted the letter before lighting an oil lamp to take with her into the kitchen to make her afternoon cup of coffee. Electricity in the mountains was as ephemeral as the colours of the sunset, one never knew when it was going to bless the homes connected for its supply.

How old was the child? Thirteen? A troubled age, but probably reasonable.

"She cares only for horses," wrote her the girl's mother, "she isn't interested in any of us, after all we've *done* for her. She is just so difficult and it is upsetting the unity of the whole family, especially poor little Stephanie who is so sensitive to these things, so sensitive to *atmosphere*. Zabeth said before we even left England that you are the only person who could possibly bring Anna into line with how we want her to be. Brian and I have so many commitments, what with his flying and his promised promotion and our imminent posting back to Malaysia. Anna says she doesn't want to come with us, all she does is mope about her father and say she wants to go back to England to be with him. Of course he doesn't want her ~~either~~, but she won't listen to me …"

Anastasia looked at the scored out "~~either~~" on the hastily written letter. It spoke volumes. And said more about the child's mother's attitude than what it had been intended to say about the father. She knew from Zabeth that Pat, having divorced Anna's father, had married a man many years her junior. To have a daughter of thirteen was not possible from this liaison, the child had to 'disappear'. To settle in a new country like Australia where the newlyweds were attempting to create the 'right' impression in a close knit military community in which divorce was then the socially unacceptable face of failure, disturbed the status quo. According to Zabeth the child was sensitive and intelligent and sadly aware that she was the cause, though unable to understand she was not the reason, for the increasing distance her mother put between them.

Stephanie, on the other hand, was a baby and woefully self-centred as adored babies are.

The group arrived in Australia and went to stay initially with relatives of Brian. Now that her father was ten thousand miles away Anna locked up her memory of him along with those of her left-behind-cat and how-it-used-to-be-hopes in her heart.

Her cousins by proxy in this new country were much older than Anna, and the family lived in the 'bush'. They were hard-faced and steel-minded and their children spoke of shooting. Anna realized they meant animals. She had never heard of anything so depraved in all her life. She thought of left-behind-Sambo and walked off sadly across the hard-baked earth whose quiescent soul had not yet begun to penetrate her own. She sat on a sun-bleached log and quietly cried to herself. A small lizard ran up her trouser leg and a green ant, disturbed on the log where she sat, bit her. She sobbed all the way back to the house — everything was so hard, so alien.

After a few weeks, when they had found a home of their own and a new school for Anna, her mother demanded she take the surname of her new husband so that the neighbours might be fooled into thinking Brian was Anna's father. The deceit repelled the child to her very essence, and, in her first attempt at assertion, Anna from that moment refused to answer to, or allow anyone to call her, Anastasia. For the name Anastasia belonged to her father, and to her father's family name, which was hers also, and which was the French connection to the Russian aunt after whom she was named. 'Anastasia' was added to the storehouse of sacred memories and hopes held within her heart.

All she could love in this new land were the flowers, and the sun. Always shining, it lit an overwhelming diversity of flowers with an intensity of colour even more brilliant, even more vibrant, than those of the Tropics. Some were as tall as herself, their strange shapes furry and soft and brilliant crimson and emerald green, and as soft as pussy paws. They were protected too, and Anna thought, in spite of its initial hardness, a country must be alright for its people to love and protect its flowers so much. When the family travelled by train across to the other side of this vast continent she missed the flowers shaped like kangaroo paws, and learnt to love instead the wild banksias looking like the wizened faces of strange creatures, and the yellow puffballs of mimosa that perfumed the air with honey in the spring. The birds, too, were like jewels, and their unfaltering cadences thrilled her heart. She knew she would love the animals too, but she never saw any, perhaps they knew the shooting was meant for them. Perhaps, too, it was only the people in this new country she had a problem with, and that included the people of her family – and her father was so far away. When she was told she was going to be sent to India to an aunt she had never even met Anna didn't really mind, for her great aunt Anastasia was an aunt of her father and she felt she might belong a little more with her than she felt here. Her aunt Zabeth had told her that if she was ever offered the chance to visit aunt Anastasia, Anna should accept it, for she would be sure to find peace with her.

Many miles and much time later, when Anna began to be 'difficult' over her name, her mother's reaction to send her away didn't come as too much of a surprise and Anna quietly said yes, she would like to go.

3

The Arrival

Anastasia didn't make the train journey to Delhi often. Altogether with bus changes and train connections it was a gruelling fourteen hours, spine-jolting for the first part of the trip as the bus swung up and down treacherous potholed roads following the ascents and descents of the mountains and valleys. The beauty of the land through which she travelled was an unending source of joy and for that part of the journey at least was a positive compensation.

She alighted at the noisy, crowded, rafter-blackened station of Old Delhi stiff with dirt and dust and bone weary. As she looked around at the milling hordes of people hurrying about their business Anastasia had the oddest feeling she would not be making this journey again, an intimation that made her smile. The scene in front of her was heightened in its apparent chaos by the blaring Hindi film music, the erratic taxis and the truculent little black and yellow auto-rickshaws buzzing about like mega-bees. The owners of the pan stalls adjacent to the station sat cross-legged, glassy eyed from over indulgence, next to piles of lime, leaves and betel nut. On the forecourt women sat in the sun applying henna with traditional decorations of swirls and curls to the dainty feet and elegant hands of pretty girls.

Outside, shrines with burning camphor flames on dusty street corners vied for space with the shoe-shine wallahs, the magazine sellers, and an old Sikh cobbler who had a tiny, sickly kitten tied by its hind leg to a metal shoe last. Anastasia didn't like to probe too deeply into the possibilities of its hapless future. Since the Asiad Games beggars were not so much in evidence now, the Government had affected a 'clean up'. Anastasia took an auto-rickshaw to her destination within the walls of the old city, was welcomed by the young woman in charge of receiving guests, shown into her simple room and left to bathe and rest until suppertime.

Anna was on a direct flight from Sydney to Delhi. It was a long eighteen-hour journey with a couple of hours pause in Singapore to stretch her legs while the aircraft re-fuelled. She had never met her aunt Anastasia and yet through the numbness that had frozen over her heart in the past years she was surprised to feel, well, a kind of lightness, a kind of singing, that she hadn't known for a very long time. For such a young child she had a storehouse of memories of trains and boats and planes – and goodbyes. When she had flown back from Malaya with her father, as a family, for the last time, it seemed to her that he had left her in deep freeze right there on the bleak English railway station, the bitter March wind stinging the tears on cheeks unused to such frozen temperatures after three years in the Tropics.

Goodbye. A couple of days before that, during a stopover en route, her father had said something very strange to her. Only later did she realize what he was really trying to convey to her – *goodbye*.

"Well, sweetie, I won't be seeing you for a while once we get to London, so I am going to leave you with a couple of puzzles to keep you busy."

They had been close, Anna and her father. His wife's unnatural rejection of their firstborn became a deeply disturbing reality with the birth of Stephanie many years later. When the family arrived in Singapore Pat left Anna to herself, Stephanie with the amah, and spent her time down at the Officer's Club tanning and flirting with the fresh young English officers down at the swimming pool. And then her father went away on long, long walks, only he didn't take Anna with him anymore, and he stopped using the secret language they had invented together, and he even teased the cat.

18

Anna's heart thumped inside her chest, she almost knew what he really meant …

"First I want you to invent a self-squeezing tube for toothpaste," he chuckled, "that's for humanity. It'll make you a fortune. Then, to keep your neurons active, get a map of England and work out a system of colouring the counties using three colours only. No two counties must share a common boundary with the same colour. Pretty tricky that one, baffled scientists for years," he boomed, trying to make light of the real meaning behind the words. The real meaning which was – *goodbye, we can no longer share a common boundary*.

That was three years ago. Anna had never seen her father again. And that awful Brian who ate bread and dripping came to their house instead, and stayed. But he couldn't help her to solve the puzzles and she was sure it had something to do with why her father never came home.

Her mother wouldn't let her bring her cat back either – "he's perfectly happy where he is, he's forgotten all about you…" but he hadn't. Because when Anna had crossed the little close, Beulah Close, to where Sambo now lived with a kindly Jewish couple he had pressed his face into hers when the tears fell down her cheek. Just as he used to in the days before the family had gone to Singapore and before her mother had given birth to Stephanie and the shouting and acrimony had rent the house and Sambo became the repository for all Anna's sadness. It was then she knew, with the advent of Stephanie, that any hope she had of gaining her mother's love or affection had gone like the wind.

And yet, and yet, high up in the clouds in another aeroplane on another journey it was as if she felt a lark singing, singing in her heart.

Now the aircraft was landing. The hostess checked Anna's safety belt and the man next to her, an Indian travelling home, concerned that such a young child should be travelling alone, offered her a boiled sweet. She didn't particularly want one, but took it anyway. Food had much to do with her inner hunger, and if anyone offered her food she equated it with love – something she craved for very much. Her mother used to deny her fruit – that was for Stephanie, Anna could fill up on bread and butter. A food offering was a love offering, and she never refused.

Her kindly fellow passenger introduced himself as Mr. Bhattacharya, and suggested that if her aunt was late in arriving at the airport he would instruct the ground staff to convey the message that Anna had gone with him to his family home. He lived in a rather better part of New Delhi, where she would be safe and welcome to rest until the arrival of her aunt. He didn't say it, but Anna knew he must be someone important.

His concern was unfounded. Mr. Bhattacharya carried a 'Diplomatic Bag' which meant, to Anna's amusement, that he was waived past the queue of people waiting to be searched at customs. Holding Anna firmly by the hand and slinging her overnight bag over his shoulder while she held her only other case in her free hand, she too was included in his exemption from delay. As they entered the waiting-lounge of the cool air-conditioned flight terminal building, among a sea of cosmopolitan faces, Anastasia's presence commanded attention.

Anna had never seen a photograph of her aunt, for great aunt Anastasia was the enigma of the family and never seemed to stay in one place long enough for anyone to pull out a camera. Yet there was in this small plump woman whose hair was as white as the snow-capped Himalayas a presence so commanding that Anna felt her heart stand to attention. Later, she was to tell her aunt of this, and of the stab of recognition so deep as to make introductions superfluous.

Mr. Bhattacharya appeared to be affected in a similar way for his manner became softer, less, *diplomatic*, noted Anna, smiling to herself. He *pranam'd* to Anastasia in that timeless Indian gesture that Anna would remember her whole life, placing the palms of his hands together like a prayer in front of his heart and bowing his head.

"Auntie", said Mr. Bhattacharya, "I have been taking very good care of your niece. I am very happy that you were not held up in getting to the airport otherwise I would have my driver return and wait for you to bring you to my home," his words tumbled into the air with great speed, "now, can I ask what is your programme? Your niece is very tired and I am thinking that you must be also, coming from such a long way. Our buses," he chuckled, "are not quite up to standard and, ahem, I must be introducing myself: my name is Bhattacharya, Prem Bhattacharya. And you, you are Auntie!"

He chuckled again and Anna blinked when she heard him call her aunt Auntie. Later she learnt this to be a polite and affectionate form of address used by almost all Indians to older women of any relationship or none.

Anastasia smiled and imperceptibly inclined her head. *Why*, thought Anna, *she looks regal!* It was such a surprise Anna wondered if her aunt really was a Russian princess.

Yes, Anastasia answered in response to Mr. Bhattacharya, she was tired, and she knew Anna would be too, so she had arranged to stay in a small centre in Old Delhi where her need for peace and seclusion had become known over the years since her first stay there. She thanked him for his concern, anticipating and refusing in one delicate sentence what she knew was coming next – an invitation to spend a day or two with Mr. Bhattacharya and his family before the two women made their long journey back to the hills. She knew offer would have both guests smothered in well-intentioned, but endless, questions and entertainment and her long established hermit existence beckoned her home.

"Then," said Mr. Bhattacharya, "it will be my pleasure to drop you there in my car. Come, come, I insist, it is no problem at all."

Once outside the relatively cool airport lounge Anna felt she had walked into a baker's oven, the heat was suffocating and she was momentarily overwhelmed. Anastasia took her hand, sensing immediately how the fifteen-degree temperature increase would be affecting her.

21

Like a vast ocean of brown faces the city taxi drivers swarmed them, all shouting their discounts at the top of their voices. Mr. Bhattacharya spoke to them in Hindi and the sea of faces subsided in a body. Shepherding his two guests across the concourse to the lines of stationary cars he pointed out his own cream version seemingly identical to the other one hundred and one cream, beige or black vehicles steaming under the sun in soldiered rows. Anna's nostrils prickled as the pungent smell of India awakened the memory of her earlier years in Singapore. Oddly enough, instead of bringing associations of painful memories of her father it made her feel excited, full of new promise. Involuntarily she squeezed her aunt's hand. Anastasia looked down and Anna grinned, her eyebrows wriggling up and down across her forehead. Anastasia thought how like Guy his daughter was. She remembered Anna's father well, a brilliant, serious student of mathematics, with a bizarre sense of the ridiculous which was to upset his wife greatly. She also recognized that Anna's resemblance to her mother, whose smaller frame she had inherited, was in appearance only. She was her father's daughter, French genes dating back a thousand years, the tiny village de Vismes still held the family history. It was apparent to Anastasia that under the sorrow weighting down the child's shoulders an inherent ebullience needed release.

As they reached the car its driver stood to one side holding open the door while Anastasia and her niece sat in the back. Mr. Bhattacharya climbed into the front and gave directions to his driver in Hindi, explaining almost apologetically to the two women with him that he was descended from the rulers of a tiny Princely State which, since Independence, had been absorbed into the area now known as West Bengal and his natural tongue was Bengali. He had come with his family, he added, and his servants and retainers to take up the diplomatic post in Delhi where he now lived. Anna, having recovered from the momentary shock of the heat-wave, was now fully attentive to the fascination of colours and sounds and smells and myriad impressions all around her. It was

22

exciting. That singing feeling in her heart was quite noticeable now, like welcoming back an old friend, the real part of her that had lain dormant for too long. Everything around her was so alive, so vibrant, so colourful. And then there were the funny little shops and bazaars, and people – so many people, and bicycles and little ponies pulling tongas, donkeys and creamy grey cows. With the hump on their back characteristic of all Indian cows, even in the frenetic traffic of the busy streets they wandered thin and unconcerned. The people here were busier, louder than those in Malaya; indeed all communication appeared to be conducted at high volume accompanied by much waving of arms and nodding of heads.

Beyond the bazaars that ran alongside a splendid Fort wall of red stone they passed once more into wide leafy lanes to turn left down the tiny avenue of Court Lane. Nearly at the end was a charming low-set quarried stone complex of bungalows and courtyards and pergolas overgrown with a profusion of flowering vines of many colours. Anna loved its enchantment at once. She had been oblivious to the conversation between her aunt and Mr. Bhattacharya during the journey, absorbed in the vitality around her.

Having delivered his guests safely Mr. Bhattacharya presented them each with his card on which was printed his address and phone number, one side in English and the other in the Devanagari script of Hindi. Anna tucked her card safely into the small interior pocket of her overnight bag and put out her hand to shake his.

"Oh no," laughed Mr. Bhattacharya, "you must be saying it in Hindi now, like this," and he put his hands together prayerfully in front of his heart and said clearly "Namaste. This" he continued "we can say both coming and going, isn't it? Now you try…"

Anna repeated it, surprised to find the gesture and its accompanying word coming so natural to her.

Anastasia also pranam'd and thanked Mr. Bhattacharya for his kindness and told him he could always find her cottage in the hills if he were to contact the postmaster of a hamlet some sixty miles from Almora. She

23

sensed Mr. Bhattacharya was intrigued, but knew with an instinct born of a culture that still respected the interior ways of life sacred to humankind, and now almost lost, he would not inquire deeper without an invitation. A knowing look passed between them as they stood for a moment together, Anastasia knew he understood she would offer no answers.

The two women stood on the verandah as the car pulled away, Anna waving in response to her new friend. Then they turned into the cool stone courtyard and walked across the flagstones to the two small rooms Anastasia had booked for three days to rest before making the long journey back to the mountains.

Mr. Bhattacharya, his left forefinger thoughtfully stroking his smooth chin, wondered with the intuition of the heart what exactly had impressed him about Auntie. Fleeting impressions surfaced to his recollection of an experience he had once had of meeting a holy man on the shores of the Ganga just beyond Rishikesh many years before. The people around the holy man called him Mast Ram Baba, the God-mad Baba, because they did not know his name.

"The true Guru," one of Baba's followers had said to Mr. Bhattacharya, "has no name and no face. Baba is an old man, and all we have are the slokas of Truth he sometimes writes, in Sanskrit, which show him to have been a great scholar. But of more, we know nothing, not even his name or his worldly history. His presence gives a luminosity and a meaning to our simple lives and he enriches our hours with his silence, teaches us by example how to live fully in the presence of the Divine Moment."

With a sudden surprise Mr. Bhattacharya realized he did not know Auntie's name; and that for some obscure reason he had not even asked for it. A fine diplomat he was, he laughed to himself. He hoped he would meet both of them again and recalled how the withdrawn Anna had responded to Auntie as if they had always known each other. He was pleased that he could perceive the timeless intuitive connection of heart to heart, a connection beyond boundaries, unconfined by time or form or space. He instinctively knew Anna had a sad story and believed it was the Will of the Gods that had brought her here.

4

The Hoopoe and the Homecoming

Anastasia took Anna to the bathroom to freshen herself after the long flight and explained to her the principle of sitting on the small stone slab and filling the large bucket while using the small handled jug for pouring water over herself. The loo principle took a genuine shift in mental gears before Anna grasped the cold water, left hand treatment, *sans* toilet paper. Anastasia pointed out that in most Indian homes one ate food not with a knife and fork but with the right hand only, the left hand being reserved for cleaning oneself. Anna adjusted easily, as children often do, to the new modus operandi once it was explained. She said she would bathe now so that she could then lie down and rest. Anastasia filled both their small water jugs with boiled drinking water cooled by currents of air in the large matka water pot standing by the open windows and retired to her own room to write and read before lunch. Anna would probably sleep on as her internal time clock would take a few days to adjust to the time difference between Sydney and Delhi.

The days passed quickly. They visited the Red Fort and the elegant Pearl Mosque; the Lodi Gardens with their timeless tombs of heroes and conquerors long past; the towering Qtab Minar recalling the soul in its aspiration to return to its Origin; Jantar Mantar with its flowing elliptical geometry. They visited the Zoo, though neither of them liked animals in captivity, but Anna longed to see a real tiger. The tiger gardens were large and open and the tigers, crepuscular creatures of the dawn and dusk, territorial by nature, alternated with each other their time in the large shady compounds. They were, thought Anna, magnificent beyond imagining, and the Royal Bengal tiger who looked deceptively docile and mischievous, was the king of them all. Among the other cats Anna fell in love with the Indian Fishing Cat, quite small, though larger than Sambo, with exquisite limpid green eyes. He looked at Anna from his tree bough day bed, and the look in its eyes remained with her for a long time. This beautiful creature had a sense of completeness in itself, a pride in its being that had not been extinguished despite its imprisonment.

On their last day at the centre Anna had tidied her two bags in readiness for their journey to the hills and was sitting in the courtyard garden when the oddest thing happened. While she was watching the group of chattering birds called by the gardener the Seven Sisters, a bird the colour of cinnamon, with wide wings of vivid black and white bars and a long curved bill settled on a stone by the lotus pool. It turned to look at Anna, raising a spectacular crest of black and white feathers to call in a deep voice "hoo-poo-poo, hoo-poo-poo." Anna was conscious, in a misty and unconscious way, of the words, softly and distinctly alongside the "hoo-poo-poo": *I've come for you, I've come for you.* She stared at the beautiful bird fearlessly looking back at her, nodding its head up and down three times until, crouching down, it pushed itself off the stone and flew away.

Later she told her aunt the hoopoe had opened a secret for her. As she spoke she was quick to notice a gleam of light pass across her aunt's eyes and once more she felt her heart was standing to attention. As Anna shared her experience of the hoopoe with Anastasia the older woman understood why the child had come to her, and why her heart had said *yes* in spite of all good reasons for saying no.

For the past twenty years Anastasia had been what she called a conductor, for people had come from all over the world, and wherever she happened to be in the world, to find the key to that peace that passeth all understanding. She had been on her own quest for this peace, this key which she knew would lead to Truth, and her ability to help others was the result of years spent with a very great Master – a Master who was the smoke of the fire others do not see, the sound of the music others do not hear. He had touched, as a poet once said, the Hem of the Garment of God and his whole life was to throw out a thread that others may grasp and follow to the same end. Very, very few found their way to the end, but Anastasia was one of them. It was through him she learnt that the earth prays and that being silent with nature drew people to wish to know the mystery of the one beyond All. The mind of most people does not know it is being led in this direction, for it is within the heartbeat of the earth that the call is felt and its response registered in the human heart. Anastasia knew that those who hear with the inner ear, see with the inner eye, are rare.

"And those," murmured Anastasia half to herself and half with the intention that Anna might also hear, "those whom He wants for Himself He marks with suffering…" for it was the suffering of the heart that longed for its Real Home.

Anastasia decided then that this little girl, who had come to her unloved and unwanted, not knowing her place and not knowing herself, would need to go to the Forest; she knew what Anna would find there. She knew that Anna would meet the Hoopoe again, the bird who wears the Crest of Truth and whom God had made the Messenger of the Way.

The first part of the journey back to the hills was by train. After an hour night fell. Anna and her aunt pulled down two of the bunks in their bogie and lay down on the light cotton blankets Anastasia had brought with her for the journey. She had brought each of them a padded cotton quilt to wrap themselves in too, and the Indian family with whom they shared the compartment also settled down for the night. The shutters on the open windows were pulled down, for when dawn came the train would be at the gateway to the foothills of the Himalayas and the air would be crisp and cool. After the train they would travel by bus into the higher reaches of the Kumaon Hills and beyond.

In the morning Anna awoke, cold. She pulled on her only thick fleecy cotton jumper and put socks on under her sandals. Anastasia said they would get some warm clothes made for her such as the hill people wore as the weather would be cool from now and during the winter nights they would need all the clothes they could put on. Anastasia wrapped herself in a shawl so soft and fine it felt like down and she told Anna it was woven from a mountain goat with very special hair. If Anna felt she would be comfortable wearing one, said her aunt, she would give her one as a gift.

An hour later, having broken their fast with cups of hot already sweetened spicy chai and vegetable cutlets – *cutlights, cutlights,* called the boy selling them from huge wicker panniers balanced on his head – the train pulled in to its final destination. From here on the two had long winding bus journeys, best forgotten for the curves and bends of the narrow mountain roads which the bus seemed to corner on two wheels suspended over chasms falling hundreds of feet below. This part of the journey made Anna feel ill. By late afternoon when they reached their own destination she alighted from the rackety old bus stiff and an alarming shade of green.

Anastasia made her sit down on a step and tuck her head between her knees, telling her to breathe in and out slowly and deeply. Anna's natural colour gradually returned, her legs lost their watery feeling and taking in an extra deep breath she lifted her head – and gasped.

There in front of her, almost blocking the sky, were the first mountains of the Himalayas. Vast and silent and white and awe-inspiring, the sight of them stopped Anna's heart for four beats. She held her breath, suspended in time at the scene in front of her. The mountains glistened with fresh snow, range upon range of them, as far as the eye could behold. Anna forgot everything at that moment, tears sprang spontaneously to her eyes at the immensity of the vision facing her.

The step she was sitting on led into a tiny store which seemed to sell everything. There was a plethora of merchandise from roughly made mousetraps, kerosene stoves, cartons of matches, light bulbs, candles, rolls of elastic, thick woollen socks, embroidered caps, quilted cotton doonas, calendars of the Gods and Goddesses of the Himalayas; to all manner of foodstuff – sacks of rice, brown sugar, flour, lentils, chick peas; packets of teas, biscuits, walnuts, apricots and shelves of sundry toiletries. No corner was spared and the dim electric light bulb suspended from a cobweb draped cord in the centre of the ceiling barely illuminated more than a couple of square feet. In the glow of its beam directly beneath the globe sat an old man, Motilal Bannerjee, who had been passively watching all that had been happening in the past few minutes.

He uncrossed his legs and stood up, wrapping his shawl around him, and picked his way carefully around and over his merchandise to stand in the doorway and comment on Anna's tears.

"Auntie," he said, squatting down on his heels on the step above where Anna was sitting, "so this is your niece? She has been touched by the grace of Haimavati," and turning to Anna he patted her cheek and said: "this is a blessing young sister, from the Daughter of the Sky, She is the whiteness within the snow and not many people come to know Her. We always say that the one whom She blesses with tears from a heart that sees Her for the first time will be led to their true Destination."

Anna looked up at him from the lower step in the entrance way of his shop. She wasn't entirely sure that she understood what he meant by 'Destination' but even she was to see the word in her mind's eye with a capital D from the reverent way in which this thin, old, man on the step above her had said it. He looked into her eyes and continued in a soft voice: "tears wash clean the windows of the soul you know, and then one can remember God more clearly, and the remembrance of God will polish your heart, like a mirror, so that everything you see will reflect His Greatness."

Again Anna listened with a faculty beyond her ears, for in truth she had never really thought much about God. None of her family really gave much attention to Him at all, and the lessons in religious instruction from her Church of England Sunday schooling, especially when she learnt she would be going to a heaven somewhere where God didn't want animals because they had no souls, appalled her. Nothing had prepared her for the effect on her heart that Mr. Bannerjee was having as he spoke about God and blessings as if they were his very breath.

Mr. Bannerjee paused, instinctively aware of the impression his words were having on the young heart next to him. He glanced up at Auntie who had the suspicion of a smile at the corners of her lips.

He continued: "We call this moment *darshan*." And then when the silence of the moment had passed his voice became crisp as he smiled and said: "Now, let me get some chai for both of you before you go on up to the bungalow." He clapped his hands together quicker than the eye could see: "Chai, Aditya, for all of us, and tell Mummy to come and say hullo to Auntie and, what is your name little sister? ah Anna. Quickly now, they are coming from Delhi itself and are *too* tired to move!"

Anastasia had settled herself down on the sunny side of the second step and rested her hand lightly upon Anna's shoulder watching Anna listen wide-eyed to Mr. Bannerjee's words, knew that Anna had never heard such a lovely story, never heard anyone speak of God before in such a way that made the given Reality of the mountains seem so close.

Anna wondered if it was the mountains themselves that made people talk like this. There was something, something she couldn't quite put a word to, was it sacred? about them. She had a feeling that if angels were real and lived anywhere they would choose to live here, in the whiteness of the mountains, and she told Anastasia and Mr. Bannerjee what she thought.

"You are right," responded Mr. Bannerjee enthusiastically, "we call them Devas, Bright Beings, the

Shining Ones, and here they are close to the Oxygen of God, the only reality that keeps us alive you know, but it isn't many people who know this anymore. People are all so-o-o busy, rushing here and rushing there, trying to make more money than they can use, convincing themselves that they need so much they are even afraid to share in case even what they think is their 'not enough' runs out. They fill their heads with commitments and their homes with noise, and they have forgotten how to sit and stare out of a window, forgotten how to weave dreams to catch the wind. They fill their children with so-o-o many facts and figures, which they will have to de-programme from their minds if they ever feel uncomfortable enough with all of this 'more of' and want to find the way to where the Truth is. And do you know, Anna, where the Truth is? It is buried here," and he tapped his heart briskly with the flat of his hand, "not here," and he pointed to his head. "Oh Auntie, you must teach this child the ways of the Invisible World!"

Anastasia was smiling broadly now: "Moti, you could put on a *geru* dhoti and sit in Hyde Park, there are so many people in western countries who are longing to hear what they can barely remember…"

They spoke of the journey then and Mrs. Bannerjee joined them on the steps in the warm sunshine. They spoke too of the beauty of the late autumn flowers, and of the need for provisions to be brought in for the cooler months. Mrs. Bannerjee took a liking to Anna and shortly after sitting on the step drinking her tea and watching the child's bright face she disappeared inside beyond the dark curtain to re-emerge with a tiny brass peacock paperweight inlaid with semi-precious stones as a gift for Anna's new life. Anna's words of thanks poured out in a tumble of confusion. "Oh, it's so lovely, thank you, thank you very much. It is like a jewel…" and Mrs. Bannerjee nodded her head and smiled, saying:

"Mmmm, it is like a jewel, but it is not for jewels we must search, it is for the Jeweller."

Once more Anna sensed she was listening to a tale within a tale, a parable in which something was hidden, something rare and precious, more precious than a jewel. She knew, *somewhere*, that the Jeweller and the Destination were connected.

It was a long climb to the cottage hermitage where Anastasia lived. High, high on the side of a mountain it perched on a small levelled block of land aglow with zinnias and dahlias and cosmos, daisies and autumn roses. Yuccas and ferns and trellises of jasmin led the eye to the edge of the land where the view of the towering deodar forests tumbled into the valleys beside and below them, and down from the mountains above the snowline behind the cottage to the garden boundary. They had been walking up, up, up for nearly an hour. Moti had called two young village boys to carry the baggage and provisions and fruit and vegetables up to the cottage with them and Nandini, from the village to the west, was there to greet them when they arrived. She came once a week carrying shopping to save Anastasia the long walk. Anastasia gave the boys a couple of rupees each and they skittered happily off back down the hill track to the village, taking only a third of the time of the upward climb.

Nandini had prepared a *subje* of potato and tomato and a leafy green vegetable together with a lightly spiced dhal for a light supper before the two tired travellers bathed in the water she had already heated in an old copper boiler over a fire of wood. She chatted to them both, teased Anna about the sounds she would hear from the forest around them, and then, collecting her woven string bags and kicking off her string house *puli's*, bid them a good rest. As she opened the door to put on her walking chappals and take leave there on the small verandah sat the prettiest cat Anna could ever remember seeing. Where Sambo was big and black and round and cuddly with huge puddly paws this creature was as slender as a mongoose, with fur speckled like a wild rabbit, eyes that shone like green peridot, and the tiniest, daintiest paws imaginable.

"Oh," exclaimed Nandini "where have you been you naughty puss? Nearly a week Auntie has been gone and you have hidden yourself in the forest. Auntie will think I haven't been feeding you, she will be *so-o* cross with me, every day I am looking for you! Now you just come in here and *namaste* to Anna!"

The cat walked in on the tips of her toes, passing Anna and ignoring Nandini, going directly to Anastasia who picked her up while Anna watched as the cat draped herself over her aunt's shoulders, her tail drooping languidly down Anastasia's back. She curved her slender body around Anastasia's neck, bringing her front paws over the left shoulder while her elegant pointed face nestled into the side of Anastasia's cheek.

"Time for introductions later," said Anastasia, "Devadasi is pleased to see me, and she doesn't look too hungry. I expect she has been keeping the mice away from my flour and rice in my absence. Peace be with you Nandini, we will see you on Tuesday – oh and I've just remembered, do please bring up a dozen boxes of matches from Motilal, we are running low and it quite slipped my mind".

Anastasia showed Anna her room, a room facing east, its outside view spanning the mountain peaks and the sunrise. French windows opened on to a small verandah filled with pots of marigolds and nasturtiums. The furniture was simple. The bed was a taut webbed charpoy base on a wooden frame on which was a thickly padded cotton mattress, a quilted cotton doona with a brightly coloured ochre and indigo block print coverlet. Near the door was a small writing table with a wooden rush seated chair. Thick rugs and dhurries lay across the timber floor and the shelves set within the white-washed wall alcoves were obviously for books and clothes. As well as an electric light from the ceiling there was a glass domed oil lamp and a box of matches, two candles and a glass on the desk. A terracotta matki of water sat just beyond the French doors, mountain breezes running over its condensation kept it cool in the summer months, and in winter it would be brought in to stand in the hallway to prevent it freezing. There was no heating that Anna could see, but after a warm wash she fell into bed and found a hot water bottle to warm her feet.

The first night she was cosy and warm, though she slept fitfully, night noises of the forest intruding on her dreams: the yapping of jackals, the wind moaning in the deodars, the distant barking of village dogs throughout the night. Then in the morning the haunting notes of a beautifully played flute, repeated over and over like a prayer, drifted to her on the wind. A cough, like a sob, pierced her heart. Leopard was close. With all her heart Anna sent it her love and thanked it for coming to her. With its blessing and the blessing from the Daughter of the Snows to fill her heart Anna knew life with Auntie would be filled with wonder.

Anastasia had come in during the night and placed a fine pashmina shawl on the back of the chair and a pair of coloured woven string slippers for house wear. Shoes were left outside. Turning slightly in bed Anna, when she woke, could see the garden, and the deodar forest surrounding the sanctuary of the cottage, and the mountains. Once again their vastness caught her unawares and she took a little intake of breath as a shiver ran down her spine. She reached for the shawl, her heart warmed by the gift, and wrapped it around herself. The sky was still dark and the mountains were glowing silhouettes. Anna recalled the words of Mr. Bannerjee: *Haimavati, the daughter of the sky, she is the whiteness within the snow…* Anna had never thought of whiteness being within, it was like a perfume, an unseen essence, or so it seemed. Her thoughts drifted like clouds as she stared at the mountain peaks and then, in front of her eyes, and so faintly at first she thought she was imagining it, the tips of the mountains took on a pinky golden glow. The sun was rising. Anna watched the colour deepen and pour down the mountain snows of Nanda Devi, the sky was still dark and the moon, little more than a sickle, shone more luminously in the dawn's light. A numinous silent stillness wrapped itself around her like a sound. The flute player had stopped, no dogs barked, the wind had died down, no birds sang. There was only the stillness, as if the whole universe had stood in prayer for the Dawn's coming and the Sun's rising. The golden pink flooded down the mountains, in its wake the glistening, dazzling whiteness of snow and ice graced the sky. As the first rays of the sun touched the garden in front of the verandah there, nodding her crested head up and down, and looking up at the house, was the hoopoe.

5

The Vision in the Forest

Anna climbed out of her bed and tiptoed to the windows. She undid the latch and slowly, quietly, opened them to step out onto the verandah. The hoopoe just remained where it was in the garden on a small rock, watching her, nodding her head up and down and lifting and lowering her crest. The sun had almost risen now and shafts of light backlit the marigolds and the cosmos, haloing them with light, flaming the buff cinnamon tips of the bird's feathers on her breast. The wind was picking up again, the silent prayer of the elements and animals to the Dawn was over for another day and the village dogs once more took up their incessant mindless barking.

The hoopoe watched her for a moment, then she bobbed up and down and once more Anna heard, perceived, the voice behind the bird's call: "hoo-poo-poo, hoo-poo-poo, *I've come for you, I've come for you*," she called, deep and soft.

The wind of the morning blew around Anna's bare legs and she drew the shawl closer around her. She watched the hoopoe fly away before turning back into the room, closing the doors behind her. She pulled on her clothes and a pair of thick woollen richly patterned socks which her aunt had laced on the chair, pulled on the string *puli's* and walked across the hallway to the small living room where she could hear her aunt talking softly to Devadasi and making familiar breakfast noises. She curled up in a huge cushion, sitting quietly in thought.

"Hullo darlinkg" greeted Anastasia when she came into the room carrying bowls of sweetened wheat and puffed rice with nuts in for breakfast: "Did you sleep well?

No? Strange noises and a new bed. Tonight you will sleep better. Now we will eat and then we can talk. I have much to learn about you so we can prepare a kind of framework for your days otherwise you will find they pass very slowly. Do you read or paint? I have some books, not many, of the miniature paintings of some of the Forest Schools near this region, though the painters lived more than a hundred years ago. You can look through the bookcases here and also in my room through that door there. Come now and take food."

Anna loved painting and drawing but she had stopped entirely. Her mother told her she couldn't draw, that Stephanie, ever so much younger, was far better and that Anna was just wasting her time. Something had died within her. She didn't tell her aunt of those secret pains, but she knew she would love to look at those books and then who knows what might re-kindle in her heart again. She had always drawn horses, much as she loved cats it was always horses who wanted to prance and dance across her page; horses with manes and tails flying, horses feeding, horses at rest, foals at play, horses with wings like Pegasus. Perhaps she just might draw again. She added the idea to her storehouse of secrets in the back of her mind. Right now she had a more important question to ask.

"Auntie" said Anna, "the hoopoe was there in the garden this morning, I'm sure it spoke to me again, but would it have followed us all the way from Delhi?"

Anastasia raised an eyebrow very very slightly: "No," she answered "it would not have been the same hoopoe, but all creatures communicate at intuitive levels higher and more intricate that the our use of words. She would have relayed your coming to the hoopoe of our garden, did she say anything else?"

"Ye-es, she said I've come for you, but I think she said forest too, though I wasn't certain if I heard it, if you know what I mean. And, you know Auntie when I saw the mountains this morning I felt like crying again. They are so pure and white and it is like they are too big for my heart to hold them."

Anastasia agreed. "Sometimes people come to me who have been marked with suffering. Many of these people are unloved and unwanted. There is a purpose in this, and this purpose you will discover for yourself. These people I send to the Forest. The hoopoe has come to guide you, she doesn't usually make herself so known, but you are young and can hear with the heart. In this whole world, Anna, there is purpose behind everything, even suffering. Some people misinterpret this, for we are vulnerable. Sometimes they use it to manipulate, for their own gain, merit in some mythical heaven, thinking their conversion of others will swell the ranks of their own dogma or creed." Anastasia, paused, watched Anna, and then: "yet even this perversion of the Truth is His Will, Anna, for if you remember nothing else in your whole life, never forget that not one leaf falls without His Will."

Anastasia inclined her head away from Anna, to gaze out of the window into a far place, her elbow on the arm of the chair and her fingers resting lightly on her chin. Anna looked at her. She wasn't certain she understood everything her aunt had said, but she knew she was being spoken to as an adult. She would respond by letting everything settle before she spoke. As she watched her aunt there seemed to be beams of a strange shimmering light radiating from Anastasia's eyes. She blinked, and the light had gone. Her aunt turned back to face her and repeated softly: "Not a leaf falls but that He wills it…"

"Auntie," said Anna, very softly, for there was a silence in the room, one of those stillnesses where she was aware of a presence in the air: "who is He?"

The stillness in the room became almost tangible, Anna felt surrounded by it, Presences pressing in all around her, like a chrysalis, and when Anastasia looked at her she sensed her whole being stood still at the words that followed.

"He is the whisper in the depth of the soul. It is He who knows the touch of the ant's foot in darkness over a rock, it is He who knows what is in your deepest heart, for it was He who made it. He is called by a thousand different Names, and He is also She, for the Goddess is the ebb and flow of the great oceans, the waxing and waning of the moon, the dancing flames within the fire, the gaze of a kitten and the crying of the curlew. This Great Spirit is within the greatest of the great and the smallest of the small, to the last blade of grass. I, who am a woman, call Him the Beloved. There is a space within my heart which can never be filled by a human love. Humans come, humans go, but that little space within the heart is the source of all our love and all our longing. This Longing, Anna dear, is the proof of the Beloved's existence. We long to be loved and to belong. But to what? Everything in the world passes away and every person we love dies. What remains? Love. It is the Longing for that Love that makes us long for the Beloved, and when we have found that great Love our Way is ended."

Anna gazed at her aunt; she knew so many lovely words, words that Anna knew sang with meaning, words whose essence filled her young heart.

Anna sat very still in the silence after her aunt's answer, she felt that her world had become so vast and her mind so focussed she could feel the very footprints of the ants across the floor. "Auntie" she finally spoke, "will I go to the Forest? It must be very important for the hoopoe to talk to me," she added wistfully, half to herself.

Anastasia smiled, and signalled for Anna to come and sit at the table to eat breakfast while it was still warm.

"I don't know, my dear, what you may find in the Forest, but being there will give you a chance to forget all you have known. Your pain, your loneliness, has led here. You have not been able to understand why your life should be so different to that of other children. One day you will know why the adults responsible for your life and circumstances behaved the way they did.

You see our Nanda Devi? She will hide behind thick clouds and only you will know she is still there! People are like that too, prisoners of unconscious motives, like veils, clouding real Vision."

Anastasia watched her niece's face: "Only when we are pure of intent, without a trace of selfishness in our actions, do those veils fall away and leave us face to Face. Then we find compassion."

Anastasia paused for a moment. Her own seriousness search meant she had never learnt the art of speaking from any level other than her own highest truth. She looked at her niece's face, saw wisdom beyond its years, and finished: "you may not understand everything I have said, but *somewhere* you know my meaning."

She allowed the essence behind her words to take root, returned to the subject of breakfast: "Will you have some more tea, some fruit? Spend the morning quietly, arrange your room how you would like it, take flowers from the garden if you wish. Our food here is very simple; I hope you will not miss the things you are used to too much. There is no hurry to go to the Forest, you have all the time in the world. Devadasi will probably follow you around the house, she is curious. Sufi's say cats are pure; they keep a watch around us." She smiled, began to drink the tea which had grown cold during her soliloquy. It did her good, too, to air her heightened views from time to time!

They cleared away the breakfast things together, washed them and left them to dry. Anna called to Devadasi, and then she called to her aunt to ask what the name meant, for she was beginning to sense that nothing was spoken of lightly here, that everything had a meaning. Anastasia replied: "Servant of the Bright One; Devas are the Bright Beings, the Angelic Ones Mr. Bannerjee spoke of. And her eyes are green, the green of another world."

Devadasi followed Anna back to her room. Jumping lightly on to the writing desk to perch like a Pharaoh's sphinx, occasionally blinking her peridot green eyes, she watched as Anna unpacked the few things she had brought with her to arrange them on the shelves. The morning passed quickly and soon Anastasia called her, lunch was ready. Lightly spiced vegetables and rice followed by fruit and *dahi*, curd, yoghurt sweeter than any Anna had known before. *It's made of buffalo milk*, said Anastasia, anticipating the question.

After lunch all three sat on the verandah in the warm winter sun, all three gazed in silence towards the mountains, all three at peace with their surroundings.

The days passed gently, the thought of the forest ever present in Anna's thoughts. One afternoon, sitting together as usual on the verandah after lunch the lure of the forest pulled at her heart and Anna knew it was time to heed the call. She glanced at her aunt and felt, rather than saw, an imperceptible movement of her aunt's head. She rose, went inside, gathered up her shawl and put on an extra pair of socks before slipping on her outdoor shoes, walked to the wicket gate that separated their cottage from the world beyond. Swinging it open she paused for a moment to sense which direction to go, there were so many little paths, each dappled with sunlight and littered with thick autumn leaf fall, and each looked as enticing as the other. She chose the path that seemed a natural extension from the footpath in the garden, heart smiling with her footfall.

Wild strawberries grew here and there, but they were too bitter to eat this late in the year. Soon the mountainous peaks in the distance were hidden by the tall deodar pines and the wind moaned softly through the branches. Anna didn't need to go far to arrive at a small clearing where sunlight dappled in patches the mossy ground below the leafy canopy. She sat down, and drew her knees up to her chest and looked around. She was hardly surprised to see the hoopoe on a branch just to the left of her head and she realized that it must have been the hoopoe herself urging her to come today. She sent thoughts to the beautiful bird: *was it you telling me to come today? It is so lovely here. But I am so tired, as if something is pulling my eyelids down to my knees! Oh hoopoe, please wait while I lay down for few minutes, I can hardly stay awake to even think properly.* The hoopoe nodded in return to the Anna's soliloquy.

Tiredness enveloped Anna like a cloak, she could no more fight off the sense of sinking into the earth itself than stand up and walk. She gave in to the heaviness, lay down on the mossy ground with her head on her elbow. Within moments she had fallen into a deep slumber.

Suddenly, through her sleep, Anna heard the pounding thunder of hooves. Sitting bolt upright she watched in wonder as the branches of the deodars trembled and parted to reveal the most exquisite miniature horse. It was not a pony, it was a perfectly proportioned, and the most perfectly perfect, horse she had ever imagined. He appeared surrounded by flames, the sky behind him had darkened to a velvet vault of deepest indigo. His coat shimmered silvery white, a thousand stars sparkling in his flowing mane and tail. Silver hooves pawed the earth in front of her and the breeze in the wake of his arrival rippled his starry mane and tail like a silken curtain. He pranced and danced in front of the amazed child, his breath like puffs of sound through his nostrils.

Anna pinched herself to make sure she was not dreaming. She had never in her wildest imagination seen such a perfection of a horse.

But, she heard, astonished, *I am not a horse such as you think I am, o-o-o-h, n-o-o-o*, the perfection whinnied, and the sound came out like a silver laugh echoed by the whole forest. *I am the Bright One, the Carrier of the Prophet, the Guide to the Way beyond the Invisible Worlds, Anna. You may love me and we can travel together, but you must never ask me to stay with you, for if you ask me that, because you want to keep me by you, then you will lose me. I am not of this world, dear Anna, and I can only come in the freedom of my wild Spirit.*

Anna was so astonished that it was some moments before she could frame any thoughts, could formulate a coherent sentence from her spinning mind. At first she could only gasp in wonder at the beauty of the Bright One (*is that what he called himself?*) until she remembered that she could understand the language of the Hoopoe this way. Just to make certain she added: *Can we really hear ourselves only by our thoughts?*

Lovely girl, said the Bright One shaking his head so the threaded stars of his forelock laughed in twinkling silver sounds: *when the heart of a child can bear no more pain there comes a moment during sleep – for even when you sleep the heart is watching – that the heart calls to the Invisible Worlds for peace to come. You don't even know that your heart has called, but we of the Unseen Realms hear it and we respond. Then the forces are placed in motion so that the circumstances in your outer life are directed solely upon you being led to Us. We are seen much more easily in the Himalayas because for thousands of years so many saints and rishis have meditated and prayed in these valleys and mountains. We take a special notice of prayers.*

Anna sat, statue still, motionless as a rock. Her heartbeat resounded to the words she was hearing. The Bright One spoke again: *On the banks of the sacred river Ganga, who begins her long winding descent from these hills, thousands upon thousands of pilgrims down the centuries have sung their songs of love to the Beloved. All over the world, it is true, the pure in heart have sung their songs of devotion and invocation, but here in the Himalayas it is remembered by so many. Here in these mountains we can be seen, and so it is that you have come to us.*

The Bright One turned slightly, his head lifted, intent on the source of the breeze or a sound that Anna could not hear. Quickened by some invisible movement he turned swiftly back to Anna and said: *Climb onto my back and wind your fingers through my mane. I will take you on a journey and you will understand many things.*

At the mention of time and far away Anna's response registered immediately. Without daring to blink in case this magical creature in front of her should disappear, she tentatively thought to him that her aunt would worry if she was not back in time for tea.

The Bright One laughed, rippling the Milky Way, tossing his head in equine amusement as he put Anna's mind at rest. *In the wink of an eye the world can be known, Anna, in less than a heartbeat the universe is seen. Auntie said you should come to the Forest didn't she? Then do you think she doesn't know? Her heart knows its secrets, she has journeyed deep into its depths, and that is where we are going!*

The Bright One stamped the mossy turf and tossed his mane, puffs of silver breath coming from his nostrils, Anna had the oddest suspicion that he was laughing at her. Obediently she climbed on to his back and wound her fingers through his shimmering mane. Kicking his hind hooves into the turf they sprang up from the ground beneath and left the earth behind them.

Anna heard the wind, though she could not feel it. She heard rushing water, like the cascades down blue mountains, but she could not see it. Everything was misty, except the fiery flames whose heat she could not feel, and the crystal moon who cast no shadow. She could smell a perfume though she could see no flowers, and she had a sweet taste in her mouth although it was empty. She was travelling through a world of essences which had no outward form at all. Her fingers held tightly onto the flowing mane of the Bright One.

She could hear a sound, very high, lilting, unlike anything she had ever known, a voice, many voices, coming from within the mountains. The thoughts of the Bright One flowed to her: *All this Universe is She who is the Mother of the World. From Her, whole galaxies are born, and the moon and the stars and our earth. She is the Mother of That which your people call God. She is the movement of Life, She is known by endless names, you know Her as Mother Nature, we call Her the Golden Mother of the World and few have ever seen Her. Some say*

She lives on Jasper Lake far beyond Kaf Mountain in a land some call Shambala.

Anna drank in his words as the pair sped towards a tiny brilliant light she could see ahead of them. She could hear once again the high lilting music of the other spheres. Even this faded as the distant light grew closer.

They stopped. The Bright One arched his neck and Anna heard him whisper:

Anna, fair one, here you must climb down from my back and walk into the light alone. It is your light and only you can walk its path to the centre. I shall be here waiting for you, go now, and have no fear.

Anna swallowed hard, swung her right leg over his back and slid to the ground. For a hare's breath of time she rested her hand on the Bright One's silver arched neck before stepping out on her own. It was odd, she recalled to her aunt later, because there was no ground to step out on. Nevertheless, she walked on into the dazzling light which welcomed her as its own. On and on she walked, until the light enveloped her, and the silver horse was out of sight behind the shining. The light was brilliant, but instead of dazzling her it was as if she was cocooned in its molten gold. Dimly at first, she thought she could see a figure far ahead of her. Then she heard the softest of voices calling her name.

Look at me Anna, look clearly into my golden form, all the gold that surrounds you is my Love, and my love is eternal. My Love has no beginning and no end, all creatures know this which is why when their earthly overcoat has worn thin they can leave it without tears to come Home to Me. It is not your time, Anna, to come Home. But every now and then a human heart is brought to Me, for the tears it has shed, even without crying, have washed it as clean as though bathed in the dew of Angels, and Angels see Me very clearly.

Anna looked into the golden light. She found if she made her gaze slightly out of focus she could see more clearly. The golden light ahead of her began to shimmer, to take form. She kept looking, her eyes drawn to where the voice

46

came from. There in the softness of the brilliant golden light she was able to see a face. It was the face of the most beautiful woman she had ever seen. In awe Anna caught her breath and gazed upon the vision before her. She felt her heart turn to liquid and melt inside her.

The voice began to speak again: *Anna, let your eyes focus ahead of you, look within this golden form which is My whole body and allow your gaze to pierce the veil that separates us, that separates you from Reality. Look within My golden form.*

Anna blinked again. There ahead of her in the brightness, and taking form within the shimmering light, was a tiny, infinitely tiny image. Purely gold, and sitting in perfect calmness, perfect harmony, cross-legged in the centre of a pale golden and pink lotus flower, hands resting in each other. She knew, in the clarity graced by the moment, that she was looking at the very purest form of her very Self. Somehow it was within the Lady who had spoken. She heard a voice dimly, through the golden mist: *Anna, I am the Angel who dwells in the very depth of your soul. All living creatures have their angel, but humans seldom find me. This is the image of Me that you carry within your heart. You can never lose Me, even though you may never see Me again. You only need to remember that I am your innermost Guide. You can trust My voice, I will whisper to you when you have need of Me.*

Anna remained in absolute stillness, closing her eyes to absorb the memory of the Vision into the very pores and cells and fibre of her being. It seemed she could hear all around her the Heartbeat that sustains the world, though she could not be sure, it was more a feeling than a hearing. The voice of the Lady could be heard very faint and far, as though from a star, telling her to return along the songlines of her soul to where the Bright One had brought her, an eternity ago.

Anna stepped away from the Vision, her heart full, stepped away from the golden centre of the light, turned and walked back along the path that she knew was hers. When she reached the very edge of the realm of gold she took one more step and the light changed, and there was the

Bright One beside her. He greeted her, whispered to her to once more climb onto his back as he spun around to the immense darkness where only the glow of his flaming iridescence lit the indigo space through which they travelled. The silence of the child upon his back told him all he needed to know.

Landing lightly back on the mossy clearing of the Forest, the Bright One let Anna down on the soft turf. *Now you have found your Self, Anna my child, you must learn how to polish the mirror of the heart with a sacred sound. It will keep the Invisible World open for you. Auntie can teach you that. And now,* he shook his mane and stepped away, *I must say farewell for other hearts are calling to me* … and Anna, forgetting his first words to her cried out: "oh please stay, please don't go, you are so beautiful…!"

Lightning split the sky and the Bright One vanished in fire and flame. Shock pierced Anna with a sense of dread made whole by the echo of her own words, the words her Heavenly Horse had warned her never to say: *Stay*. All that remained was a night-mare of loss and a desolation deeper than death.

6

The Unspotted Mirror

Anna sat up, stunned and confused. Her first thought was that she must have been dreaming, for she knew that the shock had slipped her mind into a deep healing sleep back there on the mossy ground of the forest. Yet, she knew it was no ordinary dream. She rubbed her eyes – there, all around her, were tiny perfect hoof prints in the moss. Filled with wonder Anna rolled on to her knees and looked at the impressions more closely. In the tip of each hoof print, right in the centre of the curve was a diminutive silver disc. She held back her tears and looked through the leaves above her to the rarefied world from where she knew the Heavenly Horse had come. She still wasn't certain whether she had dreamt it or if it had really happened, but here in her hand was a symbol of something precious and heaven sent, something to hold on to when time would play tricks with her memory. Anna looked up to see if the Hoopoe was still there, but no, she had gone.

The haunting notes of the flute player drifted on the wind up from the direction of the village in the valley and Anna felt chilled, the sun had moved and the dapples of warmth had gone. Slowly getting to her feet she began to walk back to the hermitage. She felt very different, expanded and somehow full. Everything looked different, as if the light was coming from inside her eyes instead of from the fading afternoon sun.

From the clearing Anna entered the forest proper before coming out in to the open air and the path leading to the hermitage gate. There on the verandah sat Devadasi, her peridot green eyes slanted and her mouth definitely curled into a pussy grin. *She knows*, thought Anna, and she could have sworn Devadasi blinked.

Anna felt as old as Eternity and as wise as Wisdom. Walking into the small sitting room where Anastasia was at her desk she sat down on the huge cushion by the bookcase without speaking. Anastasia turned in her chair. Without a word she held out her hands to Anna who walked into her arms. They held each other for long moments until Anastasia stepped back and looked at her niece. As Anna returned her gaze Anastasia knew the child's transformation, knew that she had been graced by entry into another world, a world Anastasia knew well.

The days began to form their own framework. Nothing appeared to have changed and yet everything had. Anna learned to make chapattis, soft, sweetish, unleavened bread; to clean and prepare vegetables. Nandini taught her to sort and sift pulses by tossing small scoops over and over on a flat woven reed basket letting the stones and grit fall away from the grains. Everything was done by hand with the most basic of culinary equipment and life slowed down to essential movements. For Anna even the simple discovery of putting one foot in front of another as she walked to and from the rooms in the tiny cottage became a point of pleasure in her own existence. Neither she nor Anastasia spoke much. Without interfering, her aunt watched Anna live and establish a deep accord in their relationship, an accord that revealed a maturity beyond her niece's years. Living thus removed from accustomed noise and trivial excitement made careless movement or clumsy speech stand out in extra-ordinary relief.

Anna felt she had her head in the vault of the sky and her feet rooted in the earth. Gradually this feeling passed and blended into an expanded awareness, a more integrated perception, a different way of seeing. It was then that she could begin to speak of her experience in the Forest.

"What really puzzles me, Auntie, is that even having been born to people who didn't want me is alright, isn't it. Because if it hadn't been like that I would never have gone to the Forest and I wouldn't have come to you." She paused, remembering how the Bright One had told her to "polish her heart with a sound."

Her aunt put her hands on Anna's shoulders and looked very deeply into her eyes: "the Name is the polish of the heart, we call it the unspotted mirror for it reflects Grace. We can choose any one of a thousand names for the Divine, and the Divine can be either Father or Mother, God or Goddess, Lord or Lady, for no one Name is greater than the other. Here in India all names lead to the One Name, all words become the Word. Certain names conjure up certain images; personal names like SitaRam or RadheKrishna or Jesus or Mary or KuanYin are surrounded by cultural stories which give certain concepts; but there are others to which no idea can be attached. Choose whichever one means the most to you and breathe it into your heart."

Anastasia lowered her hands and Anna stood thoughtfully, her eyes in a far country: "I would like you to give me a Name, Auntie, because all the images I think of seem to make the enormous feeling smaller, sort of my size. I want a Name that will bring the Mother of the World closer to me even if I may not hear or see Her again. I need my heart to hold Her always."

There was one of those sudden stillnesses in the room again; again Anna was aware of a strange light in her aunt's eyes when she spoke. "I will give you a Word that contains the Everything and the Nothing, the Beginning and the End, the Fullness and the Emptiness. I will breathe it into your ear." She breathed the sound of the Name into Anna's ear and the sound sealed itself into Anna's heart.

"The breath will carry the essence to the farthest recess of your soul, far, far from where the mind with its thoughts can go. Breathe in the sound of the Word when you wake in the morning and before you sleep each evening, this is the password to carry you through the journey of life. We call it *mantra*, it is like eavesdropping on the Heart of hearts. The heart surrenders to that one Word, its secret lovelier than all words."

Anna couldn't bring herself to speak, so great was the impact of the Word inside her. It had just two syllables, and as she coordinated them with her breathing, she felt the Name descending deep into her heart as if it had always belonged there.

"Auntie," she said after some moments, as if the thought had surfaced from hidden depths, "I know that the pure golden image that the Golden Mother of the World showed me was myself, and I know we are made in the image of God, but, then, why are we all so different?"

Anastasia's laugh radiated humour and joy. "Why are we all so different? Ah my darlinkg, do you think the Greatness of God has only one Face? He has a billion, billion faces – every star is a witness, to the last blade of grass! It is only humans who argue about what they have forgotten!"

Anna wondered at such a huge answer, she felt loved. When she came to speak again it was with difficulty, for the question was tinged with pain: "Auntie, this means I may not see the Bright One in the Forest again, doesn't it? Because if this Word is the Key to the Way, then the Bright One won't need to come to me, he will have other prayers to answer won't he?"

Anastasia tilted her head and turned to look out of the long windows at the setting sun: "This is true. A vision like this nourishes us for a lifetime. Whether the Bright One will come again or not I cannot say. But there will be all the years ahead of you, for I have decided that you have adjusted to life here very well, and if you would like to stay we can arrange for you to attend school in Naini Tal, it will suit you. All that you have experienced is the source of strength for your inner world, but equally important is schooling to equip you for the world in which we live. I've written to your mother and Brian, and also to your father, to propose that you remain here provided they pay for school fees, for my resources cannot accommodate schooling. The final decision will be yours of course." The expression of happiness on her niece's face gave the answer she needed.

"We shall leave the rest in His hands, though of course He has no hands! That is just a figure of speech! And now you know that He is not only He, but She! Now I suggest we have supper, and then sleep. Tomorrow is another day."

The days slid slowly into each other, and passed into weeks, and the weeks to months. The snows came and winter touched the garden, the flowers faded. The reality of their life together was in accord with a very slow rhythm like the changing of the seasons or the coursing of the stars. The transformation of Anna from an unloved and unwanted child to a young girl for whom every moment of their peaceful life together was joy, was done in depth, in the darkness of the heart, and she learnt day by day to live from within.

In the spring she went away to school in Naini Tal as a boarder. She rarely thought of her parents, though now and then a word or thought would activate a trick of light in her memory and a hurt or a resentment would be recalled. But it was true, the remembrance of the Divine Name was the polish that kept her heart pure and the all too human feelings never lasted long. Each semester end Anna would return to the hermitage and to the slow rhythm of the life she had come to love. Every Diwali, the Hindu Festival of Lights to celebrate the return of Rama, who rescued Sita from the demon Ravanna, Anna would paint a special mandala for Mr. Bhattacharya and for the Bannerjee's. Mr. Bhattacharya would come up from Delhi to visit her at school from time to time during, buy her *kulfi* ice-cream while they sat by the green waters of the lake in the Shadow of the Devi. He would tell her stories from the ancient *Puranas*. Anna learned to love the Hindu myths and the reverence the people had for everything they held sacred. She knew that throughout humankind it was through symbols that one could glimpse the higher realities. But she could find no words to ever describe her meeting with the Bright One.

Whenever she returned to the Forest the hoopoe greeted her, but now Anna had lost the ability to understand the language of the Birds. Perhaps it did not matter anymore. The Bright One never came again, but he was too much in her heart for her to feel any separation. She had the tiny silver discs with their crescent moon impression linked and mounted on silk thread which she wore around her neck, hidden from view. Only Auntie knew.

In Anna's last year at school, Anastasia fell ill. A sudden fever, and Anna, home for the winter holiday, insisted, as Anastasia refused to eat, that she call a doctor. Devadasi cried piteously and refused to leave her side.

Anna ran and ran down the mountain, bouncing awkwardly from rock to stone to turf and dislodging shingle all the way down. It was a wonder she didn't fall and injure herself. When she reached Moti's store he went with her to the tiny post office further down the valley to telegram for the doctor to come. The snows would delay him, it would be at least a day and a half before he would be able to reach them. Night was falling by now, and Anna asked the Bannerjee's if they would come up to the hermitage tomorrow with the doctor.

That night was the longest Anna had ever lived through. Towards midnight Anastasia stirred, and Anna hastened to assure her that she was with her. "I know, my dear," Anastasia's voice was very soft, but quite clear "you must not worry, I know where I am going...."

Anna swallowed her tears and bent her head closer to hear her beloved aunt whisper to herself the same words Mr. Bhattacharya had once told her were gifted to the great avatars and saints when they could see the angels before them: *My faith is firm, my doubts are none, Sivohum, Sivohum, They Will Be Done.*

The glory of her aunt's smile burned its memory into Anna's heart forever, she knew her aunt was looking not at her, but through the veils to another world. Moments passed. At first Anna thought she was imagining it, but as it became brighter she realized that the whole

54

room was filled with a golden light, a golden presence. Within the goldenness she could sense movement, as if the golden light was taking form. Unbelieving at the wonder of it Anna knew, despite her flickering surface doubt, she was in the presence of the Devas, the Bright Beings, and they had come for her aunt from the Golden Mother Herself.

Devadasi, with a last backward glance at the human friend she had loved for so many years, turned and walked out through the unlatched French window, across the garden and into the Forest. She was never seen again.

The golden light, the golden presence, faded. Too numb to cry Anna folded her aunts pale hands together on her breast. Then she too walked to the Forest to sit in the clearing she knew so well. She sat for eternity, and as the sun's rays left the mountain Anna heard the soft ululation of a hoopoe calling. Anna wrapped her shawl closer around her, it was freezing yet she was too numb to feel it properly, closing her eyes prayers streamed from her heart. It was an outpouring, inarticulate, unfocused except for one thing – a rose. The flowers in the winter garden had long died, but she so wanted to place one in Anastasia's hand as a symbol to express her wordless gratitude in being taught the essence of life. Like the perfume of the rose, it was beyond words. There were no more tears to weep and Anna held her head in her hands, empty.

She was exhausted, the numbness was beginning to wear off and the pain of pins and needles made her grimace in discomfort as she tried to rub warmth and circulation back into her stiff limbs. Hours had passed unheeded. Pulling herself to her feet Anna heard the Hoopoe call: "Hoo-poo-poo, hoo-poo-poo" and she *thought* she heard "*this is for you, this is for you*" even though she had not understood the language of the birds for a long time. Focussing on the Hoopoe who was perched on a rock nearby her heart skipped a beat, for there in the mossy turf were the tiny and exquisite hoof prints she remembered so well. Wonderingly she bent to touch their imprint and murmur *thank you* before making her way back to the cottage. As she turned towards the hermitage gate she was surprised to see coming towards her on the forest path an ochre-robed mendicant, a *sadhu*, one of those seekers of God who wander like the wind, blown like autumn leaves all over India. Anna was well used to seeing them, some looked like princes in disguise, others were in rags, but all were a living symbol of the lesson in non-attachment the Bright One had enshrined in his entreatment to her not to ask him to stay. She stood to one side to let him pass, he looked straight ahead. As he came abreast of her he suddenly stopped, thrust out his hand to her and with an automatic reaction she held out her palm, open. Laughing, he disappeared deep into the Forest. In her hand, two blood red roses.

Anna's face was wet with tears as she reached the cottage gate in time to see the Bannerjee's hurrying up the hill with a man who was obviously the doctor. Anna's face told them they were too late.

She placed the roses under Anastasia's folded hands and turned to look at the mountains, at the whiteness within the snow. The doctor, astonished, said: "But this is winter! From where are you having these roses? Such a thing is not possible surely?"

Anna, her face still turned toward Nanda Devi, said: "this morning at dawn Devadasi walked into the forest for there was no need for her to keep a watch around her beloved mistress anymore. But *I* needed something, because for me it was too great a loss. So I also went to the forest. The only thing I wanted was a flower, and I prayed to the Beloved for a rose. It came, from a *sadhu*, laughing as he passed by me. I knew it was a gift for my Aunt from her Beloved, and that it was for me too, to show me never to doubt, never to lose faith, a whisper never to forget these precious years. It was for me to give to my Aunt with love, for it was she who taught me to see through the eyes of Love. You have come too late. She would have wanted it this way. All we can do now is stand in the shadows and look at the Light she showed us."

Anna sighed softly before continuing. "I have been thinking deeply. There is no need for me to stay in India now; times are changing for us foreigners. I shall go back to Australia, although none of the family may have changed I have, and this is the gift Auntie left with me – to see with the heart when the eyes are blind."

The others in the small room where Auntie lay were moved by the speech of the young woman in front of them. The Bannerjee's loved Auntie deeply. They had watched Anna blossom over the years they had known her, and they listened to her as she turned from the window to say, looking at the inner beauty that had transformed the peaceful face of her Aunt: "This is not the time for tears – see the moon is rising, and look, look at the golden ring around it. Auntie was the moon you know, she was our moon, she lit our darkness, gave us 'insight' to the Reality within. Now" she continued, "all we can do is live with the light she gave. She lived her life luminously, inspired me to find the inner freedom to live my own life. She wouldn't want us to weep. We must share the poetry of life, the poetry that the weavers of the eternal world play out in the weft of its *pralaya*.

With your help we will put in order the things necessary to arrange now. In a couple of weeks I shall close up the cottage and leave for Delhi to organize my ticket home. Of course," she looked at the sad faces of the Bannerjee's, especially Motilal who had aged greatly in the last year, "I shall return from time to time if," she added softly, "it is His Will."

7

The Song of the Ever Free

"Auntie...." The words of a distant child whom Anna once knew as her own sad self rang in her ears as the aircraft flew over the sub-continent to her new beginning. It was the question she had asked in the first few days of meeting her Aunt. "Auntie, why did God create so much suffering? Why did He even create the world?"

And her Aunt had leant forward and cupped Anna's face in her hands and said: "Why has He created the world? That you should be in it! Why has He created you? He is alone, He needs you. Why did you have to suffer? Because otherwise you would never have looked for Him!"

Anna sighed and knew the answer to the Greatest Mystery. For the Sigh in the Soul at the heart of all beings is the Call that carries us Home.

I have no father
Thou art my Father
I have no mother
Thou art my Mother
I have no home
Thou art my Home
I have no desire
Thou art alone my Desire
I have no goal
Thou art my only Goal.

I go to the Spirit of Heaven
And I go and I go and I go
I go to the Imperishable Treasure

And I go and I go and I go
I go to the Spirit of the Void
And I go and I go and I go….

A passing photographer thought her pretty enough ... with her woollen pony 1948-9

Her father loved her - 1953   *With the Old Man of the Forest 1956*

Her beautiful French Grandmother, and wise Aunt Alice

Beloved 'Great Aunt Anastasia' – Mrs Irina Tweedie

A passing photographer 1968   *Fern – Fiji 1967*

Jasper, beloved, 1971

Roger saw her through the eyes of love   *Edna 1974*

Roger with Sir Edmund Hillary 1974

Swami Sitadevi Saraswati 1983   *1975 cats, bats and a Butcher Bird*

Dame Judi – 'faux family'   *Bhaktimurti 1994*

After being 'cooked' 1986   *Jeanine – February 1992*

Father Bede reading Jeanine's book, Silkstone, Queensland April 1992

... now let me tell you of the Black Madonna – 1995

Father Bede, a favourite photo, taken in my lounge April 1992

Fr Bede with HH Darling Lama

Secret Agent takes Ratty to Patmos ...

1995 Dad and Daughter, Silkstone, Queensland – family truths

Two Middle Aged Ladies on Walkabout 2001

The Birl – Black Australia

Quinkans at Split Rock

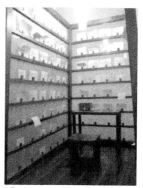

Letters to a Lost Loved One

A Royal Blue Welcome 2013

Anneke, super Supervisor

Anne, earliest mentor

Sainte Radégonde   *Notre Dame d'Ay*

Three Holy Hills

Arunacala, Tamil Nadu, South India

Cudtheringa, Castle Hill, North Queensland

Glastonbury Tor, Isle of Avalon, Somerset

– 2 –

WHERE THERE'S ROSEMARY, THERE'S RUE ...

8

The Inbetween Years

All posies of memories will include rosemary, for remembrance. Shakespeare knew well to give sad Ophelia her famous lines, *rosemary ... and rue;* for rue, regret, will always shadow certain remembrances.

Anna's mother's second marriage to a man twelve years younger than herself and only ten years older than Anna ruled out the possibility of parentage. When the newlywed couple migrated to Australia, Anna to a certain degree had to remain 'invisible', unseen as part of 'family'. Stephanie was a babe, her age was suitable, no one would question her place in the new nuclear family.

For Anna, Sundays were the most terrible; they were 'family time', except that Anna didn't count as part of it. Exiled in her room, excluded from Sunday lunch, she waited until the front door clicked, the silence in its wake indicating the family afternoon outing – and, for her then, a few hours alone. The denial of Sunday lunch every week left its emotional imprint – *she was not worth feeding.* Foraging for bread, butter, she remained hungry every Sunday. *No you can't have that,* her mother would say, banning her from the kitchen, the table, the fridge, *that's for Stephanie, fill up on bread and butter.* And fruit looked so tempting, but Anna knew each piece had been accounted for and she was a timid creature in this new abrasive land and new abrasive family unit. She spent those solitary Sunday hours lying in the hall by the bookcase, books nourished her, the characters whom she met in them became far more real than humans. At times tears would leave damp patches in the soft fur of the family cat, who always seemed to know Sundays and was always there for her. Cats, Anna knew,

knew things about the invisible world that humans didn't know, things like love and heart-hurt and timing and mystery.

In the 1950's the secret shame of divorce haunted the middle classes, was considered shameful, proof of a fall from social grace. Times had changed. Twenty years later divorce was so acceptable, so easy; many young women didn't even bother marrying.

Pat kept secrets, and Stephanie's whereabouts was one of those secrets. She made taunting comments implying how successful or how gifted or how beautiful or how modern or how *anything* Stephanie was – and how Anna had never made the grade, any grade. *Could she,* Anna ignored her mother's jibes over their few encounters spread over long years, *could she meet Stephanie?*

Pat's peals of laughter ended with emphatic denials of Stephanie's desire to ever meet a sister she hadn't known. She, Stephanie, had, so Pat proudly claimed, run off with the married French lecturer from her University to live in France. Her sister's very existence remained a mystery.

By one of those cruel synchronicities the Angels hold in store when truth needs revealing, for Angels, only concerned with truth, are impartial to the heart's hurt, Anna learned a fact that should have taught her of duplicity, but didn't, then.

She was in Sydney seeing friends, Mother's Day happened to fall on the Sunday during her visit and she took a bus to the Theosophical Manor where her mother lived in secured splendour, knocked on the great door, waiting, as always, her heart drumming, until a woman opened it. *Hullo,* said Anna, *I've come to visit my mother, Pat …* and before she could finish her sentence the woman's excited voice called down the corridor – *Pat! Pat! Your daughter's arrived!*

Pat appeared from one of the rooms off the long corridor, stopped short, saw Anna and said, with a deal of dismissive scorn weighting the pronoun: *Oh it's you, I thought it was Stephanie.* Anna, confused, responded: *But I thought Steph was in France* ... tailed off with: *it, it's Mother's Day,* ... excusing herself for standing on the door mat as the wrong daughter, her heartbeat clamouring as her mother said witheringly: *I know it is, Stephanie's come home, she left that dreadful man, she's studying Law and she's due any minute to take me out for the afternoon.*

Foolishly, foolish Anna asked if she could wait to meet her sister, after, how many years? twenty, at least. Pat's sharp refusal to invite her in to wait made Anna turn back, return to the bus stop, and to friends. *Law* ... a world of privilege, all the family lived in a world of privilege, but no, Pat was quite *quite* sure, adamant actually, that Stephanie did not wish to meet her sister.

There was a time when Anna was fifteen that her gift of seeing beyond her ken was a pain so sharp she once doubled over in the school playground, heart pierced, as she walked with two friends to the next class: *Mum and I are going shopping on Saturday,* said one, causing Anna to reel, she had never heard anything so loving. She had never gone shopping with her mother, the thought so alien she hadn't known such a thing was possible on this planet. It was such things as unmothering that bound her known world, and sent her unmothered into that world to search, it could be said, for the Mother of the World. Pain stalked her silently in those early years of her life, would ambush her in roundabout ways – brushing her teeth, posting a letter, making a cup of tea; her breath would leave her body suspended in slow motion, her heart rent in jagged shards that cut the edges of her whole being. It knew Longing, her heart, and it was that Longing that called her into the world.

Denied the tertiary education that was a given, *sine qua non*, to all the women of her paternal family since Saint Radégonde, that great scholar Queen of the Franks, had created convents and universities for women in the fifth century – no money for *you*, scorned her mother – and her father too far away in England to know what he was sending for Anna's education in that far country of

Australia was being spent on frivolities and cosmetic attempts to keep his ex-wife's younger husband's interest. It failed, and Pat married again, and again. The fiscal result? Anna was not granted the intended education but given a suitcase at the age of seventeen, shown the front door and sent to fend for herself. She had neither the guile nor the worldly savvy to succeed, but she survived. It marked her. How could her Fate, then, be any other than to search for her real Mother, the great Mother-of-All? The Mother every Catholic and every Hindu knows. Anna couldn't know, then, that mothers are a child's world for good or ill as the boundaries of that world bound her. Beyond her ken was a foreign country but she was born dream-ridden, born with wind in her heels. Anna knew as a two-and-a-half year old, clutching her little woollen pony, waddling on her chubby two-and-a-half year old legs down the garden path and out through the garden gate, leaving her known world behind her as she breathed the wider air of the world-out-there, that the world *out there* would love her, and to it she responded. She would travel far beyond the garden gate of Beulah Close, Edgware.

That was all so long ago. At seventy-two Anna had long given up hope for a longed-for birthday card from her mother. She had never received such a thing in her entire life. Her mother was most surely dead now. How would she even know? There was no one to tell her. Anna got over it on her own fiftieth birthday when no card arrived in its usual fashion: *My mother doesn't love me,* she woke and said to Self, *own it, give hope back to its Native Nothingness.* Her heart was a reliable organ, and while it would still weep over many future sorrows, it ceased right then, after half a century, to mourn its motherloss.

Anna sighed. Seventy-two was a good age from which to look down from the ridge. Seventy-two, she decided, was almost old. Her own small life, circumscribed by genteel poverty, touched with grace, reminded her always that she had, somewhere not on this earth, said the great Yes: *Yes,* to all the difficulties, the losses, the loneliness, the failures, the illnesses, the nomadic pilgrimages, the creative gifts she was barely courageous enough to make use of – much less own or utilize for material gain. *Yes,* to Everything. *Somewhere* she had asked never to forget from where she had come, had asked only to know God. And did she? Only God would know, but as she hadn't been granted the distractions of worldly wealth or success, and as her heart, as Anastasia requested it should, always turned to That which guided its heartbeat, the question didn't matter much. Over the years and through the vicissitudes of all, her Obedience to the whispers from this invisible protection became her heartbeat itself.

9

The Return

Anna was over thirty before she had saved enough to return to India. There, she travelled third class, an uncomfortable thing to do, but choice, a privilege of money, was not hers to make. Waiting on the platform of Grand Trunk Express travelling from Delhi to Madras she met a French woman.

Arlette was not given to interacting with westerners then floating aimlessly about India. These were the hippie years, the drug trail aftermath of the discovery that any twit could inhabit realms of hell or heaven by popping a pill. Arlette paid no heed to the floating flotsam from the West descending on India then. She lived seriously on a small holding close to Tiruvannamalai, moving there after she had retired from a career as a dentist in France, and was translating the works of a great sage from Tamil into French, bypassing the hyperbolic English currently available. Arlette had noticed Anna, sensed a firmer core beneath the apparent aimlessness. Against her own set of rules Arlette approached her, asked where she was travelling. She found the younger woman's aimlessness only confusion over a hasty change of plan when Anna's visit to Jammu Kashmir was thwarted by the death of its Sheikh and a ten day mourning period decreed, stopping all trains crossing that northern border. She had bought a ticket to the far south instead. Arlette smiled, she knew about synchronicities. *Perhaps you would like to follow me on to Tiruvannamalai*, the older woman said, *it is a holy place. You may visit me, after you have found a room at the ashram there. If they have one spare. Three days you are permitted to stay but if you ask for Sri Ramaswamy and mention my name you may, I only say may, be permitted longer.*

Reaching Madras Arlette led Anna to the bus station to catch the rickety old vehicle that would take them even further south. The journey took some hours. Arlette, fiercely independent, had not sat next to her and Anna was almost faint with hunger when the poor, very poor, old woman next to her undid a corner knot in her tattered field-worn sari and produced two small cucumbers. One she pushed into Anna's grateful hand. Smiles passed, a memory etched. Rounding a bend Anna's heart flipped over at her first sight of – Arunacala! The holy mountain. *Knowing* sizzled through the cells of her body. She would have the feeling again at her first sight of Mount Ararat, of Montsegur, of Glastonbury Tor, and of the pink granite monolith of Cudtheringa in the warm tropics of far North Queensland. They were portals to the *Other*, places of power time beyond mind; other lives, other centuries. Being in such places she could re-member threads and sacred footfalls.

Arlette left Anna at the small terminus of bustling Tiru, stipulating a time to visit and directions to her cottage. Anna paused at a street stall to buy bananas, deaf to the plaintive *Ma! Ma!* insistent at her elbow. She barely knew how to treat beggars and in her tired state didn't turn to respond. Instead she bought a second hand of bananas and then, turning, thrust them toward the plaintive sound. As she held them forth the old wizened beggar gazed at her, and raised two stumps. Leprosy had taken his hands. Compassion flooded Anna. Gently she put the hand of bananas onto his arms and brought her own palms together in *namaste*. She felt very small in that moment, and humbled.

Sri Ramaswamy offered Anna a large airy room filtered green and cool by large trees shading the barred windows. *Monkeys*, he said, nodding at the window grills, *and you must be locking your door every time you leave. You may stay as long as you need. Meals are in the main hall* ... on banana leaf platters, Anna was charmed to discover.

She settled in gratefully, loved the tropical air of South India, like silk it kissed her skin and reminded her of her childhood in Malaya, before acrimony had rent the innocent fabric of 'family' and had proved it a fantasy. Had she really come far in her understanding of the deeper verities, she wondered, as memories gained clarity. The memory of *grace* made her smile – yes, she *had* lived in a way others criticized as folly, but that folly was the thread of inner Obedience only she could follow. Folly, follow, fool, Fools of God – were they linked? Obedience opened her at every loss, to gain; she knew marrow deep that she could only have lived the way her own narrative had fallen: following that inner Obedience was not a choice but an Imperative. She felt she had two spirits and only one faced the world; a double lifeline on her right hand, a blueprint Anna had no choice but to live by. This was no Fate line, but a line of her own weaving, the whisper from true North to her soul.

Anna adapted to the slow rhythm of the ashram routine in the blink of her eye, loved sitting on the floor eating from banana leaves or on plates of stitched peepul leaves, thrown away after each use. She sat in the Temple as the chanting flooded her blood and woke ancient memories. Twice she did the *pradakshina* around the mountain, a three and a half hour walk, always with the mountain on her right but walking to the left of the path so the *devas* which chose to accompany her remained close to the mountain side. She discovered caves inhabited by holy men.

Mani Swami had travelled from his native village in the most southern part of Tamil Nadu many decades before. Pausing at Arunacala he had *darshan* of Ramana Maharshi, but something in his destiny pulled him north. Besides, Virupraksha was occupied in those years by a fiery swami nowhere ready to leave his post. Many years passed, until Mani Swami had a dream in which he was told to hurry, hurry south back to Arunacala, the mountain itself was calling him. He woke, gathered his ektara, his thin bedroll and few food utensils to make haste on the slow trains of the time to arrive finally at Tiruvannamalai – to hear the death chant for the swami caretaker of the Virupraksha cave who had died that very morning. Mani Swami had been travelling for three days. He walked up the mountain to where his new 'home' was waiting.

Anna sat on the low wall listening, enthralled, by his story. A chameleon sat on the wall with her, changing his colours, standing sentinel. A large black crow flew down to land at the stone lingam. Mani Swami paused in his tale, watching the crow. The crow watched Anna. Then he walked a few crow paces in his crow way and picked up a small fallen leaf. He returned to the lingam, watching Anna who was watching him, all the while Mani Swami remained silent. Crow dropped the leaf into the yoni base of the lingam, cocked his head to one side eyeing Anna, walked toward her and flew off. Anna looked at Mani Swami, who was smiling.

This crow, said the gentle old man, *is a reincarnation of Ramana's pet crow who stayed with him to his death. When the crow died it was re-born with consciousness of itself because Ramana had loved it. Love is yeast,* he continued, *it is the leavening. Because this crow was loved it will raise the consciousness of all Crows.* Anna thought of Jasper, how much she loved him, her cat of cats. Mani Swami perceived her thoughts: *When we love a creature very very much it is this love that raises the consciousness of its species, our love for them helps in their evolvement. We must all evolve,* he said, *and Love is the mystery.*

Mani Swami looked up at the sun: *Now I must go to the Temple for my biksha meal,* he said, *would you like I lock you inside the cave while I am away? You will be with the saint for more than one hour. I must lock against monkeys and tourists.* Anna said *Yes.* Whether she would like it or not she wouldn't know, but she knew that a gift like that – no one ever got past Mani Swami into the inner sanctum of his cave – demanded from her that *Yes.*

The cave inside was dark and deep. Little light penetrated beyond the outer part of the cave where Mani Swami had a small strung *charpoy* and a tidy pile of dhotis, two, she assessed, some tin mugs, a small burner and tins of tea and sugar and condensed milk. A spoon sat on a ledge, a cotton throw folded over the wooden end of the *charpoy*; a *neti* pot, a bucket and a small tin sat in the corner. Anna pondered on the simplicity of her own poverty – it didn't compare.

As her eyes grew accustomed to the dark she could make out the mound in front of her, covered with a clean *geru* dhoti and ringed with fresh marigolds at its base. It was a very large mound. Too large, she thought, to be the ashes of the saint; why, its diameter, as she looked, was at least three feet across and rose to a reasonable height. Her criticism was cursory, the legend was all, she suspended judgment. The story was four? five? hundred years old. The village of Tiruvannamalai was then governed by disparate factions each threatening warfare with the other. One day the headmen of each faction took his grievances to the holy man who lived in that cave for him to decide how to settle. The holy man was wise, he knew whatever answer he gave would not satisfy the other party. *Come back to me tomorrow,* he said, *and you will have your answer.*

That evening a strange comet was seen crossing the sky, flaring brilliantly and briefly before it sank, apparently behind Arunacala itself. The following morning the villagers made their separate approaches to the cave – to find a pile of ashes on the ledge Anna was seated in front of now. The holy man had self-immolated. The villagers were distraught, all antipathies forgotten. They had lost their beloved saint. Thenceforth the villagers united in their grief and a succession of holy men had claimed, had been called almost by intuitive divination, the right to live in the cave. Mani Swami was its true successor. Anna knew she was honoured and although meditation didn't come the time went so swiftly she experienced no cause for concern at the locked grill keeping her there.

Mani Swami returned, she thanked him and walked back down the mountain for her own lunch before walking to Arlette for a different kind of nourishment.

Anna studied many of the great myths of the mountain in the library of the ashram; this kind of knowledge came easily, as if the printed word was already mirrored in her deep mind, reflected up, as it were, from her Far Memory. She couldn't have said this then, but Arlette would hint at it, observing Anna's facility for absorption. The legend of the birth of Arunacala moved Anna profoundly with its many-layered interpretations, for myths are a wild way of telling the truth, a form of thinking. Anna knew instinctively, years before she found her Jungian analyst who helped sort out the need for her to resolve, dissolve, her mother's odium, that myth was the mirror she would look through to see the moment of severance in herself, the many cuts of her own life: divorce, death, separation, loss. Myth, she knew even then, was the lament of ancestors trembling at the edge of our vision, not only her personal vision but the earth's vision, for the earth itself thinks in myth.

The myth of the mountain sent her perception sizzling out of her own skin: Brahma and Vishnu were arguing (as male gods do) over who was the greater. Behind them was a column of fire that had no end. Brahma set a task: *I'll go to the highest heaven and you go to the deepest depths, whoever returns with a sign from the edge of Eternity beyond this fire is the greater.*

Brahma was a crafty one and took the form of a swan, but exhausted after a thousand years of never reaching the highest heaven where the flames would cease, he found a small flower, plucked it and asked it to lie to his success when he met Vishnu again. The sweet smelling flower agreed to the duplicity, and, as they approached the plane of earth and saw Vishnu ascending from its depths with nothing to show for his efforts, the lie was told – the colossal column of fire each had sought to measure exploded into stars and lightning and thunder and Shiva, first of the Cosmic Trinity, revealed – Himself. He spoke, condemning Brahma: prayers would never be offered to him. Shiva was the greatest of all the gods and all gods were born of him. As the fiery column subsided it solidified in this Kali Yuga, this age of darkness, to become the earth and rock which made up the mountain of Arunacala. Anna hadn't the woman-wit then to question the gender of the birthing of the gods from a god and not a goddess but Arlette went on to tell her something so profound it shook her womancore and settled for the right year in Anna's life to emerge from her own depths to be re-born, far in the future as she recovered from a difficult hysterectomy, as her Womanroar: *Shiva is inert,* said Arlette sagely, *without Shakti to vivify him the world would cease — Shakti is the flame of Creation, She is the flame of the Dance of Shiva as Nataraj, She is the Dance itself, She is the Prakriti that vivifies Purusha. Shakti is before all that exists, She is the Wisdom of the Apocrypha in the Catholic tradition:* Before God, I was, *said Wisdom. The west rejects this, and has divorced man from creation to the detriment of all life other than the life of that ego which man — and woman — consider supreme.*

Anna stopped writing; fingers at rest on her laptop, amazed once more at what she recalled. Chronology was unimportant, the golden threads which compelled her thinking were an interconnecting web and linear time was out of synch. Such thoughts were the tessera of her life; random and wild they would fall as they came; coloured piece by coloured piece.

The earth may think in myths of mountains and fire and floods but over her life she had seen its destruction, whole species exterminated; knew that humans no longer looked on those wild edges, humanity had shrunk into self, consumed in a central vortex of narcissism, always focused on something at the centre of the individual life, focused on a screen, a phone, a computer *her* child, *his* successes, while the beautiful earth went to hell.

We need to be dreamt by the earth, the land, to be reborn, she sighed to Self, *heaven is the great Betrayal, the biggest lie there is;. It is here in our precious earthy body, a body made up of stardust, where we must live the life we dreamt into being. The addiction to transcendence keeps us in a coma, tells us desires are absurd, passion for justice naive, that we can abuse our beautiful Earth because matter itself is an illusion. The addiction to transcendence is the ultimate heroin.*

Through her life she had met countless people, Old Faith and New Age, it hardly mattered what belief system, dreaming of a transcendence which would keep them high and self-absorbed. It translated as ecocide.

Transcendence, ran Anna's fingers on the lap-top, *is the kindergarten awareness of the first step on the path. The journey is to bring this awareness into the body, to know the transformation which infuses matter with light. Then the Earth is seen as light; body and personality become soul-infused.*

Soul-infused.

Time with her Jungian served as a springboard to open new worlds of access: *Myth is not 'a long time ago'; myth is the wild edge of truth, of Now,* she tapped out in slow fingerfalls, gathering thoughts as she typed; *homogenising and pasteurizing the world, as the west is bent on doing, only confirms the quiet voice of Hopkins, that poet of the Mystery:*

> *And all is seared with trade; bleared, smeared with toil;*
> *And wears man's smudge and shares man's smell: the soil*
> *Is bare now, nor can foot feel, being shod ...*

No God's Grandeur; now, even *the pied beauty of dappled things* was silenced. Today the poet priest would weep. Anna's fingers tapped like a mystic code on the waiting keyboard, bringing up reminiscences long jumbled in her mind.

The following morning she walked to Virupraksha to see Mani Swami, to say goodbye; her days, many more than three, were coming to an end. She knew she would return, but he was an old man and she could not know that he would be there when she came again.

The morning was cool, it was December, the breeze as she climbed higher and rounded the mountain edge brought waking noises from the village below, clanging bells from the Temple, scents of sandalwood incense and something indefinably floral. Her sense of smell, and her sense of hearing, were acute. She paused to take in the sounds and scents. A stone jutted out conveniently, she sat, her back against the mountain, as the breeze eddied and flowed with its sensual gifts. Her skin prickled as a different sound reached her – *but not my ears,* she was to say to Mani Swami, *it touched my whole body, I heard it with my skin; and it came from the mountain, is it possible?*

He asked her to describe it: *High tensile voices,* she could only explain, *almost like wind in high wires, but there are no wires, and it was inside the stones, inside the mountain ... it was inside me, I felt suffused with sound.*

Mani Swami smiled: *That sound is The Sound, the Nada Brahman, the Sound of God. I have heard it; living here, inside the mountain it comes as a blessing.*

Anna's skin prickled a zillion pinpricks. *Nada Brahman* – she knew she could never speak of it, almost forever. Forty years later Anna heard Susan Richards speak on BBC Radio 3 of hearing a forest in Russia sing; *No one with me could hear it,* she said, *it sang in harmonics, high, like wind in high wires; but there were no wires there in a Russian forest.* She had heard the World's Tonic Note.

You have a difficult Path, said Mani Swami kindly to Anna, *you will be alone and only with God. Teachers you will have but few few friends. You are blessed.*

As she left Mani Swami that last time the resonance of the Sound hummed in her bones. She had waited a thousand lifetimes for this birth. She hurried to Arlette for a last lunch together, until next time. Conversation, as all their conversations did, charted a course to a story:

Arlette's cottage did not have a beam. Arlette was a French woman of that practical bent in whom romantic flimflam was given no quarter. She had limited money, had retired early from her profession and wise investments back in France meant she could live in comfortable frugality as a westerner in India for as long as she wished. She needed to build a house on her leased land and she did. It sat, a most charming cottage of whitewashed mud brick with a palm thatched roof, in a large walled garden with a couple of wells and a small outside tank as a bath.

She had a periodic generator which provided light, and bottled gas for cooking. Her garden provided year round vegetables and an occasional gardener put in the hard graft. Wealthier western neighbours, Germans who spent their northern winter months in warmer India, lived quite some distance from Arlette and came to watch the building progress, offering all manner of German advice, none of which the practical French woman paid heed to. Especially when it came to The Beam.

Earth tremors were common in that part of Tamil Nadu and mud brick cottages had no foundations, the Germans and their mansion required beams to underpin the structure. When their house was being built to serious German specifications, over huge supporting beams which underpinned it, they warned Arlette time and again that she would need beams if there was an earthquake. There was an earthquake, not a huge one, but enough to cause more than a little damage to the German mansion. Quite a lot of damage in fact. They hurried over to Arlette, certain of being met with disaster. All was in order as Arlette greeted them. *But*, the Germans said in surprise and more than a little miffed, *you have no beam, how is this possible?* Arlette smiled benignly and said: *I do have a beam you know, it is the Beam of Grace.*

Arlette championed Anna's peripatetic search, they corresponded from time to time, met twice more in those early years. Learning of Anna's dysfunctional family Arlette firmly said: *Your family's standing in the world and your own – barely crawling – is irrelevant. Trust the golden thread that guides you. You will be judged by worldly minds,* twice Anna had heard that, in the space of one day, *you will fall short of all worldly expectations; it will be hard to justify an existence supported by government but remember that you are supported by Invisible Means, just as my cottage is supported by the Beam of Grace. They are the same. You will learn to walk in a sacred manner.*

A sacred manner – how did one walk 'in a sacred manner' Anna thought for a moment, but not too long, for life was knocking her sideways with blows falling at her from left and right and behind. Smiling *now*, but not *then*, she looked though her own kaleidoscope to see a Very Straight line emerging from dodging all those tsunamis. She had no choice: *'Keep walking'* was the Imperative: *There is nothing to trust, the only way is to keep straight on.*

She was nearly old. From time to time she did think she was blessed. Her grass roots travelling had shown her truths from which to assess a strange privilege of birthright. Anna did not have the emotional and inherited security of women in the villages of Tamil Nadu or the Taurus mountains, women who were poor materially, but who knew their family and their place in the world about them; nor of the black nomad tents around the foothills of Mount Ararat of Kurdistan; neither the networks of extended families throughout India, wealthy or no. All those women knew their community and their position in it. Extended families were their world. Anna had none of these, and then, nowhere to lay her head. She could have died anywhere and who would know? But, she had a kind of freedom and her numerous and quite legitimate passports permitted her to travel wherever she was Called. Not for her the camel trains and porters and cooks of a Freya Stark or a Gertrude Bell, or even the young companion of Alexandra David-Néel, much less the lifelong financial support from that traveller's long-suffering husband! But the privilege of her passports, she held three different nationalities at various times, allowed her to walk anywhere in the world. *They* were her birthright.

10

Weaving

Before meeting Arlette, before her trips back to India as an adult, Anna returned to England to search for her father. Deep-frozen inside her were memories; striding over the Sussex Downs while her father expounded binary sequences, which she understood at the age of six by seeing the pictures in his head as he spoke – and losing all comprehension of such lofty matters the minute he changed the subject to something other. When he spoke of math and music it was the language of math with which he spoke. He told her of the farthest stars, of infinite integers, rational and irrational numbers, and the elements of atomic particles. He spoke of mathematical symmetries deeper than mind or matter. Anna 'saw' all he said, by osmosis and the shared blood in their veins.

He treated her as an equal and she loved him, he was her sun and moon and stars but he couldn't save her from the cruelty of her mother. He couldn't save himself from the cruelty of his wife either. Anna was twenty going on twelve when she returned from Australia to England to look for him but time had changed all their lives, there could be no going back to that innocence she had stored in deep freeze. Her father's second wife wanted no part of his earlier life, would block, for fifty years, every attempt of Anna to re-establish any bond with her father. She re-connected with her two aunts, her father's much older sisters, Alice and Zabeth, doughty spinsters living richly fulfilling and rewarding lives. Neither was able to breach the blockade, though each tried. Memories of Alice, the more eccentric of the two, warmed the cockles of Anna's heart.

In her later years Alice indulged in an afternoon nap, occasionally reflecting on why the English (her mother was French, after all) resisted simple pleasures like siestas and winter heating twenty-four-seven and double glazing and snow tyres and down duvets and cooking mushrooms with white wine and butter and garlic. Life here was so *puritanical* at times, she tut-tutted to Anna, and Anna, aghast at seeing her aging aunt bent double as she washed sheets by hand in the bath tub, insisted she buy for herself a washing machine. Perhaps that puritan need to suffer, *suffering is good for you,* was the inheritance her aunt unwittingly carried. Cromwells had successfully destroyed Merrie England just as Calvin, a similarly humourless man, had discoloured her aunt's homeland. Alice's French mother had married a Swiss, a *protestant* Swiss, her lack of washing machine, a Calvin denial.

It occurred to Alice in her older age that what she loved about Catholic France and Orthodox Greece was their open devotion to the Mother of God, and in Hindu India, God as Mother, a *Goddess*; a devotion lost in protestant lands in which the four-letter words of Mary, Mass, Pope and Pray raised many a hackle. In France, Alice knew, the feminine expression of daily life, a love of fine food, a good kitchen, flowers, children, warmth, dance, music, *abundance,* was quite apparent. The Calvinist church of her parents fitted well in puritan, Protestant, England. Her father, long time Pastor of the Swiss Church in Endell Street, held visions of a religious unity and tolerance far beyond his pulpit, his inheritance to Alice an underlying spiritual generosity, always reaching out to other faiths, other races.

I am a Stately English Galleon in Full Sail, Alice smiled and her tiny Bengali lover agreed, though he knew she hadn't a drop of English blood in her veins. A pharmacist, they had met fifty years before, named her his Great White Goddess; she tucked him under her arm like a packed lunch when they travelled to Calcutta to meet his eminent family. Alice adored India and the Indians she met loved her. Unable to bear him the children that Indians so love, she had refused to marry Santosh, he had married a mutual friend who, with an equally generous nature, sent her husband to his first love every Thursday for the rest of their lives. *She is Indian in her heart,* said his wife secure in her knowing that Alice's dedication to the flotsam of children she collected was absolute and made the marriage inviolate.

Alice established Homes for Autistic Adults, for which she was awarded an M.B.E. in her seventies, an honour that deflected her much younger brother's teasing of her ample form and more ample heart. Alice had known 'Anastasia', their shared love for India with its spiritual heritage enriched their interior lives.

When Alice had met Mrs Tweedie for the first time Mrs Tweedie had stood up. Alice was framed in the doorway behind her niece. Tweedie and Alice *flowed* towards each other across that room, people parted like the Red Sea, and watched amazed as the two snow-haired octogenarians bowed to each other, palms together in that timeless Indian gesture of greeting. The air in the room pulsed with Presences: the two women *knew* each other, other lives, other times.

That first day Alice remained in meditation long after the half hour and Mrs Tweedie asked Anna: *Bring your aunt back, she has gone too deep this time.* Later, Tweedie sent Alice to a private group, a handful of people, in the nearby home of Margaret, a woman who shared Alice's vocation with autism. It was a blessed meeting. Fine people gathered around Margaret, people who went to deepen their relationship with God in the anonymity of her home. They were rich years for Alice; who would attend until her death. Dame Janet Baker went there when she could; she described Tweedie in her autobiography as: *A Sufi and a Saint.* Mrs Tweedie would say: *And when Dame Janet sings the Angel in The Dream of Gerontius her voice is infused by the Angelic Realms.*

Alice was a generous celebration of a woman, her tiny flat in Bound's Green with its bright orange-walled dining room was open to all comers, including an opportunist from Nigeria who fleeced her of all but the darns on cardigans. Guy found the blatant abuse of his sister's generosity galling, but the flaw in Alice's nature included a white gene of guilt towards the emergent black race and this particular sallow-faced Sam – his name *was* Sam, and his sallow air the result of his dissolute nightlife – had insinuated himself into their church to pounce on spinsters. When Alice died Sam, flying in first class from Geneva where he lived, bedded in to her flat like a squatter, demanding £25,000 to move out. He didn't win.

Alice thought it a tragedy her niece didn't speak her family tongue. French was so much more nuanced than English and she and Zabeth always spoke it together. She consoled herself with the fact that she and her niece spoke Cat exceedingly well, in that language of the heart which all cats understand. She had little affection for Guy's first wife, Anna's mother: *A difficult woman,* she said, *didn't like her own mother, you know; she didn't like us much either, and she certainly,* she paused before she could even admit it, so beyond her own thinking was it, *didn't love you. That burden, blood carries karma, the Biblical sins of generations ....* Alice picked at the darn on her cardigan, a frown rippling her broad forehead.

She looked up, watching her niece's face: *I couldn't have children of my own. This is why I love the little damaged ones, why I have this school.* She paused, took a quiet breath, and: *I have never told you this, but when you were born Guy was so excited he came straight from the hospital to Zab and I and told us to get our coats and go back with him:*

Now! P-P-P-Pat's had her baby, he stammered!

He drove us madly back to the hospital, so excited he was. But your mother ... Alice paused, sighed, continued: *Pat had turned her head to the wall, the nurses didn't know what to do, she refused to hold you, refused to feed you... refused to touch you and ... she refused ... to let any of us touch you; even your own father. None of us knew what to do, we wanted to cuddle you. We weren't allowed. The nurse couldn't override Pat's refusal. You were so alone, so sad, looking at the ceiling as if you knew where you had come from. Guy and Zab wouldn't see it, they were too upset, but I knew you wanted to go Home. The reason you have come was washed away by the flood of oxytocin in Pat's womb as you were born.*

Anna sat very still, very very still. She found herself in a place before she had language. Abandoned. After the loss of her own daughter she had suffered soul-loss, again. It would take much of her life to integrate her mind into herSelf; even longer to integrate into her *body*. Hugging people was anathema, she would roundly resist all save hugs from very dear people, and they were few. Never cuddled as a child, never touched, never held, Alice's words were too sad to hear. Anna, when she had grown to almost teenage, had tried to hug her mother, had seen her hold and cuddle and kiss Stephanie. Her mother's eyes, as she shook off Anna's attempt at intimacy, blazed cold, lazer-incised. Ice *burns*.

It had fallen to Alice and Zabeth and an eccentric Swiss governess to bring up their younger siblings when their mother had died. Guy was eight, youngest of the six children born to the beautiful Frenchwoman. Their father, the Swiss pastor, died, it was said, of a broken heart too few years later. Decades later Guy himself was found in a ditch having swallowed a bottle of pills in an attempt at suicide at his wife's leaving him for *that young Hicks*. He later married the straitlaced woman from the Borders whose Baptist version of God was made in the image of man, a rather small-minded man. Alice's breadth of vision was a conversational challenge at family gatherings. Anna's breadth of vision, coloured in *geru*, put her beyond the pale.

Alice offered her passerine niece the sofa bed in her lounge as a temporary perching place whenever she came from Australia with her suitcase of hopes, but Guy was slow in getting to know his daughter. They met three or four times a year in various tearooms, he took her to Kenwood House. Anna needed to believe, like Sally Bowles, that her father loved her.

Anna was excluded from her father's house from the time she had found him again at the age of twenty. Four decades later she was still waiting in the wings when he died. Alice and Zabeth had died years before, no one bothered to tell her at the time, she learnt the news after the two funerals. She focused on the only family funeral she had ever known of to attend – her father's.

When she learnt of it Anna was paralysed with indecision. The family had excluded her for more than half a century, a hurdle of consequence she couldn't overcome alone. She deliberated until a friend said: *If the second wife didn't exist would you attend your father's funeral?* Anna's *Yes* was the answer she needed to hear from Self. She went to stay with a friend in north Wales. Bolstered by Penny's cups of tea, sound food and solid insistence Anna was able to drive over to Stafford and attend that funeral. *He's your father,* said Penny, *and nothing changes that.* It was a challenge. Yet Anna was, after all, her father's firstborn, and she loved him. It would require all the courage she could summon. She went, and arrived early. The woman funeral director walked her to the front pew. *I know families, and some,* said this no-nonsense woman in a ringing voice, *are terrible. You sit – here.*

The funeral parlour filled, and filled, and filled. Her father, long-retired, was held in high esteem by his old students of UMIST, by members of Woodland Trusts, National Trusts, Mencap, Remap, Chess fraternities, Musical trusts, Math brains, students of the world and a whole universe of intellectual interests. Anna learned more about her father in one hour than in her whole lifetime.

Her father's coffin was there in front of her, slightly right of centre. In due time the congregation stood to sing the final hymn. Suddenly the heavy blue curtains parted and her father's coffin began to glide into a space beyond sight and the hefty curtains closed behind it.

Something snapped in her. *That's my father!* Anna's heart howled, and its cry shook her soul. *You can't take him – I, I don't know him yet,* and she stepped from her aisle seat

94

in the front row and in an instant parted the curtains to enter the space. The curtains fell heavy behind her, all sound blocked. She put her hands on the coffin. Words whirled around her head, she collected a few and said softly the ones that were right and true. A sound, as clear as a crystal bell, sounded from the ceiling above her in the small but sacred space of the dead, coalesced into a voice she *knew*. Anna stood astonished at the amazing grace which only she would know: *Sweetie*, said the voice, using his so-familiar address, *I am so glad you came*. Anna looked up in wonder. The booming, smiling, voice faded, her face softened, she could say goodbye.

Anna parted the curtains and came out to hear the last verse of – *Amazing Grace*. She barely registered the round O's of astonishment that made up the rows of people who had witnessed her; people who didn't know their departed friend had a *daughter!*

Anna was last to go out, which meant she stood first in the family line-up as people filed out of the chapel. *And the last shall be first* – and she *had* inherited her father's thespian inclinations. Small and plump, fine hair elfin short, even he remarked on his daughter's resemblance to the great actress. The pith of Anna's memory of that day became her Judi Dench Moment. She *felt* her father smile. *We didn't know,* said all the members of all the Trusts and all the Associations and all the Fraternities her father's passions had supported over long years, as they filed past, shook her hand, to hear a smiling Anna introduce herself by name as her father's firstborn from his first marriage. Members of the second wife's family gave her a wide berth, shot her looks that would curdle cat bile. Anna's tears, when she shed them later in the safety of Penny's company, were of regret, regret for the failure of ever establishing the relationship she ached for. When her heart's wellspring had dried, the memory of her audacity at her father's funeral brought a Cheshire Cat grin to her aging face and, she would admit it, a purring comfort to her soul.

Out of her loss came an unexpected gift – a hare and a hoopoe. They demanded to be painted, to be *birthed*.

They were sacred beings, the Hare to the wild edges of its landscape, for the hare has fairy-blood coursing through its veins, and the Hoopoe, central to Attar's parable *The Conference of the Birds* and to Anna's time in the Forest when the Heavenly Horse came to her. Their execution came under the guidance of a brilliant wildlife artist at two live-in workshops and, with no previously known skills, Anna had been obedient to every brush stroke. That she had too little money to continue under his inspirational tuition bothered her a little, but not hugely.

Anna loved the landscape and the legends of mid Wales, that wild country. There, hares have long been associated with magic and the ability to walk between worlds and to connect with the Other. They danced at a slant to the universe. St Melangell lived at a slant to the universe, differently, she changed the mindset of the Prince of Powys back in the fifth century. The hare was a totem of mystery and misunderstanding, the hare may simply do things *differently*. The persecuted, dear hare, the cat-o'-the-woods, stands out from the sea of sames – does things her own way. Anna did things her own way, aslant to the universe and it was the Hare who came to her after her father's funeral, and after it the Hoopoe, demanding of her unpracticed hand their own holy portrait.

11

Thinking

Reminiscences, other deaths, other lands: Fern, France, Benedictines and ... Bataclan. 13th November 2015. The world had shrunk by the time of Bataclan. Anna's worldly wanderings had set her, in her late fifties, down in Glastonbury to bloom where she was planted. She felt the tragedy of Bataclan penetrate marrow deep. France was her father's mother's blood. After his death Anna's unresolved relationship had shifted from a major to a minor key with the awakening that she, too, was more French than English in her appearance, in her sensibilities and in her crisper communication with all. She had not inherited the English gift of phatic communion; a Frenchman had once alerted her to: *Viva la difference: the English are too polite to be honest; we French are too honest to be polite.* The difference explained that common English animosity to the French – Anna had a friend who still spat arrows over the Norman invasion a thousand years before.

The aftershock of Bataclan compelled her to go to Paris to pray in solidarity with Parisians, with all of France. The city was subdued, quiet, as people continued to go about their days just as they did before Friday the 13th. On the morning of that same day, Friday the 13th November 2015, ten thousand miles away on the other side of the earth, her oldest friend died. It was morning there, and she died just as the world was learning of the tragedy to the beloved city she had never seen.

Far away and long ago it was Fern who had given Anna back her name, the *patrimoine héréditaire,* denied her by her mother when she had left Anna's father to re-marry *that young Hicks*. The new family had migrated to Australia and in the transmigration Anna was, under her mother's obdurate coercion, morphed into a new identity, told to take her mother's new surname. The pretence repelled Anna who had thenceforth set her own name in deep-freeze. *Nigelle* was the name her father had given her at birth; her mother had no name to give the baby she didn't want. Eleven year old Anna searched for a first name she could team with Hicks: *Carole*. With an 'e'. *Carolicks* in the Australian vernacular was *truly* ugly. Anna lived with it through all her Australian school years.

Brisbane 1962. Anna was seventeen and living in Lady Musgrave Lodge, a sprawling old Queensland mansion run by two eccentric and elderly sisters providing a safe haven mainly for daughters of gentlemen graziers needing a city base. On the first morning of their first meeting Fern walked up to Anna with a smile that would melt tundra and exclaimed that with a face like hers she wasn't about to tell her that her name was Susan or Sheila – or *Carol*, was she? Haltingly, letting her tongue round the unfamiliar sound, Anna said slowly: *No; no, my name is ... Nigelle, Nigelle de Visme.*

At this point I pause, confused. Should the child 'Anna' from the Heavenly Horse now assume my own name? Should I continue in first person? Finally, knowing I want to give other players in my story the ability to think their own thoughts, I decide to remain Anna, third person. All is true – and the thoughts of those other players hover in the wings, accessible in the All is Now. I return, then, to the name of 'Anna'.

Fern's wide smile widened – you're *French!* Anna wasn't wholly French, only half, but the half which had been severed suddenly resurrected and her niche, and very French, name thawed, *sounded,* plumb-bob deep. The delight in Fern's voice silenced the facts of Anna's childhood; no need to spoil the fantasy of that pure moment. The two young women were so different, so alike. They shared the pleasure of cream teas in the Shingle Inn, French films at Alliance François, stories of tropical childhood, Fern had grown up in Fiji. Fern introduced her to Dagmar Nemeçek, a poetess of many names, a Czech refugee haunted by terrors only she could see. Dagmar, a generation older, expanded Anna's cultural world, recognized a kindred spirit, took her to simple soirees at the riverside home of Pavel Forman; Pavel, elder brother to Miloš whose own remembered horrors of 1968 would eventually birth cathartic others: *One Flew Over The Cuckoo's Nest,* his most evocative.

Now, over half a century later Anna was in Paris. She and Fern had never made it there together over their long friendship. Told as a young girl she would not have long to live, Fern had gone on to live long. She outlived three surgeons; survived them all, survived with only half a lung, the other one and a half removed when she was eleven, survived with no spleen, numerous new knees, hands clawed with arthritic cruelty, transplanted liver. Her smile remained. But now, on this morning of memory, her featherlight body had given up the ghost under anaesthetic while waiting for yet another knee replacement. Fern had died almost the moment the terror of Bataclan shattered her beloved France a world away.

Notre-Dame de Paris rose high on the other side of the Seine, the queue to enter stretched an hour or more across the plaza as people and handbags were scrutinized by security at its great doors. Anna doubted she had the wherewithal to stand in a queue that long. So soon after Bataclan the holy place was armisticed with security. The whole of Paris was armisticed with security for COP21.

In time she ventured across the bridge and hovered, uncertain, by the front end of the endless queue. A strange magic shadowed her uncertainty: a large man approached to transect the queue. As he did so the couple he passed in front of stepped back to let him through without pausing in their conversation. In that nano-second a small black-coated invisibly-old woman stepped sprightly into the space he left. Conversation continued; no frisson of curiosity alarmed anyone of her interception. Three people ahead of her ... and then she was at the door, her bag, an apricot pacsafe, explored, a smile, and a wave, and Anna was through.

She moved to the right and walked down the side aisle not knowing quite where to leave the book she had brought as her gift of peace, a book she had written, or where to sit and pray. Anna walked slowly, glanced left across the nave ... and fell out of her skin. Breath ceased. Her feet took root right where she stood. She became an amalgam of goosebumps. There, right along the nave hung vast tapestries of such splendour, such colour and fine detail, their beauty took her breath away. They were the living tapestries of the postcards she had carried with her for more than twenty years – since her Obedience to the task set her by a very holy man almost quarter of a century ago.

12

Setting the Warp

The Black Madonna. The Queen of All Creation. The Para Shakti. Avyakta Prakriti. What vast cosmic realities Anna's small life had been blessed to receive. *Obedience,* she said to people who asked how she had come to know of such things, *Obedience with a Very Capital O.* But, she would add, seriously: *How low can we bow in surrender to Obedience, to life?* She would tell some, very few, of her friends of the task set her by a great and holy man who had asked her to follow his 'journey to the Black Madonna' over porridge at breakfast one morning. Porridge had never tasted so good. He recognized, long years before she did, that Anna's journey through Indian metaphysics made her heiress to his penultimate experience. Anna acknowledged the thought a quarter of a century later when, as an old woman, she felt again the benison of India.

Father Bede Griffiths. How they met could only have been, Anna reflected, guidance by Grace. By then she had been gifted yet another name, Sitadevi, had become a swami, a teacher, in a traditional yoga order. Sita was born from a furrow when the earth opened; Anna's newly given name should have alerted her to *something,* a hint that her small place on the planet listed at a distinct degree to the universe at large. She saw things. Felt things. Had been born with a caul, her fontanelle, under it, remained a soft, pulsing membrane at the crown of her head as vulnerable as a papered window in a storm; a gift, said some, which granted second sight. A broken and hanging branch of a tree would call her as she walked to school, diverting her journey by a street or two to touch the tree and apologize for the roughness of the boys who had mindlessly snapped its branch in passing. A kindle of abandoned kittens in a grass verge dumped by a busy road, taken home and found loving homes for; a fledgling fallen from its nest; an emu shackled by nylon rope cutting into its leg, proud flesh growing over the killing capture; a goat trapped in quick sand; moths beating against window panes, glowing lamps – all came under her aegis for protection, for rescue, and all creatures great and small called to her. She heard them. Hadn't the Hoopoe and the Heavenly Horse come from Other Worlds to guide her?

When she was given the name Sitadevi her mouth widened in her customary O of astonishment: *How did you know?* she asked the small, feline-graced, Indian swami who had looked above her head for long moments, looking at *something* she had no cognition of, under the fiery Australian sun at his ashram north of Sydney. How *could* he know that on the other side of the planet over a decade before that moment Anna had asked for a rare book to be brought up from the archives of a City library somewhere in the north-west of England, a bleak and cruel place with coarse accents and even coarser food, and had sat reading it all day? The day had fallen out of its framework in that library, had become a world and in that world an entire tableau had unfolded before Anna's eyes as Sita and Rama played out their cosmic drama in a mythical forest in India, far, far from where she sat reading. In that wood panelled smelling-of-polish and thick-with-silence Reading Room Anna was no longer Anna, or even Nigelle – she was a Shadow of Sita. And here was an Indian giving her a name she already knew in her soul: *It is meaning devoted to God,* said a visiting Indian woman, smiling at Anna's astonishment that the Quest for Sita echoed a Quest for Self.

Anna had then, as Sitadevi, made the journey to India where she had met Arlette; Arlette, who had seen how ill Anna really was after her months in India eating food as she found it. Arlette's unbidden rescue of Anna saved her life. She fed Anna fresh eggs from her hens and steamed vegetables from her garden until Anna took on a healthier hue. The respite was only temporary. When the time came to fly home to Australia two gazelle-eyed Indian Airline hostesses propped Anna up between them like a sandwich as they came through Perth – anyone ill and flying in from 'unhygienic' India was made to disembark at the first airport any plane landed and Perth was a continent away from Sydney where Anna needed to be. All the passengers were sprayed in the aircraft of course, though that discourteous Australian regulation did little other than insult those coming in from first world countries. Once Anna reached Sydney the sunglasses hiding her jaundice-yellow eyes came off, the hostesses left her and Customs ambulanced her straight to an isolated ward for infectious tropical diseases at Sutherland Hospital where Anna lay undiagnosed, and in a semi-coma, for weeks. She was not permitted visitors, and remembered nothing of those weeks except the reverse culture shock of the dazzlingly clean hospital toilet bowls. The first time she saw one, after her experience of the unmentionable squalor of India, she fell and hugged it, managing a weak laugh at herself as she struggled in her weakness to rise.

The staff asked for her next of kin, foolishly Anna answered their question from her haze of quite painless semi-consciousness. She knew her mother was living in Mosman, in the old manor house of the Theosophical Lodge along whose hallowed corridors had walked Mary Lutyens, Leadbeater and Krishnamurti, less than an hour's distance from Sutherland in that vast continent. Her mother's reply that she was *soooo* sorry, she was *far* too busy to come, and, no, she couldn't help her daughter with accommodation, but she would send a tin of Sustagen ... appalled the hospital staff. It was beyond their capacity to compute. Mothers love their children, right? Wrong.

A staff sister called a friend of Anna's, living with her ailing husband and three children in a three bedroom timber cottage in Heathcote, near the hospital, on the edge of the Royal National Park. Katharine would make room for Anna, somehow, despite her own concerns. Born deaf was challenge enough for Katharine, but now her husband

Ray had a rare blood disease requiring constant attention and monitoring. Katharine and Anna waited for the Sustagen which, like her mother's final promised sandwich decades later when Anna, in a wheelchair and told she would never walk again, never came. Anna no longer apologized for her mother and her piecrust promises.

Anna left when she was able to, collected Jasper, frail now, from friends, and went to Pearl Beach where she had been offered a room with Aub, who didn't mind cats at all. After a further week or three she was up and seeking nourishment. These were sun-filled days, she walked the beaches of the dazzling blue water-silk bay, climbed slowly the rocky boulders horseshoed around the sea separating Pearl Beach from Umina, Patonga, Woy Woy.

Anne had a beach house, a two room timber cottage with a huge front verandah and a bush garden home to wild birds and bandicoots. Anna saw Anne as a mentor, older and very wise. She was Australian and Irish and Catholic. She had married Gavin, a Scot and Gaelic. Anna met Anne in the space between her two loves, for Anne and Gavin had divorced after many a year and parenting four uncommonly bright boys. Anna took with her to Pearl Beach two books to enrich her convalescence and introduced them to Anne: Gavin Maxwell's *Ring of Bright Water* and Kathleen Raine's earliest version of *Collected Poems*. Instantly attractive to Anne for many-layered reasons, Kathleen's *Love Poem* moved her to tears:

> *Yours is the face that the earth turns to me,*
> *Continuous beyond its human features lie*
> *The mountain forms that rest against the sky.*
> *With your eyes, the reflecting rainbow, the sun's light*
> *Sees me; forest and flower, bird and beast*
> *Know and hold me forever in the world's thought,*
> *Creation's deep untroubled retrospect.*
>
> *When your hand touches mine it is the earth*
> *That takes me--the green grass,*
> *And rocks and rivers; the green graves,*

And children still unborn, and ancestors,
In love passed down from hand to hand from God.
Your love comes from the creation of the world,
From those paternal fingers, streaming through the clouds
That break with light the surface of the sea.

Here, where I trace your body with my hand,
Love's presence has no end;
For these, your arms that hold me, are the world's.
In us, the continents, clouds and oceans meet
Our arbitrary selves, extensive with the night,
Lost, in the heart's worship, and the body's sleep.

Anne and Anna met at the heart of the tragic relationship between Kathleen and Gavin, his passion for otters, their love of wildlife and the spiritual insight of Kathleen's poetry. *A Ring of Bright Water* became Gavin's legacy of his complex life, the tragedy of his otters.

Anne's friends were the Coburns, the Serventys, the Williamsons, Marea Gazzard, Margaret Olley, Jill Roe, Barbara Thiering, names making up the Who's Who of Australia at the time, and all part of Anne's charmed circle. Anna met them, was not too gauche to know she was only part of their virtual reality in Pearl Beach and far from their actual world of various successes back in Sydney. Vin Serventy referred to Jasper as her familiar; Barbara Coburn thought she might knit the pattern of his pretty chocolate pointed face into one of her brilliant jumpers. Her fame was silkscreen but she had recently bought a knitting machine and loved experimenting. Her husband John quietly contemplated designs for his abstract tapestries, murmuring to anyone in earshot that when he could merge all into a single point he would have understood God and the world. He had worked in France for some time, Aubusson wove his cartoons. His Curtain of the Sun for the Sydney Opera House was breathtaking in its colour and abstract simplicity. Perhaps he and Dom Robert may have met in one of the Aubusson ateliers, recognized each others' way of understanding the world and Nature, linked in their Catholicism, each processing the Great Mystery by ever refining and defining their art to a single expression: *l'ombelle,* the humble cow parsley or Queen Anne's Lace, for Dom Robert; the Still Point of the World for John.

Something profound struck Anna as John spoke of the Still Point. Something inchoate in her feelings about the world and her misfit in it: the complex and many-faceted confused her, her longing was for unity, Unity, a Still Point from which and out of which she could feel strong, secure on her own feet as the person she might come to know; a person who wasn't blown thither and yon in her search for that – *still point.* She felt the same about music too, the grandiose jangled her, where the profound simplicity of plainchant or the slow Hymn to the Devi soothed her and gave meaning to *calm;* Pärt's *Spiegel im Spiegel,* she felt, came distilled from the tears of the soul, Beethoven's 4th piano concert haunted her heart. The purity of a single note could send shimmering silences through her. In an entire book of words the power of a single well-turned sentence would cause her to stop reading, look up from the page, lost in something beyond herself. During a maths lesson at the mention of Infinity, applied to random numbers never reaching it, Anna's brain had parted company with her body for whole moments. Infinity! Why, that was where the Heavenly Horse had taken her.

There was a mystery about Sound. Words reverberating in the cosmos cause all kinds of repercussions. One must be careful, Anna knew, of their spoken force for words have a deity all their own, an unrelenting Goddess for good or ill. *Vāc* was the wife of Vision, Cosmic Sound. Anna saw sounds in colour, spoke words and sentences in coloured chords, synaesthesia. Every letter had a colour, subtly changing hue according to the colour on the letter next to it, but always retaining its foundation colour. Whole words married their own colours: Monday, maroon; Tuesday, smoke grey with golden green flecks and so on. She knew Sound became Vision – in the Beginning was the Word – and Creation, *was.* God spoke one Word: *Kun! Be!* and the world *was.*

When Sibelius was asked by the painter of his kitchen what colour green he would like the great composer answered with a musical note. Anna had seen green when a friend, an opera singer in Brisbane, had hit a mythical high note – it had leapt from her mouth, Anna watched amazed as it floated to the ceiling, began to descend an electric green that dazzled; *elf* green. Beethoven's fourth piano concerto, that liquid opening; Mitsuko Uchida called it: *Unbelievably spiritual, Beethoven dares to look up, he seeks for the Light.* This Anna understood. Mystical Sound became Body-Physical-Flesh.

Anna remained through that summer in Pearl Beach recovering in scintillating company. She grew apace, recounted whole diamond-bright conversations. Ideas blew through her mind like tornadoes. It alarmed her now to trace the long and obstacle-strewn path that led her to intellectual freedom and the gift of independent thought as she slowly developed a short-fuse against galloping assumptions, received opinions and categorical syllogisms. An irresponsible and interrupted schooling certainly helped, awaking as it did a bravado of freedom, quite necessary to survive her ignorance of each new curriculum in eleven different schools of schooling over as many years and nearly as many countries.

One light morning over breakfast on Anne's salt weathered timber verandah, Margot, visiting from Canada where she held two Chairs at McGill, charmed Anne and Jill with: *d'you know, Knut,* – Margot's current love, nephew of Dag Hammarskjöld – *went out last weekend and bought a Newspaper!* She didn't mean the Danish equivalent of the Sunday Australian, she meant an Entire Empire. Margot and Jill dazzled Anna: Chairs in triplicate, at least one AO and an Emerita – she could barely get her homespun little head around such luminosity. *But,* she said later, *they tolerated my ignorance and I learned and learned.*

Observations made in such company delighted Anna, less for their subject than the way word were used: *Like the Ancient Mariner X fixes one with a glittery eye and there's no escape* ... and: *Librarians at Balmain Library are so-o-o humourless, for a start they're all dressed in high fashion from Dachau ...* and: *Meals on the Indian Pacific catered for an amalgam of considerations ... pumpkin, sausages, pie — and passing through the smokers' carriages to the dining car was like the aftermath of Chernobyl.*

Anne had Anna's future welfare at heart. She saw Anna's life as a meandering art of improvisation and did not approve of such profligate waste of the intelligence she knew Anna was unaware of and fully capable of developing as a sensible, and financially stable, foundation for Life. *You need a five-year plan,* said Anne, smiling at Anna's wide-eyed astonishment of such an audacious appropriation of Time. Anna's life, unstable from the time she was born, could barely embrace the next five days of stable possibilities, much less a Five Year Plan. Anne bought newspapers, encouraged her to look for jobs. One carried an advertisement for places at Nepean College for Teacher Training. Anne convinced Anna she would walk through it. The same newspaper also offered a live-in position for a cook-housekeeper in the same town, and so Anna met the Parers, became the children's Mary Poppins, blown in on the wind, lived in her caravan at the bottom of their large garden where the Nepean River ran alongside.

The slow days passed, carrying away loss and abandonment. Mandy Parer's goldfish died and the river took its small goldenness with rites and prayers. Padre Parer was not amused at funeral rites for a fish. He didn't like cats either. Anna was fired, forestalling her career as a future teacher for, homeless again, she was unable to continue at the college.

Anna's beloved Jasper, so old, so frail, had died while she was there and the children honoured his passing with poems and a soft blanket to enfold his frail form. The vet had visited: *He is only alive because of your love,* he said in his thick Yugoslavian accent, *I come tomorrow, be with him one more night.* The next night Ivo returned and, while Anna held her beloved cat, gave the lethal injection into the gentle, tired creature. He left her holding him. Minutes late

108

a sharp rap on her caravan door and in rushed Ivo, tears running down his face, saying: *My keys! my keys, I left my keys!* Anna, dazed and uncomprehending, turned her head to the fridge, where sat the keys. *Ivo,* she said, *Ivo, I don't think Jasper is dead* ... Ivo stopped in his tracks, taking in the cameo moment: *My dear,* he said softly, *never have I seen a cat love so much a human. His love for you kept him alive much longer than his body should have. He is dead, I gave him enough for a thirty pound animal – he weighs three pounds. Please, you must let him go now.*

Anna listened but couldn't hear, said goodbye to Ivo. She sat with Jasper in her arms until the children, one by one, came down to see her. Caf had written a love-letter to bury with Jasper, Mandy had written a poem for Anna, Bugs brought down a soft pink baby blanket to wrap around him.

Johnny dug a hole, deep, by the mulberry tree and Mooch, the children's little dog, sat watch the whole night. Then Anna's tears began, sleep did not come, the sight of Mooch each time she looked up from weeping would unbend her again. Her eyes burned red with weeping the whole night, her loss was absolute. Jasper – he had been her lifeline, her line to life. Ivo never sent a bill. This dear, unseeing, Siamese cat had been given to her, unwanted when its human family got a dog. Anna and Cat, with the Cambridge graduate who had loved her in her woundedness, sailed back on a cargo ship to Australia.

13

Entrez, les Chats

In the 'Seventies Anna lived a while in Bristol. The spectre of the Three Day Week shadowed Britain and, after the magical interlude in Stratford upon Avon had ended with the death of Roy Rich, she was fortunate to be offered work in the newly created Professional and Executive Recruitment Department of the Civil Service, almost by default. In eleven years of schooling Anna had attended nine around the world and, coming new to each curriculum, failed every necessary examination: 11 Plus; O Levels; Intermediate; Scholarship; whatever its name, she failed it. P.E.R. refused to believe her, she was just what they were looking for: *bright, attractive, personable*. Eighteen months later a new boss demanded she show proof of an education she didn't have. Anna had nothing to show. Being fired was the only option, but ...

One morning a very large young man came to be interviewed and sat at her desk. Anna asked him what work he would like to register for. *Husky driver,* he replied. She smiled, a little.

They explored the employment possibilities for a Cambridge Blue with three years experience of mushing huskies in Antarctica and now residing in Fishponds, Bristol. Husky driving up Park Street was, Anna was pretty certain on that score, not one of those options. When he rose to leave, the chair rose with him. He was wedged. He was a very large young man with very twinkling honey-brown eyes. As he wriggled out of it he invited Anna to lunch, then dinner, and in due time immigration back to

Australia. She would return to that far country if Jasper could come too, she replied.

Roger was accepted for a teaching post in Australia on the strength of his Cambridge Master's degree: *They give it to us automatically for being a good chap for three years once we come down; I went off to the Antarctic and couldn't be anything but good,* he chuckled to Anna, the degree ensuring his name was top of the interview list.

Decades before the ease of internet only sleuth work would reveal travel possibilities left of centre and somehow Roger found them work supernumerary to the crew on a cargo ship, paying them one shilling a week each if they would look after thirty-one dogs bound for Sydney. Jasper would have separate quarters and could travel with them. The dogs were mostly pets, much loved, yet not one owner had thought to leave an item of clothing with the comfort of a family smell in the wooden cage, nor a cushion, nor a toy. Roger and Anna had little between them but they quartered the garments they had with them to give each dog a sleeve, or a back panel or a front or a leg of their clothing for the dogs to adopt, sleep or chew on. Roger, used to the critical assessment of stores for the Antarctic where corner shops were thin on the ground, was disturbed to discover as he did his own reckoning of provisions, that the kennels responsible for the dogs' travel arrangements had seriously underestimated food – it would run out before reaching the Cape. Great Danes ate more than Miniature Schnauzers, a factor which hadn't been factored in. A large, articulate man whose handsome presence commanded attention, Roger went straight to the Purser and the Captain, requesting to see them together, to insist the ship augment its stock of dog food in Hamburg; it was too late now to stock up in Tilbury or to castigate the meanness of the English kennels. Reluctantly, it would come from the ship's funds initially and Roger didn't care how they eventually reimbursed themselves as they stocked up in Hamburg as demanded, and by as much again, for the six week voyage.

The dogs arrived in Sydney well and groomed. Keeping a snowy white deep-furred Samoyed pristine as they exercized along tar-caked decks took some effort. *As happy a cargo as ever had been,* said the Captain to the breeder of salukis who met the ship, and: *We've never seen our imports free of haematomas before,* said Bill the saluki breeder to Anna and Roger, and: *Where are you staying?* Roger, who liked the small wiry Australian on sight, said: *Probably a hotel* and Bill invited the new arrivals back to his large property south-west of Sydney for their first week.

The animals were taken into quarantine for three months and Anna and Roger were able to visit Jasper frequently. Often the girl in charge of cats would have him draped around her shoulders: *He's special,* she grinned, *I bring him cooked chicken.* The cattery section had huge open-air cages with mezzanines for sleeping and tree trunks to climb up. Situated along North Head, on a natural amphitheatre of land along the Harbour on a site with large gum trees and cool breezes it was as idyllic a place as a quarantine station could be. It was as idyllic a place for a human to be, too.

In due time Anna and Roger travelled on from Sydney with Jasper to the Gold Coast where Roger's teaching began. They found a home to rent, a tiny bush cottage, hand adzed, without a loo or electricity but Roger's survival skills saw full expression and together they made it charming. All creatures great and small found sanctuary there, or were found; each had an attendant story of a timing miracle.

Driving back at dusk from Guanaba to Coomera one evening a flash of pure marmalade dashed, slinking, in front of their car. Roger braked at once. They climbed out to follow the flashing direction to a large culvert and peered inside to see a cat, terrified, one eye pustulate and hanging from its socket. Anna suspended a gasp, whispered to Roger to get the milk they had just bought at the Guanaba store and fashion a bowl from one of the other shopping packets, ditching its contents if necessary, and bring it to the entrance. They sat, murmuring encouragement for over an hour until the cat ventured as far as the milk. It began to purr. Sickened by the sight Anna and Roger assessed it as a large and, at least until its recent fortunes changed, well fed and probably loved pet ... but they would take it to the American vet on the Gold Coast who made all their rescue cases well, or neutered them, without charge, if Anna and Roger would home them. The injury horrified Ed: *Looks like a boot.* Abuse was the lot of many cats in the climate of Australia at the time, Ed could write a book. He kept the cat for three weeks, Anna or Roger visited daily for the first five days, giving the cat confidence as Ed fed him to build up his strength before he would operate to remove the eye, and then daily visits for the long recovery period. The cat was a beautiful creature, with a gentle nature and would become, because of the speed at which he would spin around when someone or something approached his blind side, Dillon, after Matt Dillon the fastest draw in the West.

Dillon was soon followed by Tweetie Pie and her brother, found on the Highway shoulder, thrown out of a speeding car, too stunned and injured to move. The little male died, but Tweetie Pie survived, a pretty soft tabby colour, always remaining a little aloof. Next came Muttons, who would pee in Roger's shoes with sheer happiness at seeing him when he returned from work. Mutti was a mite unbalanced.

One day Anna and Roger had driven to Brisbane intending to attend a concert being offered in a school, the information had come through his school grapevine. The venue was closed. They thought they had mistaken the time so they hung around. In the quiet afternoon the cry of a kitten was clear to those attuned to such things. It wasn't a comfortable cry but one filled with pain and distress. The venue was a kindergarten and looking through the window all Anna and Roger could see was a colossal coke machine but nothing else: *Surely*, they looked at each other, *the noise wasn't coming from that?* Investigation was demanded. But how?

Roger saw high-set windows on the far wall and doubted he could shimmy through, but Anna could. Lifting her high, she squeezed through and dropped like a cat to the floor, walked slowly over to the coke dispenser murmuring comforting kitten noises, to which the invisible creature responded with loud howls of anguish. She followed the cries; they were coming from behind the coke dispenser. No way could she shift that, and she couldn't position her head against the wall at any angle possible to peer between the wall and the back of the dispenser to see anything. But the cry was very loud, from right there. Anna walked back to the high windows beyond which Roger, now out of sight, would be standing. *You'll have to break in,* she called, *the kitten's trapped behind the coke dispenser, it'll need all your strength to shift the machine to free it.*

How did they do it? Anna wondered now; did they leave behind a broken window, a broken lock? It wasn't the concert timing they got wrong, it was the day itself, just as well for the kitten. She couldn't remember anything but the distress of finding it with weirdly broken legs and huge pleading eyes. It wasn't exactly trapped, just paralysed with pain and fear. Between its huge round-as-button eyes was the telltale M of a real tabby, instantly he became Buttons=Muttons=Mutti. Roger reached in, long-armed, gathered the kitten in his large hand. The kitten erupted into purrs. Back in the car he handed it to Anna while he sped back to Surfer's Paradise and to Ed who was always on call for them. Ed frowned as he examined the kitten. *Looks like he's been used for football,* he said, *but his soft bones are setting in their crippled position and I can't operate to reset them. Build him up with food and vitamins and he'll be okay, bring him back in a couple of weeks, I'll check him over again.*

Mutti moved in to the cottage with them, too small then, and crippled, to climb up on to the bed with the others, he first slept in any one of Roger's shoes until one night Anna and Roger were wakened by his button eyes and loud cries and a distinctly warm, wet feeling between them on the pillows. Mutti was agitated. It was also the first time he had scaled the bed with his lopsided deformed legs and he was simultaneously proud and perplexed. Sleep bemused, Anna and Roger rose, comforted Mutti, went to the kitchen for a cloth and there in the dim light of dawn stood in surprise. Along with a colony of tiny bats, a possum lived in the roof. With cavalier disregard at its increase, Anna had watched a stain

114

on the kitchen ceiling growing larger and larger. *Possum pee*, said Roger, *co-tenant.* Mother possum was peering down through the hole left by baby possum now sitting wide-eyed on the kitchen counter, missing its mother and wondering where she had landed. She had dropped through as the rim of wet-softened ceiling hardboard collapsed; it was their nest patch. Mother possum was a friend of Mutti's, their huge eyes linked them as kindred compadres and at dusk the pair could be seen scampering in each of their ungainly ways together across the yard towards the huge Moreton Bay Fig under whose vast spreading limbs the cottage nestled. Marvelling at Mutti's story-telling pee to convince them both to get up and rescue baby possum, they did just that; Roger reaching up to hand baby to a relieved mother before boarding up the hole with a sheet of ply found outside by the corrugated iron shed.

Then came Baby, an exquisite tortoiseshell and white kitten sitting frozen in the centre of the four lane Pacific Highway carriageway as traffic sped by. She too had been thrown out of a car window. An uncommonly bright kitten she had, like Jenny-any-dots the Gumbie Cat, just sat. Anna, with incredulous disbelief, saw her somehow coping with the tornado slipstream of cattle road-trains and juggernaut containers of overpowering force, just sitting. Anna, always a slow driver, pulled over and got out, mindlessly waving frantically to the traffic on her two lanes to: *Stop! stop!* while she juggled her way to the centre painted line, swooped up the kitten and navigated herself back to the relative safety of her ancient station wagon. Baby purred. That's all. Baby, tiny and plump, had a confidence in herself that defied Death and she would dominate all the cats, all the bats, the possums, the horses, the emu, the sugar gliders, the snakes – and the goannas who eyed her up for lunch.

Misty was just one too many mouths to feed. Roger found her by the turn off to the cottage track on the way home from school, how she got there remained a mystery. He picked her up, turned the car round and headed back to Surfer's, 20 miles away, resolving to take her to Ed to put down. Misty curled up on his lap and slept in perfect trust the sleep of the just. By the time he reached Ed Roger knew he could not end the life of this pretty long-haired smokey-blue cat. He patted her, she wriggled with pleasure, he could feel her fragile bones and too thin body under all that fur, sighed, turned the car round and headed back to the cottage. Misty moved in and, with Dillon and Mutti, claimed Roger as their True Love. Jasper, devoted to Anna and increasingly blind as the retinue rods failed, though his eyes would always retain their clear pale blue of newly born stars, hated them all. Anna belonged to *him*.

A young ruffian from the Gold Coast, how did they meet? called by one day with a sack. *Just found these at the dump,* he said, *couldn't let them be killed in the metal crusher, thought you'd take them.*

Three kittens. Exquisitely formed, obviously well bred on one side of the family but mother, regardless of pedigree, had gone a'rovin with Tom. Where the mother cat was now nobody knew, Anna hoped she would escape the metal-crusher.

Dillon found a way to balance on the curve of the bull-nose corrugated roof of the verandah for life's latest distraction. Bats. Hundreds of tiny, tiny bats lived in the roof alongside the possums. The cottage hadn't had human tenants for decades. Each evening the bats would fly out through a single hole along the soffit. Dillon, with his one eye, watched, fascinated, *thinking*. Roger found him up there, spread along the soffit and watching the bats fly past his face and out into the evening to swoop and feed. When it came time for them to return his game would begin. Up went a paw to block their entrance hole, plop would fall a surprised bat into the gutter as it rolled down the short bullnose. And plop! again, and again, and again. They would pick themselves up, dust themselves off and fly in again. And again. Dillon's round orange eye watching, his plump furry smile obvious, until he tired. None were hurt, none were caught, the game was the thing, a badminton of bats.

During a particularly long walk one evening Roger and Anna saw an emu standing strangely static in a far paddock. On their return it still hadn't moved, something was up, emus didn't hang about when humans were around. Anna and Roger crawled through barbed wire fences and slowly made their way to – horror. The emu had been tied with a nylon clothes line to a stake, its leg had grown proud flesh over the nylon, this would need serious surgery. And a horse box to transport it. God knows how long it had been there but it was still alive and standing. Anna assured it they would return and the pair hurried back to the cottage, hopped in the car, they had no phone, and sped to Ed. Ed, closing for the day, spun into miracle mode, phoned a mate for a horse-trailer, and, all in place and taking no more than an hour, followed them back to the cottage where the two men abandoned Anna and their car. Roger continued with Ed to the emu. It was a grizzly rescue. First Ed tranquilized the bird, not easy, but the bird was too weakened to do damage, and with one leg so injured anyway it couldn't kick out. Roger cut the nylon rope, somehow they got the bird into the horse box, drove back to the cottage where there was water and Ed set about cutting away the proud gristle and flesh to reveal and remove the embedded rope. The putrid flesh smelt gangrenous. Even tranquilized the great bird shuddered as the nylon rope was eased from the pink living under-flesh of gristle. Washed clean, the proud flesh removed from the deep wound, Ed packed it with Sulfanilamide, then sat back to contemplate the bird's immediate future. The cottage had a home paddock with reasonable fencing, the bird needed feeding up – what did emu's eat? It survived, grew strong on foraging the paddock and drinking copious amounts of water, and one fine day leapt the fence and left. Anna missed its low boom as it strode the fence line each morning calling their attention. But free is best, and she sent a prayer for its safety.

Boo. *Boo boo boo boo boo* is the litany of a baby Pied Butcherbird before it learns its own sublime coloratura. Anna found a fledgling on the road, the nest was dozens of feet up a slash pine, the tree itself one of a stand of escapees self-seeded from the wood chip plantation further inland. She took it home, fed it egg yolk and tiny worms and it grew and grew. Nine cats lived in that two room cottage. Nine. All natural predators of birds. Anna spoke to each of them in turn: *If you touch a feather on this bird you'll go right back where you came from*, she said, sending pictures of their Awful Lives Before Rescue. Not one of those cats attempted to harm Boo, who grew.

The cottage was unfurnished when the two immigrants had moved there and furniture was expensive. Anna took to trawling the local dump. Australians in those days were the most profligate of folk and astonishingly good things were to be found on dumps in the days before councils and greedier folk set in place licenses to forage. Anna found treasures, old and new, one such was a chair, flock-covered, circa 1950, with wooden arms. The springs had gone but she could fix that, she still had her upholstery gun from a short stint working with an upholsterer on the Gold Coast, she knew about such things then. Mutti took the chair for himself. The hollowed seat was perfect for his uncomfortably set limbs to fold into and it became his. Until Boo recognized with his growing bird brain that the flock pattern on the chair was a *tree* and on its branches were *flowers*. With loud and assertive, aggressive really, *booooos* as he sat on the chair's arm, bullied Mutti into relinquishing his comfort. It became Boo's preserve as he frustratedly pecked and pecked at the flock forest.

Dillon came in for a serve. Always hot in the bush beyond the sea's breeze of the coast the kitchen back door of the cottage remained open, the open glass louvered windows of the front verandah drawing every whisper of air through the small middle room. Dillon would sprawl by the door, with his head to the prevailing air, air too breathlike to warrant calling *breeze*. Thus positioned, his blind side was exposed, his good eye to the wall. Boo perched on the top of the door, far up, *thinking*, as Dillon dozed. Anna heard the bird-brain cogs turn as she quietly worked in the kitchen. Silently and stealthily Boo would choose the moment to swoop down and land by Dillon's blind side to screech with huge laughter: *Boo boo boo boo boo,* always in fives, right into Dillon's ear. Dillon would leap a foot from the floor and spin mid air for his good eye to see – nothing! Boo had flown back up on the safety of the door.

Anna knew butcher birds would only mature as their baby boos developed into the thrilling coloratura, cadenzas that contradicted the natural instincts which had gained them their whitefella's name; *Butcher bird*. But fledglings learn by imitation, and in the three weeks the bird had been growing no adult butcher birds had appeared. Anna sat, thinking. Roger had bought her a tiny portable battery-run cassette player and from time to time she played her few operatic cassettes until one light bulb moment as she focused on Joan Sutherland's mad scene. Lucia, swooping up and down the scales, gloriously mad, her notes impossibly positioned high and low, extended or curt, listening, echoing – well, that caught Boo's attention, rivetingly. He flew to the top of the gas powered fridge where the little black cassette player warbled its apparent butcher bird aria. Boo cocked his head this way and that, almost jumping up and down, feathers trembling with excitement. Anna repeated and repeated the track; Boo *boo'd,* in repeated recitatives of five the whole afternoon until, just as Roger returned from work, Boo threw back his head, filled his throat and poured out his own cellular imprinted aria – *exactly like Lucia's.*

Roger walked in to hear it. It was a holy moment. For the whole of the following day Anna patiently replayed and replayed Lucia's astonishing coloratura as Boo answered with his own. Evening came, Boo sat on the top of the kitchen door, alone now and singing with all the power of his inheritance. The following morning he ignored his breakfast, sang two arias and flew far over the back paddock to live his own life. Mutti reclaimed his hollow chair, Dillon relaxed by the open door once more and the Boo chapter of their lives closed.

The back paddock became home to horses rescued from journeys to abattoirs, rescued pet ponies ended their days with them, all shared with Emu. But all the while ghosts and spectres rumbled restless in Anna's depths and would not sleep.

Anna loved Roger. But ... back in Australia the sunshine cast in sharp relief the anguish of her years in England, her fruitless attempts to connect with her father, the loss of her daughter – too hard, too hard to speak of – carved on her soul in sorrow that story remained an area of her life too complex then to share, explain or discuss; she was swimming in unshed tears for years. A caul had grown over her heart; humour a lost joy for too many years. All the concealed demons of her psyche rose up when Roger asked her to marry him. They had come to Australia on that promise to the Australian Embassy, her childhood there no assurance of her new migrant status. But their marriage wasn't a marriage and Anna was disconsolate with guilt that she couldn't respond to such a dear and attractive man. She had no reference for human contact. Never touched or cuddled as a babe, she had lain in her pram 'being' the dappled shadows of the tree canopy above her, knowing that beyond it was Home. Where, then, was she? Certainly not in her body. She was so emotionally damaged her body remained out of reach somewhere below her head for decades, until she walked the whole Camino de Santiago at the age of sixty-eight and far in the future when she came to appreciate that sturdy little body which served her so well. With Roger she was incapable of being in touch with her own body, much less being touched by someone other, or permitting intimacy after the loss of her daughter. With monumental sorrow, Anna left Roger; it would take more courage than she could summon to remain. He would be the very best of the few men in her life. Roger took Dillon, Mutti and Misty; Tweetie Pie died horribly, Anna took Jasper. Baby went to friends on Springbrook, the three exquisite escapees from the metal crusher to a friend on the Gold Coast and the acquisition of most of Coomera by Dreamworld obliterated the pretty historical cottage, sprawling its nightmarish dominion over the acres they had loved. The chapter with all of its stories closed.

Roger saw her once more, in the distance. He had driven up to Springbrook where Anna had gone for refuge. He loved her, was so willing to talk things through. She was too damaged to know such a thing was possible. She, misery numbing every one of her five senses, unaware of him, was walking Lyre Bird Ridge, far ahead of him, wearing a long black dress, the lowering sun glowing through her fine hair. The image made him think of a candlewick on whom grief burnt like a flame. He watched her walk on into the winds of her Fate, a storm hidden in every fold of her dress as she walked further on. He wanted so much to save her... but turned his car, knowing her unhappy solitude could not sustain a breach. Eventually he met a young woman and they lived happily ever after.

But now Jasper had died. He had been given to Anna thirteen years before by a husband, her own, a helicopter pilot who liked Great Danes. A fellow pilot, whose heavily pregnant wife wanted a dog, needed to re-home the pretty Siamese. Anna loved him at first sight. Life with Paul didn't last long; a Cranwell fast-track graduate he resigned his commission to study architecture at Bristol University where he was waylaid by a young man. The pair went everywhere together except university. Anna didn't know the newspeak word *gay*. She didn't recall either of the men being very gay at all. By the time she learnt that the pretty little word she had known all her life applying to light-hearted happiness had been annexed by newspeak to apply, willy-nilly, to someone behaving as oddly as her ex-husband, she and Jasper had moved to the other side of the planet with the Antarctic explorer who loved her, despite her baggage.

Roger and Jasper lay behind her. India had opened a chink in her heart where light was beginning to illumine a future before her. Being with the Parer children, whose affection embraced her in those desolate days, was little short of a miracle. Michael Parer, the children's uncle, lived further up the Blue Mountain range. Michael and Mally welcomed their nieces and nephew whenever they came, their home had an open door and a wonderful library. Michael loaned Anna a book, on the cover was a photograph of a tall, white-bearded man clothed in two orange cloths, *dhotis*, walking down a forest path somewhere in India.

14

Threading the Weft

Anna moved on to Wollongong where she was offered another garden for her caravan to perch in for a while. She accepted a six month contract as an Arts Coordinator within the University for an independent community arts group spear-headed by Judy, the American wife of Edward Cowie. Edward was a renaissance kind of professor who went on to found the School of Arts Fusion at James Cook University in Townsville, and returned, eventually, to Dartington in Devon from where he retired. A musician and artist he composed motets for Bellbirds and Lyrebirds, symphonies for the Earth and choral music for Gaia. His paintings of birds added illustrations of musical notation, they enchanted Anna. Edward found symphony in Nature, found *'tongues in trees, books in the running brooks, sermons in stones, and good in everything'*. Nature fed his pen and his musical and artistic expression owed everything to it. He too was defining simplicities to describe creation. His dynamic presence left its mark on all the universities he passed through.

Next door to her office was a small unit for Aboriginal culture where Anna befriended its Koori staff. Wary of *whitefella*, the women accepted Anna, shared a poem with her, noted her response, a response which opened a bond between them: *You are a child of the Dreamtime People* its first line ran ... and Anna wrote the poem into her first book. She was invited by the women to a Dreaming Place far off in the bush, across rugged country, but, they told her, she must ride blindfold all the way. The cave was in a secret place on forbidden-to-access government land, but they ignored the signs and the barbed wire and continued to venerate their ancestral gathering ground. Jolted and bumped and blindfolded Anna journeyed deep into Koori Country, humbled by the spiritual significance of what she would see when the rough jeep arrived and her blind was removed. She added its memory to her amalgam of initiations.

A decade later she discovered the writings of Max Dulumnum, an Elder whose *Heart Gone Walkabout* placed spirituality firmly in the body, the earth, the *now*. His ancient spirituality was light years from the enfeebled interpretation of spirituality popular in the Western world, blandly indigestible as 'New Age'. The grist of Max Dulumnum was tough fare:

I will not live if I do not eat meat and blood, Max wrote, *a fellow is dry without meat, will die without meat. Breathing and existing come from having meat. We eat blood and it goes everywhere through us.*

Meat is the quintessential health food. We give our own blood to our sick, children or adults. It is therapeutic. Only meat and blood can save them. Today our blood is sick, it is sick with sugar.

Kangaroo meat is not a fatty meat. It is very lean, good for us. Cattle fattened on some sort of stuff, salt, all this takeaway food, this garbage, we Aboriginal people can't eat this stuff and be healthy. This stuff is whiteman's disease.

Our spirit, our life, is in our kidneys. Our people have special names for kidneys. We don't want new kidneys, we don't want another fella's spirit put into us.

Now our kidneys are sick with white man's food. We don't have bush tucker now; grog and sugar make us sick, then we have no spirit, we are empty. We live on as unwell people, with whitefella medicine.

Now factory farming denies all respect for all kine, the global cruelty to creatures of the Give-Away ensures no nourishment can come from their imprisoned suffering and slaughter.

Under and beyond the moral dilemma of meat, whether as substance or metaphor, or liver, or kidney, or spleen, or hand, or tongue, are the metaphors of words, an essence now lost. Words for Anna were soul-food, she had rued the loss of countless words within her own lifetime, knew that true meaning could enrich a sentence, a metaphor could sing a soul out of its sickening, a well-turned sentence heal a heart. English language once used metaphors of liver, of kidney, to include temperament, nature, constitution, disposition; arcane references for personal attributes resonate with the Aboriginal understanding of which Max wrote. Who, like Shakespeare, could now say "that are of my own kidney"; "think of that, a man of my kidney" for who, nowadays, would know the meaning?

Meanings are lost, forgotten, as American 'English', becomes the norm and English education within its own motherland, anodyne. Substituting the rich and ancient forms of expression of our mother-tongue, jettisoning the words of our language with their immeasurable richness to make way for newspeak, predictive texts, incorrect automatic spell-check, diminishes all the grace of a perfectly nuanced intent, reduces our expression and limits conversation and colour to monosyllabic minimalism. Will it matter, when all is said and done? The ancients invoked a leavening of hubris in their caution: *Memento mori*, remember death, the wisest of ancient truths, has now become *momento* mori. Sinclair Lewis, granted the Nobel Prize, failed to know the difference between rites and rights when referring to sacred dance.

Words, those minute particulars, had fed Anna when her mother hadn't, words were her Sunday lunch; poetry and prose nourished her soul. Words, wrongly used, prevent real understanding.

Once, during a debilitating bout of depression when she lived in Glastonbury, Anna had gone to her favourite GP to explain herself, her lassitude, her wish to go Home. The depression was more circumstantial than innate – being poor and homeless she had been housed in a small mews of council bungalows where, for years, her neighbours then were a mix of drug addicts, alcoholics. The courtyard itself, with no security in place around it, became a drug run for the dispossessed and dysfunctional of the town, used as a nightly escape route from the adjacent park, a chosen pitch for drug dealing. For her first nine terrible years there – three thousand nights, more or less, until her relentless appeals for gated security, at the very least, was put in place – Anna's sleep would be broken night after night by shouting and drunkenness an arm's length beside her low bedroom window, an arm's length from her *pillow*, its assault frequent as offenders ran from the park for the exit on Magdalene Street. Confined to two rooms, a bedroom and a sitting room of diminutive dimensions – she had no kitchen other than a space for a fridge, sink and oven, no work surface on which to prepare food, eating became a demeaning experience, the bungalow had no back door, no rear windows – she saw no sky, no sunrise, no sunset, her view was the six foot picket fence surrounding the communal washing lines. It was soul-destroying, and as her soul was being eroded she could find no voice to sing. Sleep deprivation, a known form of torture high on Amnesty's list, due to the drug run outside her window each night, added to her despair.

The young doctor listened intently, waited as Anna paused, to end with: *I feel I've fallen off the last 'e' of hope* ... before gently responding with: *Part of the trouble is that you are so articulate no one believes you can feel the way you do ... who, then, can you talk to?*

You, she managed a rueful half-smile, knowing what he meant, and took a prescription of ciprinol to get her through the badlands for a couple of months.

Wollongong was built on mining. D.H. Lawrence had lived unhappily in Thirroul; Anna's caravan was a block away in Austinmer, birthplace of Sydney de Kantzow who founded the airline of Cathay Pacific; irrelevant coincidences. Wollongong University was a ten minute bus ride away.

Settled in her new rôle as Arts Coordinator Anna wanted to use her six months wisely, mindful of Anne's faith in her. She applied to Deakin University for an external degree in Comparative Religion. Her Indian professor marked her first essay with a High Distinction. It was a stepping stone – but something deeper rippled on the littoral of her mind. Anna didn't wish to know *about* God from a variety of comparisons, she wanted to *know* God. She wrote a grateful letter, grateful to know that despite her mother's assessment of her as stupid the academic world had disagreed: a High Distinction was not to be gainsaid; her grateful letter was many-layered – its gist, she wished to withdraw from the course.

A week later the next month's assignment arrived from the University. *Darn,* thought Anna, *our mail's crossed.* Curious, she opened the pack. Turning the pages of the A4 booklet of assignments she found a full page in black and white of the same white long-haired gentleman on the cover of the book Michael Parer had lent her. Father Bede Griffiths, for it was he, was visiting Australia in May. She reached for the telephone to call the Melbourne phone number and book her place, dislodged some papers, there was the letter she hadn't yet posted to the University cancelling her degree course.

Anna gave her name as Sitadevi and the flustered voice she was speaking to asked if that name belonged to: *er, um?* Anna helped him out: *Satyananda Ashram north of Sydney?* An audible sigh of relief followed. The young man replied that Father Bede had specifically requested a visit to this ashram but they, his organizers, had no idea where it was or how to get there, or even what an ashram was. *I'll take him,* she said, *I have a car, I know the ashram very well.*

A sigh of grateful relief filled her ear. Anna replaced the phone in a daze. She would chaperone Father Bede. Over the next decade she would come to know Father Bede very well indeed.

15

The Will of God and a Flash of Geru

Much had been written of this holy man though little of his *katabasis* understood. *But that is the way of all history*, said friends, reminding her of the apocryphal story of Jung, oft quoted: *Thank God I'm Jung and not a Jungian ...*

Shirley du Boulay had known instinctively that Father Bede's experience of the Black Madonna was: *Beyond the Darkness*, the title of her biography. She told Anna that she felt 'overshadowed' by Bede during the writing of it, yet Shirley had never met him in person. She was wise and insightful and Father Bede came alive through her words. In 1990 the world had called his experience a stroke, but when he returned to consciousness a week later Father Bede knew it as something quite other.

The ancient Greeks understood it well: *katabasis* – a journey through the underworld of one's unconscious to reach those great Eternal archetypes, Cosmic archetypes. Father Bede 'returned' and expressed his experience as being: *Overwhelmed with Love*. He spoke of journeying with the Mother, the Mother of All Things, the Divine Feminine, the Ground of Being. Few around him knew what he meant as he revealed the essence of his experience: *She is the Para Shakti, you know*, he would say, to anyone and everyone whether they knew what the Para Shakti was or not. *She is cruel and destructive and all-loving and all-nourishing; She is the rocks, and the earth, and the trees, She is the whole of Nature and All That Is.*

On his final world tour of lectures in 1992 Father Bede asked to break his journey of the southern States of Australia to spend four days with Anna in southern Queensland. Anna's pretty cottage, built a hundred years earlier of timber and raised on stumps for coolness, its wide and shaded, lattice-lined verandah running the span of the building and looking out across the garden, welcomed her honoured guest. Anna had not lived there long, her half-acre garden was being established with 'rooms' of roses and crinums and blossoming trees and woodlands.

The spiritual circuit of Australia was small; everyone knew who was who and what was happening across the divide of differing paths. Word got round that Father Bede was breaking his southern schedule to make an unscheduled visit to southern Queensland for a personal visit, and the intentional muddle of timetables for his arrival at Brisbane airport alerted the priest who had generously paid for Father Bede's journeys. The Christian Meditation Network (then known as the CMC) wanted him, *there*. Father Bede wanted to be *here*, with Anna. Father Doug, responsible for initiating the tour, phoned Anna with some urgency: *Can you get to the airport now?* he said, not realising she lived fifty kilometres to the west, *the CMC have brought Father's flight forward in order to take him to one of their homes, he insists on going to you, but no one 'knows' where you live. You must get to the airport to intercept their intentions.*

Anna drove the busy highway to Brisbane airport intoning green-light prayers all the way, swung into the hugely filled parking area with her usual mantra: *Hail Mary full of Grace, please find me a parking space*, and threw a thank you to Her for finding one so close to the Arrivals terminal.

Like a small whirlwind she blew into the domestic airport, noticed a huddle of people, mostly women, grouped in close conversation standing beyond the few seats available. She knew from their no-nonsense, middle-Australian clothing these were the hijackers. Ignoring them she made for the portal leading to the jetway through which Father Bede would walk. Seconds later she heard: *'Sitadevi! Sitadevi!'* and, there they were! Father Bede's smile of delight shone high above the smaller, stocky, Christudas who was calling to her. Should she hug them? Delight rippled through her, Christudas hugged her, she pranam'd to Father Bede. The holy huddle unravelled, morphed towards Father Bede, crowding him, pushing Anna away from their proprietary claim, telling him he would be staying with them, somewhere. Father Bede demurred in his gentle manner, looked at Anna/Sitadevi, and quietly said, no, he would be staying with Sitadevi, and he would be happy to come with the group to the lunch they had prepared but Sitadevi would come too and take him to her home afterwards.

Anna watched. Silently. She was ready to do whatever Father Bede preferred, even letting him stay with the lionizing CMC if it was his wish. It wasn't. Lunch over, she apologized to her passengers for her small and elderly and unairconditioned car as she drove her two guests westwards to Silkstone.

Her small cottage was given over to the two men, each having one of the two bedrooms while she bedded down on a daybed on the sweeping rear verandah. A public talk on Saturday evening had been hastily arranged by the CMC in Bardon, at a church – what church was it? Anna raked her memory. Did Anglican churches have sacristies? or vestries?

Sitting at his feet, in her swami robes, in the uncomfortable sacristy of Bardon church on the night of his talk, Father Bede had just been given an envelope containing an insulting $500 by M. of the Christian Meditation Centre while the donations at the door were filling every tin, box and then, grocery cartons; unimaginable sums as donations poured in from those who loved him. Christudas watched as hundreds of people gave in gratefulness that Father Bede had come to Brisbane on an unplanned schedule. Like bush fire the last minute advertisement in the media had spread and people were flocking there from near and far. Anna went to the sacristy to be with him. Father Bede said to her: *You are one of us; you must sit with us when I go to speak.* Just then M. walked in: *Out!* she bellowed at Anna, *you, out!*

Father Bede looked stunned, his eyebrows and his hands rose simultaneously against the force of her words. He knew of the contretemps over the change of his flight arrival. But M. didn't know that a saint's Word is so aligned to God that: *Thy Will will Be Done.*

The impromptu lecture in Brisbane's Bardon church was a real money-spinner for M. and the CMC. God was having none of it. M. claimed the money of course, which caused tears from Father: *What does she want with that amount of money?* he said wistfully, *it would do so much for our village – we would build a school and pay a teacher for years, we would build new wells and bring them water* ... More than $20,000 had been counted from donations of a thousand people who filled the church, the aisles, the nave, surrounded the building, crowded at the windows and who gave donations in notes of $10's and $20's and $50's and $100's all for Father Bede. Christudas had been at the door, had seen all. Father Bede was given the $500 before the lecture, *fait accompli.* Father Bede confessed then that the Christian Meditation Centre had arranged the venues all round Australia and had done the *same* thing.

His pain was raw the following morning, he had been truly used. Later the priest who had invited him to Australia wrote letters to the CMC asking for a percentage of the donations to be returned to Bede. He received a curt reply, lying of the amounts taken. Doug hadn't mentioned amounts, had asked only for a percentage of the donations and the lies sat ill, the biggest of all being their 'expenses'. They had none. Doug had paid Father Bede's airfares and travel costs from his own pocket.

M. and the CMC didn't have it all their way that night. In the face of her rage Father Bede gently placed his hand on Anna's arm to stop her leaving: *But Sitadevi is one of us,* he said again to a glowering M. whose body filled the doorway, *and I want her to sit with me when I speak.* Christudas had just come in to tell Father of the money he had watched being donated: *Filling grocery boxes Father!* Now he stood to leave too. *You stay!* shouted M. and Christudas grinned at Anna, raised one eyebrow. He knew one didn't mess with saints. Father Bede sat in palpable discomfort.

Out 'there' M. had cordoned off the first four rows of pews on both sides of the aisle for her cronies. Two nuns on the aisle edge of the fifth row squeezed up even closer to invite Anna to sit with them. People were pouring in like a river, unstoppable, filling every space along walls, aisles, nave, hanging in through the windows, a thousand and more, the pews themselves squeezed by humans quite forgetting their anglo-saxon need for spatial distance. Not a feather could find its way between them.

As the river of people thickened to suffocation one of the other matrons of the CMC stood on the raised dais, took hold of the microphone, announced that there was room for people to sit on the floor behind Father Bede. Swifter than lightning a flash of *geru* flew to sit at Father's feet. Christudas stood behind Father and giggled. M's face turned an unbecoming shade of aubergine. Bede smiled down at Anna warmly.

Father Bede, transfigured since his *katabasis* two years beforehand, had become light, Light itself. He had always been immersed in Christ, now he was *merged* with Christ. Hindus know, as no other race does, that when one is merged with the *Ishta Deva* only the *Ishta Deva* is present and the human ego has dissolved. When Father Bede said to M. that Anna was to sit with him it was Christ's Will *within* Bede. It had nothing to do with Anna, it had nothing to do with Anna as Sitadevi either, but it had *everything* to do with the Will of God blowing through Bede, now a hollow reed. So God sorted things out just the way His beloved Bede wanted it to be. The sad post-mortem on Mammon and M. over the familiar comfort of porridge at breakfast caused sombre reflection. Father Bede's white prophet head shook in disbelief as he recalled their black profit. For once even Christudas couldn't find words. He knew well the poverty of the villages surrounding the ashram of Shantivanam, and a couple of wells, as well as a school, would have changed lives for generations. He knew, too, the insult of the $500 thrust into Father's hand before the talk.

The next morning, after the breakfast post-mortem, they spoke of Mrs Tweedie: *Her story – Chasm of Fire – was most impressive, most impressive, we have it in our library, you know,* said Father Bede. *And Jeanine's book, oh, oh, this is a wonderful book you know ... her vision ... it is a gift from God ... it was worth coming to Australia just to find this book ... the whole of Christian theology needs to be re-defined in the light of the Vedic Revelation you know. The Black Madonna you know, I feel She is the Para Shakti,* and he paused.

Father Bede walked around Anna's garden with Christudas when they first arrived, had paused by the young Crépuscule rose bush which had not yet matured enough to flower. Did Father Bede know this rose? Anna asked. It was exactly the colour of his *kavi* robe, pale crepuscular apricot. As he stood there he murmured, more to himself than to her, that he would need eight blossoms for Mass at St Mary's in Ipswich on Sunday morning; he would give Mass in the traditional Indian way by offering flowers to the Attributes of God, to Time and to Space.

After the breakfast post-mortem Father Bede asked Anna to bring flowers for Mass, any flowers. April was moving to winter in the southern hemisphere and not much was flowering. Anna walked down the high verandah steps hoping, without much conviction it must be said, that she would find eight flowers, somewhere. She glanced at the Crépuscule and stopped short – it was dotted with roses. She stood for long moments, not in disbelief exactly, but in amazement, a holy amazement which prevented her from asking: *How?* She recalled Saint Francis: *Saint Francis looked at the almond tree and said – speak to me of God; and the almond tree blossomed.* Anna collected eight perfect blooms and laid them on the breakfast table.

Father Bede paused for some time, silent in his own reflections, his gaze remaining on the perfect roses. He finally spoke: *You have the consciousness of the holy,* he said, porridge over. *I would like you to complete my journey with the Black Madonna.*

Anna's skin prickled, it was a huge ask.

Father Bede named her home and hermitage Shakti Bhavan, the House of the Divine Feminine Energy just as Anna's cat, Shakti, turned her peridot eyes on to Father Bede and gave him her pertest, prettiest, cat smile. She had already chewed up Christudas's hand when he bent to stroke her, now she fell on her back again. Father Bede bent over to stroke her. At his touch she purred.

On their way to the airport Christudas asked to stop for a Chinese meal. He ordered a beer: *Have some beer, Father? No? Thank you very much, then I will have some beer. Sitadevi, have some beer, have some beer ...* Father Bede interjected with uncustomary irritation, the wake of being used to make so much money for a materialistic organisation bent on self-promotion really, *really* hurt him.

Drink it yourself, he spoke sharply, *Sitadevi is a sannyasi, you are only a priest.*

At the airport, goodbye, *namaste.* A hug from Christudas, words of blessing from Father Bede, and his slender *kavi* robed figure, bent with age, like a windblown oak alone on a peak of its own, passed out of sight. Anna felt a *frisson* of bereavement at his leaving, as if part of her had gone with him. She almost knew she would not see him again.

New Camaldoli Hermitage,
Big Sur, CA 93920
August 29th 1992

Dear Sita Devi
   Please excuse me for not writing before, first of all to thank you for our stay with you which I shall always remember and then to tell you how much I appreciate Jeanine Miller's book on the Vision of Cosmic Order in the Vedas. She has an extraordinary mystical insight into the Vedas which makes her unique among western scholars and I doubt whether any Hindu has such a deep insight. Sri Aurobindo comes nearest to it.

... I have had an interesting time in the U.S. not giving talks so much as spending time in silence and prayer, especially at a beautiful place in Oklahoma, modelled on Shantivanam, where they have small 'cabins' among the woods. I expect to leave here later in September and to be back in Shantivanam by the 20th.

I hope that all is going well with you. I shall often think of your place and the association with Jeanine Miller, whose book which you gave me is among my treasured possessions,
With my prayers and best wishes
Yours affectionately in Christ
DBede

By the time Father Bede came to stay with her in the early nineties Anna knew she was walking in a sacred manner. She knew that true Intention came not from herself, a self with all the frailties of the ego any human was heir to, but from her Self. At times, given a thought that made her smile at its far-from-holy impishness, she would grin wide and murmur to Self – are you sure you want me to do *this?* and then: *If every first thought comes from You, then I must.*

Anna was careful to own mischievous elements as her own, coming from those human desires found in everyone. Food was always a *bête noir*, having so often been denied it as a child. Now it would be recognized as child abuse, but then – mothers were perfect, right? *Wrong.*

The power and pull of food governed many decisions in Anna's life. Was she *worth* good food? Was she worth *good* food? How many times over her life had she collapsed, been found on park benches, when her sugar levels dropped alarmingly? At seventy her good doctor had finally diagnosed possible diabetes as a probable cause. It was the nearest diagnosis western medical practice had got to: *Erratic sugar levels,* he said, *at last our blood tests have captured them!* But it was a lifetime of feeling unworthy of *feeding,* of asking *herself* for good food that reflected the effect; the cause lay far away in the cavern of memories:

No! this fruit, meat, chicken, these vegetables, soups, the whole kitchen is for Stephanie, you fill up on bread and butter.

Her good doctor made diabetes sound plausible, and now she had a name to explain those terrible mood swings that puzzled friends as midday arrived every day and lunch was late and her bio-chemical fight or flight kicked in to replace the fallen sugar levels and Anna would have *killed* to eat something – NOW. *Now* she could say to lunch invitations that she ate *at midday, not ten minutes past,* and it worked. Friends took a named diagnosis seriously. Those who didn't slid under Anna's radar. The discipline she thenceforth ate by would lead her directly to the Taxi Driver.

She strode deeper and deeper
into the world,
determined to do
the only thing she could do,
determined to save
the only life she could save.

words by Mary Oliver

Discrimination, she'd learned from life, was not discarding one thing to embrace another but the art of taking beauty from a broken world, from deformity; finding order in chaos, extracting justice from wrong and choosing love, not hate. It was a long time learning and choice was an astonishing revelation. Hate was not the opposite of love, each were a force of *energy*; the opposite of love is – *indifference*. It was her mother's chilling indifference that froze her; hate had heat, heat had the possibility of transformation; indifference hadn't.

There was a moment in Father Bede's company when Anna observed the inherent purity of *love*. It happened during his first talk in Sydney in the 1980's.

The church chosen for Father Bede's talk was filled to capacity and Anna, in her Swami Sitadevi robes, had been ushered to the front pew as his chaperone. Father Bede spoke for over an hour, spanning entire cosmologies, without a note as reference. There was silence afterwards as the audience processed his breadth of vision to summon a question or two. Father Bede sat quietly, hands resting one over the other on his lap. Sitting slightly forward in his chair, alone on the dias, he waited, relaxed and calm and radiant.

Suddenly there was a scuffle and then a terrific banging and muted shouting was heard from the back of the church, coming closer and closer at a speed too fast for anyone present to act. Anna was in the front pew. She turned to see a very large, beefily built man, middle-aged, barely dressed in stubbies (workman's shorts) a dirty singlet and thongs (flipflops) on grubby feet thundering up the aisle, and looking murderous. Anger bristled out of his body, mesmerizing the congregation, who were paralysed with shock. Anger poured out of his mouth. He reached the slightly raised dais, paused momentarily adjacent to the pew where Anna sat. He was about to climb up to Father Bede and do heaven knows what to him. Father Bede leant towards the man, offering a hand. The man suddenly stopped short of climbing on to the dais intent on doing whatever he was intent on doing to Father Bede, halted by that gentle gesture. He dropped to his knees, his voice fell to a broken whisper, Anna and those closest heard him say: *Father, I am a very angry man.*

She heard Father Bede's quiet response: *I understand, I know, please come and see me in the sacristy ...*

The man fell to his knees and he wept.

Anna would see this compassion, this complete absence of personal fear, in Mrs Tweedie. Mrs Tweedie always left her front door on the open latch from three o'clock every weekday for those who came to quietly enter and find a place to sit with her. On this particular day a highly disturbed young man was brought to the group by a German member despite Tweedie's warning that such a thing must not be done. *The spiritual energy could destabilize a mind already unstable and create a madness,* she said. He was a very unbalanced man, young, large, maybe six foot two inches. Mrs Tweedie was five foot one or two.

He went into the large carpeted drawing room to meditate. Anna had never before meditated in there, preferring to stay within Mrs Tweedie's personal aura. She was sitting under the bay window when the large young man came in, sat down and began, apparently, to meditate. Within minutes he took a violent fit. Locked into the demons of his own mind he flailed about, waving his arms and shouting murderously. No one could 'reach' him. Gesticulating wildly, erratically, shouting abuse and threats, it was his internal world he was wrestling with. Then he began the foaming at his mouth. Someone near the door slipped out to call Mrs Tweedie. By this time the young man was raving uncontrollably. Everyone moved as far from him as possible or left the room.

Mrs Tweedie came in, sat down in front of the young man who was now attempting, ineffectually, to rise. He was still in a place far beyond reach, battling with horrors only he could see, his arms wildly hitting out at thin air. Mrs Tweedie offered her hands. Very softly she began to repeat: *Give me your hand, you are safe here; give me your hand, you are safe with me.*

The man lunged at her, eyes crazy and rolling. He had no awareness at all. Yet slowly through his madness *something* in him responded to the words she was repeating over and over. Slowly, he put forward one of his flailing hands. When it touched Mrs Tweedie's outstretched hand his entire body jerked back. She held up her palm, allowing his hand to fall into its comfort again. It became still. She closed her palm very gently over his hand and sat gazing into his rolled back eyes, pouring compassion into the disturbing terrors within his mind.

There was a tense and anxious waiting while other people asked if they should call the police, the ambulance. Mrs Tweedie gestured *no!* She softly demanded he 'return' from his inner hell. Slowly slowly the young man became calm. His hand relaxed in hers. And then the small miracle of lifting his other hand and placing it in hers, and opening his eyes, flooding with tears, bathing his face, suffused with the miracle of acceptance, of being known and of being loved. He wept as he saw his hands in Tweedie's.

Living without fear translates as living with no ego, for what is there to harm? Mrs Tweedie would say: *I do not see you as men or as women, I only see you as souls in front of me.* And who can harm the soul? Certainly not this wild madman in front of her.

Once, sitting with each and listening to them speak, Anna had them 'disappear', only light ringed the space where she knew their body was. Blinking, trying to bring Father Bede or Mrs Tweedie into focus, she thought it was her eyes that were playing tricks, she was aware that no one else seem to notice anything strange at all. She kept the visions to herself, protected from humans. Hadn't Christ said: *If thine eye be single thy body shall be full of light?* Shamans and Mahayana Buddhists said it too. When one's speech is in pure accord with one's mind and heart the body itself disappears, *dissolves,* from its earthly plane to its alignment with Self, and Self has no Form. When conversation becomes 'normal' the person regains his or her familiar condition.

16

Interlude – Daffodils

It was the daffodils which bound Anna's heart to Father Bede beyond death. On Saturday May 15th she woke with a pain locking her shoulders from left to right: *As if I was bearing the weight of a cross on my shoulders*, she said afterwards. Driving was not possible. She could barely move. She was due to drive to a training workshop for volunteers with Karuna, the newly formed Home Hospice agency in Brisbane, but pain caused her to call and cancel her place. At 3pm the pain lifted: *Just like that*, she said, afterwards. She had time then to run down to Woolworths to buy food for her cats just as the staff were filling huge bins with bags of daffodil bulbs whose planting date had expired.

Daffodils! A 'host of dancing daffodils' was a bit beyond the budget, so she settled on a few good-sized clumps. Daffodils were Father Bede's favourite flower, Wordsworth his favourite poet. Tomorrow she would plant a Father Bede garden of dancing daffodils amongst her old heritage roses in memory of his four day visit the year before. The following morning, a Sunday, a friend phoned and told her to quickly switch on her radio as Father Bede was speaking. The sound of his voice touched her more deeply than the words he spoke. After some minutes the announcer returned to say that this beloved man had passed away on the previous Thursday, the 13th. His funeral took place at 3pm on Saturday 15th May. Anna now sat, at the same table where the two of them had spoken over porridge, unable to assimilate his passing – he was *here*, still. She felt his presence, he had not gone anywhere.

She walked down the wooden steps of the wide verandah and into the garden. She knew why she had bought the bulbs. Knew why she had been paralysed with pain until 3pm; knew why she had to go down to Woollies at exactly that moment. She spent all day planting the bulbs in the heavy black soil of Silkstone. Exhausted and satisfied at the end of Sunday afternoon she sat by the newly planted bed of bulbs and pondered on how life would be without the knowing that Father Bede was somehow always 'there' for her. A great stillness surrounded her; a kind of 'presence' enveloped her. A wisp of wind came over the rose bed, not apparent anywhere else. Her skin prickled. Out of the blue, out of the blue, blue sky, Father Bede's voice came as clear and audible as if next to her: *I shall be with you till the end of days…* the very words he had written on the back of the postcard of her dream.

During those first weeks with Father Bede, long ago in the 'eighties when she followed him at his request after being his chaperone, to Shantivanam, Anna had shared her family story in brief. Father's face acknowledged her pain: *The pain*, he said, *of not being loved*. There was a question Anna longed to ask, coming as it did from her analysis with a Jungian analyst and centred, as Jung developed, on dreams.

Where do dreams come from, Father Bede, she asked, awed by their symbolic perceptions and wisdoms throughout her analysis. The peacock was crying on the palm-thatched roof of the small ochre mud-brick hut as Father Bede leant back in his chair: *Some dreams come from the subconscious,* he said, *and some dreams come from the unconscious, and some dreams come from …* and he stopped, mid-sentence.

Anna did not ask more. *You must go on to London,* he had said, *find Mrs Tweedie; her book – is the finest I know of written about kundalini.*

Anna went on to London, found Mrs Tweedie, who welcomed her. Six months later when she had 'received' Father Bede's postcard dream of a small boat moored on the bank of a holy river in India, on the reverse the words in Father Bede's handwriting and familiar blue Quink ink: *I shall be with you till the end of days, and in dying, THY WILL BE DONE*, she had, after three days contemplating it, told the dream to Mrs Tweedie. Mrs Tweedie lifted her gaze to something above Anna's head, remained silent for some time, before looking into Anna's eyes and saying: *You must go at once back to Father Bede.*

Anna had sent a telegram to let him know of her imminent arrival, had cashed in the return part of her ticket back to Australia, bought a cheap flight with Syrian Airlines and left four days later. Stepping down once again from the Trichy-Kullitalai bus at four in the morning, her heart as light as the breaking dawn, she walked the sandy path through the coconut groves to the ashram arch. She went straight to Father Bede's hut where she knew he would be writing before early prayers. He had not received the telegram, it would arrive in two days time, but he greeted her as if he knew. *Come to see me after Mass,* he said. She would take him her manuscript and paintings of *Patrick and the Cat Who Saw Beyond Time.*

He welcomed her, once more the peacock on the palm thatch cried its haunting cry as Anna handed Father Bede her story. His delight in *Patrick* and in the paintings, mandalas which accompanied the small book, jewels of colour, registered octaves of happiness in her heart. Mrs Tweedie's own response to the painting of Om, the Silver Moon Cat, had been to gasp, place her hand over the painting, command the attention of the group to say: *Look at this, friends,* lifting her hand and holding up the painting, *Sitadevi has painted an archetype. This Cat comes from beyond Time,* and, returning the small painting to Anna, said: *Your book must be published.*

As Father Bede held the paintings and the story he suddenly sat back, then leant forward, placed his elbows on his dhoti covered knees. The peacock ceased to cry, the wind stopped, 'presences' gathered, palpable in the room.

In the silence as the world listened Father Bede finished without any prompt or thought from Anna the sentence he had begun a year before:

And some dreams come from God ... It was a holy moment.

Many years had passed since then, now Anna was in her own garden in southern Queensland, planting clumps of daffodil bulbs, Father Bede no longer on this earth, and yet, everywhere. When Father Bede's voice came as clear and audible as if next to her: *"I shall be with you till the end of days..."* his words from her dream remained suspended in the air; she knew he was *there*.

Anna sat for a long, long time. The light faded. The wind stopped, the 'presences' dissolved. She rose, walked back up the verandah steps, picked up a pencil and paper and began to draw. The design for her leadlight door, over which she had been struggling for months, flowed from her pencil. It was for Father Bede. Supercharged with Shakti Anna completed the whole project in four days, working sixteen hours a day, cutting, setting the glass, soldering the lead. When she sold the cottage three years later, 'his' door would go with her to far North Queensland.

A month passed. She received a letter from Christudas:

> *My dearmost Sitadevi,*
>
> *How are you my dear? Hope you are doing fine. Really we are all very very sad always due to the death of our Fr. Bede. He was sick almost five months and May 13th 4.30 p.m. he died in my hands. Very peaceful death. Actually nobody could see the pain of death. Such a peaceful way he breathed his last. Even though he is not present bodily, his spirit is always very present. We had two Masses, one by the Bishop and another by local parish priest and others. The sun was so hot but exactly at about 3 p.m. on Saturday 15th May it became dark everywhere, terrible breeze and heavy wind, the trees were pouring its leaves to the*

cemetery. People from the villages surprised to see. And
said, this man was a great saint. Anyhow, Father
Bede is a saint and he will be with God. We too will
be with him one day. Really I am very much despond
and feel like an orphan. What to do? How are you my
dear? Are you o.k.? At least you had a good chance to
be with Father Bede last year and he blessed your
meditation room etc. Really it was his last days. Who
knew all this? He had a wonderful time with you.
Such a wonderful time, I will never forget my dear. So
wish you all the best and pray for you and pray for me,
Your unhappy Fr. Christudas

On that first Easter Friday two thousand years ago didn't
the sky grow dark for three hours? When really great
people die Nature responds. Two streams of light poured
up from the room in which the great Benedictine,
Hildegard von Bingen, lay on her deathbed on the 17th
September 1179. Didn't a colossal blue comet appear over
Arunacala when Ramana Maharshi died? When Sri
Anirvan the great sage of Samkhya died lightning struck
and cleaved in half the tree by his hut. When Carl Jung
died lightning struck the tree he loved at Bollingen in the
same way. Now Father Bede had died and an inexplicable
wind whipped up a storm as the funeral rites were being
performed and the trees overhead rained leaves like hail.
When Sita died the Earth opened and received her body.
At the funeral of Gurdjieff, sage or magus, who knows, the
electricity failed and only the small candle of each of those
present served as light. Stories abound of saints and sages
being honoured in their passing by Mother Nature. She
knows Her own. But who records these mysteries?

It was time to fulfil the task given her by Father Bede.
When he had told her to complete his 'journey to the
Black Madonna' the gravitas with which he spoke brooked
no hesitation on her part. The 'how' would unfold in due
time.

17

Shock – and Shakti

Time passed. How to fulfil the great task asked of her? How to get to France, from Australia? and what, really, would Anna be looking for? She pondered these things, and now, looking back, reflected how Time had warped the tapestry of memory. Details of 'how' assumed a chimera, shape-shifting around the core facts she could lay claim to.

She frowned as she always did when concentrating, a groove riven deep into her forehead, not from anger but concentration. She recalled making an application years before for a certain grant and, having no reply, assumed she was unsuccessful. Father Bede had stayed with her in 1992. In 1993 Anna was invited to a conference in Bangalore to mark the twentieth Mahasamadhi – anniversary of death – of Père Henri le Saux, the French Benedictine monk known as Swami Abhishiktananda. Attendees were invited to propose a paper on Shakti and Pneuma. Shakti was a subject Anna now knew marrow deep. She examined Pneuma and found she could relate it to spirit, Spirit, masculine in Latin. She knew also that in the earlier Greek *pneuma* – the Breath of Life - was feminine. The Church of the Occident now used the masculine, Latin, translation, to the everlasting detriment of women. She would compose her papers around Shakti and Pneuma according to her own understanding and sent off her reply. But how could she get there? Father Bede's task remained on the back burner for the time being.

A few days later Anna received another letter, one which sent shock waves through her. It wouldn't shock most people, for most people she knew, everyone she knew actually, had the security of home, career, education, family encouragement and more, or less, of the privileges of the western world. But this letter struck at the deep core of her earthly experience – rejection, homelessness, abandonment. It was from a government department questioning something to do with her application for a First Home Owners Grant. It told her she must phone them as soon as possible. Anna read the first three words of the departmental title and fear blocked all else. Why, she had only been into Brisbane that very week to pay her monthly dues – what can have happened?

Whenever Anna was afraid she became very, very still. She *was* afraid. She sat for a long long time. Then she put the letter aside and allowed herself to go through the worst scenario. Homeless – *again*. If that was to be, then she had better gather all her faltering courage and make that phone call. Just to be on the safe side of all possibilities she took out last week's receipt with the governmental phone number heading it as proof that she hadn't defaulted on her payment. She dialled the familiar number. Each month when she went in to pay she always commented on how hugely grateful she was to live in a country that supported its indigent and unmoored poor. It was the money the department staff paid in tax that meant she had a roof over her head. Her appreciation drew warm smiles from everyone she came in contact with there, and she meant it fervently every month.

The man who answered Anna's call was more than puzzled. He remembered her, she had never defaulted. Furthermore he didn't know of any letter going out from his department in that vein, even by mistake. Anna picked up the letter in question, read it to him. *But* he said, gently in response to the rising panic in her voice, *who is it from?* She read the departmental name at the top of the letter. *Well,* he said, *that's not us! We're the First Home Owners Loan department. The First Home Owners Grant section moved to Melbourne a couple of months ago, here, I'll give you their freecall number.*

Anna burst out laughing. Thanking him profusely and chiding herself for her unfounded panic she dialled the freecall to Melbourne.

En route from Brisbane to their new office, the man on the end of the phone told her, the computer with her original 1989 application on it coughed, or something like that, and when the computer was re-connected up popped her original application. Puzzled that there was no record of her receiving their response the officers assessing the applicants sent her the letter in question. The First Home Owner's Grant of $3000 – or was it $5000? – *had* been granted to her in 1989 or 1990, the sum to be paid over a few years. The government was *paying her ...*

The following day, having slept on her life with its current needs – the fare to Bangalore at that moment – Anna phoned back, emboldened by their error. *Could I possibly,* she had the temerity to ask, *have the arrears paid all at once?* The man went off to ask his superior. They agreed as it was their error that she could have the whole amount by Friday. It was Tuesday. The next morning she woke again with thoughts about her windfall. The grant was meant for household goods. She phoned again to appease any possible guilt over her plan for Bangalore. *You know,* she said, *I am enormously grateful for this windfall but in the years since my application I have bought all the bed linen and all the saucepans I need. Do I have to buy household goods with it?* The man asked her to hold a moment, and then returned to say jovially, *We've taken so long about giving you this you can use it to go on a holiday ....*

The sum gave Anna plenty enough for return flights to Bangalore and a little pot of gold left over for France, or at least some part of that next journey. In Bangalore the next golden thread appeared. She gave her talk. She could sense some of the women present bristle. Some were religious and some were not, all were from Germany or Switzerland or Austria or England. Each was famous in her field, whether as a nun founding an ashram in India or as an expert on Henri le Saux or as an academic in anthropology. Anna felt uncomfortable, she knew they simply didn't like her, they were *real* scholars and they knew she wasn't. And true to form in those far-off days when she knew she was not liked and had no way of redeeming herself – or of escaping the discomfort of the situation she found herself in – she would adopt the rôle of a silly female; one who couldn't possibly read a *proper* book let alone produce a work of scholarship. It was, anyway, never her resolve or vocation to solve theological antinomies but to live from within, in an authentic way. It was her own life she had to save. She was, at that time, tentatively synthesising Spirit and Matter; something she was beginning to discover that intellect and western theology had moved far away from, had separated, to the detriment of Women, Nature and her beloved Earth.

Papers read, the day over, Anna remained alone, chatted to the gardener, went to her room after supper. There was a knock on her door, it was dark, darkness falls early in the Tropics, and she opened it to find one of the priests, a gently spoken Spanish Jesuit, who had spent decades in India and deeply understood the ancient texts of the Tantras and of Samkhya which enshrined the living experience of which she had attempted to speak of. Anna invited him in. *I felt compelled to come,* he said, *though it may be slightly out of order for a priest to visit a woman after dark, but I want to say your paper, it is the most powerful of any I have heard, I felt deeply what you were saying.*

He wanted her to know this, because she hadn't presented it in a scholarly way. *It was real,* he said, *an authentic experience, not academic.* The words of this wise and gentle priest touched her. He told her that in Hebrew the word for 'she' was interchangeable with the word for 'abomination'. His words hit the pit of Anna's stomach where her womanroar still lay dormant. She wished she could remember now much more of what that dear priest had said, and even more, what she had written. So long before she owned a computer on which to store such things, the handwritten notes had long disappeared.

She closed the door and sat quietly in reflection of her understanding of Shakti. Her visit to Lizelle Reymond years before had revealed depths. In an exquisite small book of essays on Shakti this great Swiss woman had written of the West's discovery of atomic power and the West's ignorance of Shakti other than the mere word: *Shakti is this power*, she said, *and to capture it, to use it, is to perform black magic on a grand scale*, Anna's mind was then still inchoate on the subject, and she absorbed Mme Reymond's wisdom uncritically: *risking what will happen when forces are unleashed without knowing how to neutralize them. Assuming the rôle of God to satisfy unrestrained egos will only lead to chaos.* The world was travelling fast toward that chaos, but it would not be the chaos of potent creation, Anna reflected sadly, but the chaos of self-destruction. She would live to see it.

As if reading her mind Madame Reymond had then continued: *The bija-mantra the great gurus know establishes contact with the divine vibration, contains the principles of centripetal and centrifugal forces; if the Sound dies, the earth will die.* Madame Reymond, paused, offered Anna chocolates, Swiss chocolates, and when Anna accepted said briskly: *Swamis don't eat chocolates, become a woman, it is your birthright in the West. We need enlightened western women to carry the wisdom of India to us, we do not need swamis; by looking different, by calling yourself a 'swami' you are separating truth from appearances. What do you want to do with your life?*

Anna didn't know. Anna didn't know very much about herself at all in those days. She wanted God, but she held that back. What *was* God? She knew innately the essence of Power, of Shakti, of Obedience, but did all that add up to God? She wasn't sure Madame Reymond would be satisfied with *that* answer. This little Swiss grill was more challenging than Anne's Five Year Plan.

You are a seeker, she continued, *a hundred thousand seekers take the road; one, perhaps, may reach the goal. All seeds do not germinate, those who do not will become humus, but what fertile humus to feed those who follow, we must make ourselves good humus. The humus, the goal, the seeker and what is sought makes up the spiritual atmosphere so characteristic of India. Failure is not spoken of, for all effort springs from the law of Obedience, that subtle yoga which sustains the traditional family unit, a yoga frequently misunderstood by those outside it.* Mme Reymond suggested three rules to live by, rules given to her by the rishi she had written of whose wisdom had brought Anna to her door:

> *Use the least possible number of objects, for that is freedom from externals;*
> *Expect nothing from tomorrow, for that is freedom from time;*
> *Go to sleep each night in the arms of Yama, for that is to be reborn each morning.*

Madame Reymond softened, she was a little bird like creature with a wondrous mass of greying, but not too greying, Anna observed, marvelling, hair piled on pile atop her head: *When these truths are in your blood, the minutest cells of your consciousness will be transformed,* and, turning to the bookcase extracted a hard cover copy of her book to give Anna, with: *Please take these roses,* pulling a large bunch from a vase and wrapping them well, *I am leaving in the morning for Paris and there will be no one to appreciate them here; flowers need to be appreciated and loved if we are to pick them.*

Anna accepted the blood red blooms and the precious book, and the remonstrations, bent down a little to hug the very old woman. Madame Reymond returned the embrace warmly, and with affection wished Anna a fond farewell for her journey through life. Anna knew she was being hugged as a woman; swami's wouldn't hug, would they? Becoming a woman herself would take many, many years.

Our earth is dying, we are killing it by degrees, Anna confided to her journal that evening. She was staying in Geneva with her aunt, a difficult woman as unlike her sister Alice as could be. Their fourth sister, Odette, had been brought back from South Africa to attend a Swiss hospital; she was shortly to die from a brain tumour. Irene, the fifth sister, was making ill-timed advances to Odette's chevalier and the tension in the small apartment was suffocating. Anna mostly remained in her room and was chided for that too. How could she reconcile Shakti as the Mystery of mysteries, the Void, the Dazzling Darkness, of all religions when such anger ricocheted through the very walls around her? If Shakti was spirit-matter, matter-spirit, and all matter 'inspired' by its creation and infused by it, was even the war going on in the next room, *Shakti?* The thought-form of a M. Renault in creating the gearbox is 'inspired', matter and spirit fused; cause and effect are Shakti; consciousness, Shiva, is inert without Shakti to vivify. *Shakti*, the very word caused the heart to tremble at its magnitude and here Anna was caught in the maelstrom of its individual power.

Ten minutes or so passed. There was another knock on her door. Anna opened it to the Canadian priest who, years later, was to write a short and profound appraisal to her small book, the book she was to leave at Notre-Dame after Bataclan. He came in and said much about her paper; how moved he had been. He had sensed her discomfort in the presence of the scholars. Anna longed for the privilege of education. When he left she thanked the Divine Shakti for being present. A kind of oracular veil would part in moments like that and close again before consciousness could embed the words.

The following day one of the women from Switzerland stood at the lectern to share her research on the existing images and statues of – *the Black Madonna.* Throughout France and in particular Einsiedeln she had seen them all. This was Anna's epiphany moment. Even now, writing of it, she felt her breath catch, her skin prickle at its memory. She recalled how her inner voice honed, and intoned, the words: *Listen! This is for you.* Now she knew such things she could attempt to fulfil the task of Father Bede.

That evening Anna recalled Philippa's book, she too had been confounded by her life, true, her life was chaotic in a different way to Anna's, but it was that chaos that drove her to a powerful conclusion: *Tantra and Catholicism were intimately holders of the same secret knowledge.* Pre-Reformation Catholicism contained all the ingredients of Tantra and Philippa, far from being Catholic herself, used authoritative examples. At the height of the Victorian Raj a remarkable English High Court judge in Calcutta, Fellow of the Calcutta University and appointed Tagore Law Professor, Sir John Woodruffe, adopted an interesting nom-de-plume to disguise his research into Tantra: *Arthur Avalon.* The combination of myth, mystery and the esoteric enshrined in his choice drew the attention of Orientalists and Theosophists; his weighty tomes were to pre-empt the western embrace of the eastern mysticism he was exploring.

His thesis was simple and profound: the male and female principles found united in Tantra: Siva-Shakti, Purusha-Prakriti, Sita-Ram, Radha-Krishna, where the Shakti principle is the primordial Word, are mirrored in Catholicism: Christ-Mary or, as carved in the stones of the great Abbey of Glastonbury where Arthur was buried on the sacred Isle of Avalon: Jesus-Maria. *No Mary, no Jesus,* said Mother Teresa simply to an English reporter for whom Mary had been extinguished from his ancestral cellular memory since the carnage of Cromwell.

The great symbols of Catholicism are the yantras upon which to focus the mind; the psalms and the prayers chanted in rhythmic plain-chant are the mantras; the churches and cathedrals of the pre-Deformation are symbols of the body running from the font, representing Mooladhara, up through the nave, the choir and the corona to the Rose window, the Sahasrara, the thousand-petalled lotus.

After the conference Anna took a train to Tiruchirappallai, going on to Shantivanam for a week to be alone with the spirit of Father Bede, Swami Abhishiktananda and Père Monchanin each of whom were buried there; well, their shrines are there, and so their spirit. It was now December. On the 17th of the month the ashram would celebrate the anniversary of Father Bede's birth. He had died in May that year, just a year after leaving Anna and Australia. Her affection for the sincerity of le Saux's spiritual quest and her affinity with Bede easily ameliorated for Anna their marked differences.

Christudas welcomed Anna sadly. The anguished letter he had written to her after Father Bede's death was a *cri de cœur*. He gave Anna the key to Father Bede's hut, a rare privilege, for very unspiritual things had happened when the world heard of his death – is it possible to believe that some wealthy among his followers descended on the ashram from Germany, from England, from Switzerland, from America, to steal what they could as souvenirs? Poor Father, he owned virtually nothing yet even his beloved fountain pens had been stolen. What to do? Christudas felt helpless. Even with little left in the hut, to be given the key was a rare trust. *You can go to Father's hut*, he said, *at four in the morning and meditate sitting on Father's bed just as he used to. You will feel his presence.*

She helped Christudas sort out the little of what the thieves had left behind of Father's papers and writings and then he left her. By Father Bede's bed, on the floor, lay a slim manuscript that Bede may have been reading before he died. Anna picked it up. Goodness! It was *hers!* Father Bede had written the Foreword to *Patrick and the Cat Who Saw Beyond Time* and a year later Anna had sent him the manuscript of its companion volume: *Anna and the Heavenly Horse*, her own *cri de cœur*. Father Bede loved both stories. Anna picked up her manuscript, smiling to herself that no one had considered it worth stealing. As she put it to one side a smaller, loose, page slipped out. She looked at it closely and her heart leapt. In Father's own hand, written in pale blue Quink, was the prayer he had written when he felt death call. What should she do? He had hidden it in *her* manuscript. He knew Anna was coming to Shantivanam because they had discussed it over porridge. Anna decided he had deliberately placed his prayer inside the pages of *Anna and the Heavenly Horse* for he knew some words of his final prayer just might be expunged by those who didn't have the consciousness of the holy, of the Para Shakti, of the *Mother Goddess*. In his own hand he had written:

*In the name of the Father, the Son and the Holy
Spirit. Amen.*

*I dedicate myself to total love for the Father, the
Ground and Source of all creation the Origin from
whom all being comes, the One beyond name and form;
beyond word and thought, the Infinite, the Eternal, the
Absolute unchanging, unmanifest, unconditional,
Source of truth and love.*

*To the Son, the self's manifestation of the Father, the
Creator, the Preserver, the Word and Wisdom of the
Father, the revealer of the Father's love, the Form of
all forms. The Truth and the Life, the Light of all
lights, the Sound from the Silence of the Father, the
Supreme, the Model and Exemplar of all personal
being, the Redeemer and Saviour, the Deliverer from
all evil, from all attachment to matter and form, to time
and space, to change and decay, the expression of the
Father's love.*

*To the Holy Spirit, the Breath of love, the outpouring
of the love of the Father and the Son, the love energy in
all creation, the Presence of the Father and the Son in
the stars, the sun, the moon, the earth and all plants
and animals, the Heart of all creation, the breath of
life, the power of love, the Indweller in every heart, the
Inspirer of every good thought, the Sanctifier, present in
all true religion, inspirer of all true scriptures, source of
all enlightenment, the Mother, the Bride, the Womb of
Creation, the source of all energy, of life to plants and
animals, of love in human beings, the Virgin Mother,
manifest in Mother Earth and the Mother Goddess
and the Virgin Mary.*

*I offer my life through Mary, the Virgin Mother of
Jesus, the Saviour to the Holy Trinity, Father, Son
and Holy Spirit.*

There. He had said it. *The Mother Goddess.* After his vision
of the Black Madonna as *Para Shakti* Father Bede had seen
Her in All, as All. The All that he would also name Mother
Goddess; but to whom could he say this? Anna had not
yet been embraced by Her. That was in the future when

the golden string guiding her along the labyrinthine ways of her own particular path would bring her to Glastonbury and to Avalon and to a landscape sacred to that Mother Goddess, whose ancient cosmology was being re-vivified, re-imagined, by the vision of Kathy Jones. Later still Anna would see the whole earth as sacred and wounded, *then* it would demand of her discrimination, the gift of making beauty out of the broken world, out of the chaos man was making in his hubris. A sacred footprint would be demanded of her. The whole world, the whole earth, is 'eco-fragile'. An empty truism now coined for conference titles all over the world while her beloved Earth was being plundered.

Anna offered a prayer in that beatific space where Father Bede had lived and died, tucked his written prayer back into the leaves of her own manuscript and walked guiltlessly back to her hut. She trusted his words and his vision of Her implicitly, knew that few others could or would. His words, written in his own hand and revealing his penultimate experience, would simply *disappear* unless she kept them safe.

Anna spent the week at Shantivanam in prayer, meditation and in quiet reflection with Christudas. Mrs Tweedie was always in her heart. She mentioned to Christudas the book which she had given Father Bede in the eighties, when he had asked her to leave the ashram at Mangrove Mountain and accompany him to Shantivanam. Christudas told her *Chasm of Fire* had caused much controversy in the months leading up to Father Bede's final stroke for he had chosen it to be read during lunch, a traditional Benedictine discipline to encourage silent reflection during mealtimes. Anna's imagination took flight thinking of some of the acolytes, brothers and guests, while eating rice and curry, listening in astonishment and probably acute discomfort at Mrs Tweedie's graphic description of the sexual nature of the raising of Kundalini – hers!

More poignant was Anna's discovery that her copy of Jeanine's book, given to Father Bede during his final visit when he could neither put it down nor finish

155

reading it in four days, had also been stolen. *Vision of Cosmic Order in the Vedas* was now out of print and costly now as a collector's item. *Chasm of Fire* had vanished from the library too. She could replace the second but not the first. It saddened her. She treasured a photo of him reading it on her verandah, after the porridge for breakfast. When Father Bede had stayed with her the previous April, the April of 1992, Anna showed him the newly published book Jeanine had brought with her as a gift, had pressed him to take it to finish. She would collect it from Shantivanam later that year. Father Bede and Jeanine had not met but over the years he used her translation of Sanskrit texts when writing his own books: *Her translation is the finest I knew, her rare mystical insight brings the wisdom of the Rishis alive.* But her precious book had vanished with the *homo trium literarum*.

Anna had known Jeanine well. Mere weeks before Father Bede's visit she had sat on the same chair on Anna's verandah in Silkstone on her own final world lecture tour with the English Theosophical Society. From the same green chair he was to sit in just weeks later Jeanine wrote Father Bede a postcard saying how much she regretted that coming so close after all these decades of admiration for each other's work their timing was just weeks short of a possibility to meet.

Jeanine shone, she glowed from within. Jeanine was a shining memory. Philippa Pullar, whose singular presence warmed into friendship when Anna had sat next to her in Mrs Tweedie's kitchen one afternoon and complimented her on the attractive smell of wood smoke emanating from her woolly jumpers, was another. She lived in Barnes, rustically so, and adored cats. Their rapport deepened when Philippa learnt Anna loved a Kurd and she regaled her with hilariously insightful anecdotes of her own thwarted journeys along the border mountains between Turkey and Iraq hoping to research the Kurds, and riding a *donkey!* Philippa was loveable, distant, and, so Anna from Australia and completely ignorant of such things, discovered, Famous. A Writer. Philippa had warned her Kurds were tribal: *It will be very difficult,* she said, *for Yahia to adjust to Australia. I wish you both great happiness ... you certainly wouldn't survive in a Kurd village,* she had added solicitously.

Knowing women like Jeanine and Philippa lifted Anna's spirits to a higher level of awareness, added an éclat to her abiding memories of meditating for four years sitting at the feet, as the Indians say, of a great teacher. Mrs Tweedie would shudder at 'Teacher', but for Anna she was truly that. She had once tentatively asked Mrs Tweedie if she was her Teacher and Mrs Tweedie drew herself up in her chair, filling her whole Russianness with superb grandeur to say, *I am nobody's teacher, I am a disciple. Ahead of me is always my Teacher's Teacher's Teacher.* Anna had infinitesimally gasped, and smiled: *What a teaching,* she thought and knew then that Tweedie, as she always referred to herself, was *her* Teacher! Her beloved Teacher.

When Anna followed Father Bede to Shantivanam after their first meeting in the 'eighties when she had given him a copy of *The Chasm of Fire* he told her she must find Mrs Tweedie. But how? Resource, a characteristic that led her where Angels feared to tread, inspired her obvious recourse to write to the publisher, Element. Anna didn't receive a reply, but arriving in London in 1986 and spending time with Alice, and with friends in Devon, she learned of a private house in Mitcham owned by Doriel Hall, a follower of Satyananda, who offered rooms to homeless swamis. Anna was accepted. She liked Doriel but not Doriel's smoking, blackened toothed, East End boyfriend. Try as she might she was unable to reconcile the refinements of Doriel with the cruder fabric that made up Jimmy. Anna spent as many of her days as she could by going to the little Jesuit church in Mayfair, discovering Farm Street by chance; or to Ealing Abbey. Meeting Father Vincent, Isabelle and Peter Glover, felt like coming home to a home she'd never known. The soul, she discovered, was where she loved, not where she lived.

Father Vincent had known Father Bede, had spent a whole year at Shantivanam, regaled Anna with anecdotes while she listened affectionately; he and Anna spent hours together, he opened for her the ways of the whole mystical generosity of the Benedictine tradition during tea and cake on Fridays. It was almost inevitable Anna would become Catholic then, received into the Church on Easter Saturday 1986, in the ceremony of the Easter Fire calling the Dawn to Earth, lighting a Way for the Renewal rich in the symbolism she understood so well. Anna became a Catholic on Easter Saturday between the Death and the Resurrection.

Her father and her two aunts came to the Easter Saturday to support her reception into the great tradition and it moved her beyond measure that Isabelle Glover would welcome Anna and Guy as house-guests, open her home to Anna's aunts over the whole weekend, cook vast cauldrons of wondrously tasty food to share amongst all. Anna's experience of this kind of generosity and this abundance of food was a revelation unknown in her own life lived on the edge. She sensed an unconditional love from Isabelle as well as an unspoken love, an acceptance, from her father and Aunt Alice and Aunt Zabeth in coming to a Catholic monastery, accepting her decision to revert, in the historical anguish of the religious persecution of their own forebears, to the older Church. Dressed in her geru dhoti and kurta, as yet her only wardrobe, she walked carrying her own Easter candle down the great nave to be received by the Abbot who had said earlier, with kindliness twinkling behind his eyes: *We give all our strange ones to Father Vincent!*

Father Vincent had given her a passage from Paul to read as part of her introduction to Catholicism. Anna was not enamoured of Paul. Father Vincent had to give her a bible too, and she read the homework dutifully and seriously, somehow in an altered frame of mind which revealed a deeper side to Paul than the misogyny she mostly attributed to him. When she returned on the following Friday to give an account of her reading Father Vincent flung himself back in his deep tweed covered armchair to say: *In all my decades as a priest I have never heard such a depth of insight – I think we'll just enjoy tea and chat for our future meetings!*

Anna couldn't recall either the insight or the Pauline verse which occasioned it, but the pleasure of tea and scones in this delightful monk's company was something she looked forward to every week for three months.

Anna saw herself as a Catholic without portfolio, a kind of flying buttress to her chosen church, supporting it from without rather than within, but as a Benedictine she could embrace it. She loved it and knew it as the only church holding sacraments and angels and saints and Mary. She learnt that Mary's birthday fell on her own, a particular revelation that deepened over the years. The feminine force, *Shakti*, became the *raison d'être* to Anna becoming Catholic at all, the Marion mysteries led Anna ineffably to that great Shakti whose thread she was unconsciously following. Father Bede had made her an Oblate of Saint Benedict, little knowing how it would define her understanding of the Black Madonna in the years yet to unfold.

One afternoon Anna returned to Mitcham to be given a phone message. Jimmy had almost refused to write it down, he didn't like Anna any more than she liked him, but, with that magic which courted her life, another swami passing along the hall heard mention of *Sitadevi* and interjected to say he would give her the message. Thus the details, circumventing any whim of human forgetfulness, were passed on. The message was from Mrs Tweedie!

It was also thrilling! Mrs Tweedie lived in north London, far from Mitcham, and opened her door at three o'clock every weekday, welcoming those who came to half an hour meditation, 'tea and gossip'. Anna went the next day and fell in love with Mrs Tweedie the moment she beheld her, stood for several dozen heartbeats, awed by this small, sturdy woman in front of her. Tweedie, as she referred to herself, was uncompromising, the very embodiment of that promise of security which only a person grounded in truth can offer to another, especially another so uncertain of her own truth as Anna. Could Anna say Tweedie changed her life? She could, and would.

A beautiful young woman came to Teignmouth Road from Spain. Mrs Tweedie welcomed her, called her to sit close. The beautiful young woman had fantasy in her eyes, and love, and hope. She spoke: *Mrs Tweedie, I read your book, it changed my life.*

Mrs Tweedie leant forward, cupped the beautiful face of the young woman, barely more than a girl, in her hands. Then she sat back and laughed: *Friends!* her voice rang, *did you hear this beautiful young woman say she has read my book and it changed her life?* Mrs Tweedie paused, then looked down at the beautiful upturned face in front of her to say: *That's wonderful darlinkg, you read my book and it changed your life? It has taken me twenty-five years.*

Anna 'got it'. So did the beautiful young woman. Mrs Tweedie sat back upright in her large chair. She spoke of The Hint. Of how one must be always alert for the Hint from God, and how a word or a sentence spoke to one may be meant for another. Out of the window the white cherry blossom filled the view of the garden, a blackbird sang there, a breeze stirred the flowers, Anna stared and stared as an image of Christ metamorphosed from within the blossom. Mrs Tweedie had looked at her quizzically when Anna told her she had become a Catholic. No word was said, Anna was still being given the silent treatment, but the Face in the cherry blossom was all she needed to know, then.

Anna returned to Australia from her sojourn in India filled with the presence of both Bede and Abhishiktananda, but still unsure of how to plan for France. She didn't speak her father's language, had no clue where to begin. But, like Voltaire, she concentrated on creating her large garden in Silkstone, south-east Queensland. A curious thing happened. Her cottage, slightly more than a miner's cottage, more middle-management for the coal mining community of Ipswich, built on the crest of the hill, had an old picket fence of unusual design from a century ago. Made from ironbark it was unassailable by borers, flood or fire; however, it was in a wobbly state of disrepair and the half-acre garden bereft of all life when she moved there, other than the solitary mango tree ubiquitous to all Queensland suburban gardens of the era. Slowly Anna planned garden rooms, free-standing trellises for climbing roses, tropical corners, a graceful Jacaranda, weeping peppercorns on the wide grass verge in front of the cottage, jasmine bowers – and three Wilhelm Reich drainpipes set upright to draw rainclouds at the bottom of the property; a trick she was taught by Serge Kahili King, the Hawaiian shaman visiting Brisbane from Kauai.

Anna had once travelled alone down a small mountain in Himachal Pradesh to Dharamsala in the company of an itinerant Nyingma Pa lama with thigh bones in his wild hair, wearing a necklet of skulls, spectacles the thickness of coke bottle bottoms, and, with a huge snaggle-toothed smile, he informed her by signs that he was a rainmaker. He called the clouds through his large conch shell with ritual and prayers. Not conversant with Tibetan Anna nevertheless clocked the gist of his magical powers and had faith enough in genuine shamans to know those potential powers as authentic.

She had gone, then, to the local plumbing supplies, each pipe was to be six inch ID – inside diameter – she said, claiming trade talk, and: *Please cut them each exactly twenty-seven feet long.*

Whaddya gonna use 'em for? asked the young salesman, and blinked when she replied: *I'm going to call rain.* Anna was small, but the authority with which she delivered her ideas carried authenticity, even when speaking of drainpipes. There had been drought for pretty well nine years out there in inland Ipswich; the town denied the sea weather that brought rain to Brisbane merely forty kilometres east.

The young man had a brother Out West. Things were seriously dry out there. Could she guarantee rain? he asked. *Well, it's not an exact science,* Anna said, *but it's worth the cost of the pipes to try.* He delivered them free of charge, and, helped by Darren, put them up propped slightly tepee style and firmly tied. Darren had come to her first meditation evening some months before, *après le Kurd,* and during it had seen himself sitting in the Hand of God, having come off a bit of a drug run a month before that. He'd stayed ever since, a godsend to her, her penury, her home, her garden, her car and, furthermore, loved cats.

Three days later it rained. After *years.* And continued for three days. Not enough to break a drought, but enough to bring the excited young salesman back to thank her for a great idea to pitch to his brother Out West. He liked her picket fence too, which, with great good will Darren had raised up, sanded down and painted the colour of buttermilk. The resurrection of the fence began a ripple effect in Macquarie Street as neighbours forked out various sums for variations on replicating turn-of-the-century picket fences to replace the ghastly chain mesh currently in situ and so alien to the charm of old timber Queenslanders up and down the old street. As her roses and her trees and garden rooms grew so the same neighbours stopped to talk over her pretty, and unique, swagged picket fence to ask what and how and where questions. Gardens were taking shape behind those newly erected pretty picket fences when a young woman from the top of the road, a new resident, introduced herself, wanting to create a garden too. She had a French sister in law. Her French sister in law knew all the seven French families in Ipswich, and very soon every one of them was fascinated by Anna's fantasy of France and her Quest for their Black Madonnas. They all had connections, families, in France who responded with information and encouragement. They translated for her, organized hiring a car for her from Paris, wrote to monasteries and convents for her. All that from a fallen picket fence, Voltaire's admonition to tend her garden, and her faith in a Nyingma Pa lama's rainmaking.

One evening Anna had gone as usual to the regular meeting at the Thesosophical Society in the old timber heritage building on Wickham Terrace, a place of charm and calm. A woman, whose back was to her as Anna entered the upper room, was speaking with E. the

162

president. Anna hadn't seen that back for *thirty* years but she knew it: *Mother!* she called delightedly, *I didn't know you were in Brisbane ...*

The woman turned – and passed out flat. E. caught her: *Steady on, Pat,* she said in her no-nonsense manner looking curiously at Anna who had been a member for the past four years, well-known, but for this! Anna had never mentioned her mother. Pat went very quickly into the kitchen. Anna sighed to Self: *Hmmm, that was a lead balloon,* and found a chair in the circle, put her purse on the adjacent chair to reserve for her mother. Pat, holding a glass of water, came from the kitchen and chose to sit opposite her daughter. Anna's sigh doubled, she removed her purse.

Ben came to sit with her. *Is she really your mother?* Anna nodded. Ben knew that Anna had no mother in the real sense of the word, knew she had been denied any contact with her sister. The woman was lecturing on Near Death Experiences.

Pat, said Ben, *was so unconvincing. I knew she couldn't be speaking of NDE's or she would have been radiant. She'd had an Out Of Body experience during anaesthetic for varicose vein surgery, but an OOB doesn't change you. If she'd had an NDE she would be smothering you with love and asking your forgiveness! NDE's change people big time. OOB's just give them a party chat or two but the heart isn't touched or changed a jot. I had no idea she was your mother. Now it all makes sense; are you okay?*

Anna was okay, though shaky at being rejected so publicly. She would make one last attempt at communication when coffee was served. By this time Pat's *savoir-faire* had returned. Anna said, with genuine enthusiasm, she would love to visit her, and invited her to her home in Silkstone. Pat couldn't drive, or had no car, another odd lie Anna was to discover, but surrounded by wise people Pat succumbed to suggesting a day for her daughter to visit her. She had moved up from Sydney, Stephanie was a lawyer now and lived near the RBH. Anna clocked that one, only millionaire heritage homes were in strolling distance to the great hospital. Steph owned a series of smaller houses too, rented out to students, Pat lived in a cottage in the garden of Steph's heritage home.

Darren came with her for the visit. Her mother spent the entire time sitting in her signature position sideways, speaking throughout to Darren, all the while provocatively dipping and swinging her dainty foot in his direction, making sure it could be seen under the large newspaper Darren was doing his best to hide behind. She didn't acknowledge Anna for a nano-second. As visits to reconcile mother and daughter went, this was a non-event.

As they walked back to the car Pat handed Darren a book on the black arts of psychic attack. He dropped it. With great hesitation he picked it up again, dropped it on the back seat. Out of sight of Pat's cheery: *Come again,* addressed to him, he pulled up by a rubbish bin and binned the book.

Your mother, he said, struggling to find words, *is so nice I ... I never want to see her again!*

The psychic devils inhabiting her mother made a strange attack on Anna from across space and time that night. Darren, fixing himself a late-night whatever in the kitchen, heard a wild scream from Anna's room. Anna never screamed at night, wasn't beset by nightmares, this sound chilled his blood. In four bounds he was there. In the dim light a sight electrified him, like an electrical charge he sprang across the room, grabbed the recumbent Anna and threw them both onto the floor. Anna woke at once. They sat where they fell, against the old tongue and groove timber wall. Anna was trembling. Darren was gathering breath and words to shape what he saw: *I saw the Hound of Hell* he said, *I know what it was, you screamed and I ran in. This, this, creature, huge with slavering jaws, was hovering over your bed; you were trying to sit up, I threw myself through the apparition and grabbed you. Momentum carried us to the floor. I've never seen the like but I knew what it was and it was from your mother.* It was true.

That night now flashed through Anna's mind as she recalled it. She hadn't seen the 'creature' but had been lost in a nightmare where, at the foot of her bed, she could see vast stone creatures gathering menacingly, knew they were aiming for her, an odd thought reflected through her terror that they were *stones from her motherland*. She felt her very entrails scream but heard no sound.

Minutes passed, Darren switched on the light, nothing had been disturbed; all was calm in the pretty room that Father Bede's presence had blessed. Both knew they had won then, that her mother could never hurt her again. Soon Anna would turn fifty, she would wake *that* morning with the long-coming knowledge that her mother didn't love her.

Two phone calls later that day confirmed Anna's growing wisdom on the matter of mother. Ben, to ask if she was alright, he had woken, worried during the night. Phoebe, quietly observant of the Pat-E. moment, had been at Pat's evening talk, sceptical that Pat had known the difference between Near Death and Out of Body experiences. She had shown none of the *metanoia* that accompanies true NDE's: *The radiance was missing – your mother's eyes*, said gentle Phoebe, an artist, *they'd suck the living Christ out of you*. Phoebe's words shivered through Anna. Pat was her mother, did she really have eyes like that? The only time she had glimpsed it was in a large portrait Pat had commissioned, the artist had seen through the glamour and painted true. Anna was impressed that hand paint and eye could capture such vivid reality. Pat loathed the finished painting and apparently destroyed it.

The remaining pot of gold would see to her travels around France but the fares to reach there from Australia ran to four figures, she had to think outside the box. She bought Ean Begg's gazetteer: *The Cult of the Black Virgin*. The book fired her courage; she knew she must make a pilgrimage to all the shrines she was reading about and taking heart from all the local French encouragement began to plan, *seriously*. France was that magical word, world, of her own name, her father and her grandmother; France was the other half of her soul. India and France – the great Meher Baba, whose Avatar's Abode just a few hours' drive north was a regular sanctuary of calm for Anna, had written that one of his *masts*, those wild God-mad men of India, was the spiritual charge-man of France from the highest plane, that France held the spiritual seed of all Europe.

France: a little more of the sacred thread Anna was following unravelled, untraveled. Anna was weaving it around the world, answering the Obedience that called her toward France, to the Black Madonna, and forward into the future where India and The Tiger and the Taxi Driver waited with their gift of A Lavender Codicil.

18

Demiquaver – from Dhoti to Dotage

Anna's third arrival in England, in the late 'eighties, before her final homecoming, found her with only her dhotis as garments and she soon discovered charity shops to augment her need for seasonally suitable clothing. Nothing as common as charity shops existed on Mitcham Common and black featured heavily in Tooting and Tooting Bec and Brixton, but anything was better than red-white-n-blue or lolly pink, the preferred English colour-code. One afternoon Anna had returned to a phone message from Mrs Tweedie, telling of meditation at her home in north London every day of the week between three o'clock and seven o'clock. At last, an answer to her letter to Mrs Tweedie's publisher. And an answer to a dream neither she nor her corduroy clad shaman analyst, Brian, could properly interpret at the end of her analysis in Wollongong. In the dream Anna had been invited to a group, a meditation group which met in a private home in north London between the hours of three and seven, where the wise white-haired woman at the centre of the group said to those who came: *Welcome, here we drink the Wine of the Beloved*, and the garden beyond the French windows was a place of paradise.

A woman had made Anna ugly; another woman would make her beautiful, and would give her back *herself*. Mrs Tweedie. In *her* presence the emergent womanly wonderfulness dormant in Anna, woke up.

Anna had gone to Mrs Tweedie on the very day following the phone call; the garden beyond the French windows where sat wise white-haired Mrs Tweedie was that same garden of paradise. Mrs Tweedie welcomed her: *Come in, darlinkg,* she said, *here we drink tea and we meditate together and then we gossip.* What tea! What gossip! Nectar, ambrosia, depths beyond her sounding opened Anna's heart.

> *As a white candle*
> *In a holy place,*
> *So is the beauty*
> *Of an aged face.*
>
> *As the spent radiance*
> *Of the winter sun,*
> *... a woman,*
> *... her thoughts as still*
> *As the waters*
> *Under a ruined mill.*

> *The Old Woman by Seosamh MacCathmhaoil*

Mrs Tweedie, oh how beautiful she was! Anna sat at her feet, absorbing her every movement, every word, every gesture – for four years.

One freezing, snowy day in January, just days after her first visit, Anna arrived too early. Two buses plus two different Underground lines from Mitcham to Willesden Green were chance affairs of timing, mostly she got it right but this day connections were seamless and she arrived very early. She settled herself coldly on the low snow covered wall of 35 Teignmouth Road. The winter of 1986/7 was the coldest winter in forty years. Almost at once the front door flew open and Mrs Tweedie's voice summoned her in. Confusion caused Anna to demur, she had read Mrs Tweedie's book, knew how she had suffered with climate; perhaps, ran the subliminal message through Anna's mind, Anna should suffer too. Perhaps it was a Test. Mrs Tweedie responded to Anna's silliness with: *Come in at once, you cannot sit out there in the snow!*

They were alone. Mrs Tweedie sat in the big armchair by the French windows, beckoning Anna to sit close to her. Anna had one burning question. It seemed presumptuous; she turned it in her mind until it became a statement that didn't require an answer. First though, Mrs Tweedie asked where she had come from, and on learning Australia Anna quickly assured her that she was on a one-way ticket. She wasn't, actually, her ticket was open-ended but her words screened the Longing that brought her *here;* it was too big a Longing to bear rejection now. In her silliness, her confusion, her not-knowing her place in the world and her life-sized lack of self-confidence Anna was inclined, in those years, to offer silly comments to cloud all pain-filled facts, facts which lay all-too-close to her surfaces, with *silliness.* After she had said *one-way ticket* Anna had followed her words with the silliness of: *A bit like life really.*

Mrs Tweedie was Russian. Russians do not do silly. Their sombre Slav temperament runs along serious, Slav humour belongs to an altogether different key. Mrs Tweedie turned her gaze to Anna, a charge of energy passed from her, she saw Longing writ large in those hazel eyes looking up at her, belying all silliness, aching with seriousness and pain and loss, before returning her gaze to her garden. Anna was mesmerized, two beams of Light shone from the eyes of the woman seated by that window. Her own silliness, she knew it for the smokescreen it was even as the words fell from her mouth, dissolved. The very air was charged, filled with Presences. Anna's courage found its way from her heart to speak softly the burning words: *Mrs Tweedie, you know in your book when Guruji was speaking of his father who was the midday sun, and his uncle who was the rising sun, and you asked if the setting sun would mean the end of the System?*

Mrs Tweedie made an infinitesimally small movement to sit ramrod straight, turning to look intently into Anna's face as she continued: *and he said there would always be the moon — you are the Moon, aren't you.* It was a statement.

The air was electric. Anna almost suffocated with the tension of Presences so close just as she had with Father Bede when she sat with him in his hut and he spoke of dreams, her dream, coming from God. The silence was palpable, the pause before Mrs Tweedie spoke, long. When her words came she spoke softly, turning her gaze once more across the garden: *Yes*, she said, *I am his Deputy for the English speaking people.*

The Presences relaxed and imperceptibly, it seemed to Anna, dissolved. Mrs Tweedie turned back to her and said words that burned into Anna's heart: *You are welcome, you are one of us.*

It was three o'clock. Mrs Tweedie rose to open the door for the long queue of people waiting in the snow.

For the next months Anna went almost daily, sitting quietly, loving Mrs Tweedie who quite simply ignored her. She was used to being ignored, it was imprinted at birth, her core wound, but unlike the cruel rejection charged by her mother this was an altogether different quality of being ignored, more a balm, an enfolding, a space of safety and belonging. Nourishing. No one took any notice of Anna, and she noticed no one – except Jeanine, wise, dear Jeanine who came to know Anna/Sitadevi well, came to know her knowledge of Indian spiritual texts, came to know of her closeness to Father Bede who used Jeanine's Sanskrit-to-English translations for his own references. As Sitadevi, Anna felt embraced between the most special people in the whole world – Bede and Tweedie and Jeanine. *Spiritual life*, Mrs Tweedie would say often, *is commonsense, more commonsense and more commonsense. It is so simple*, but *it is never easy.*

Once, after a dream, one of those Jung referred to as a Big Dream, Mrs Tweedie whipped up a *lila* of busy conversation amongst the group sitting in the room, to mask her words to Anna. It was in the future when the Test of Anna-being-ignored was over and Mrs Tweedie then often asked her to comment on dreams from others of the group. Mrs Tweedie had leant forward in her chair – as usual Anna was completely fixated on her – and gave an infinitesimal shiver of her shoulders. Instantly every single person in that room began talking to the person next to them. It was uncanny. Anna's nose tingled as she stared at the beautiful woman-of-power one row beyond her. Mrs Tweedie leant forward, over the heads of the talking row of oblivious people at her feet: *And you work with me in the night, but you do not remember. Father Bede works that way too. Once we were together*, she said to Anna. Anna felt shot through with a thunderbolt. She saw the *lila* and was awed. She also knew it was true that she was unable to remember, did not bring the recall through to consciousness though just occasionally she would wake and retain a fugitive glimpse of something she knew was not a dream. Mrs Tweedie sat back in her chair, another infinitesimal movement, and silence fell like a caul over the chattering group. No one had noticed a thing.

Someone mentioned marriage, Mrs Tweedie smiled. *Ah,* she said, *yes, I could take a lover ...* and the *frisson* of shock horror rippled through every male in that room as Tweedie's eyes ran slowly around those who stiffened. *She couldn't mean me? Could she? No! oh no!* could be 'heard' from every male present. A smile curled Mrs Tweedie's mouth, she was playing cat'n'mouse: *but,* she sighed with theatrical timing, *He wouldn't let me!* The release of tension was palpable. *What a lesson in attachment and appearances,* thought Anna, and wondered how many of the men present had 'got it'. Where would age and wisdom sit in their fantasies of youth and beauty?

One Saturday afternoon, many weeks into the Test of Being Ignored, Anna went into London to explore the British Museum, that great Institution which had granted free access to the world since 1763; the very thought of such generosity made her proud of being one of Boadicea's Daughters, born as she had been in that great and ancient City where Cats like Dick Whittington's, and Sparky from the Great Fire, and Hodge, so loved, had plaques and statues to honour them, stories to enchant those with sensibilities to appreciate, and pubs reflecting the grin of the legendary Cheshire Cat. A good place to visit, mused Anna, quite as charged with excitement as any Alice in Wonderland. Returning, hours later, to Charing

171

Cross, having honoured Demeter and the great Lion of Knidos, Sekhmet and Bast, Shiva Nataraj and the magnificent Tang horses in their astonishing glazes, Anna stopped to buy stamps at the Post Office, to drop off postcards of these treasures to send to friends Downunder.

There was a woman ahead of her, her young daughter with her. Anna stood, silently appraising her, knowing her. It was Judi before Dame. Nearly twenty years and too many lifetimes had passed for Anna to reminisce with the great actress over her two beautiful tortoiseshell cats who lived with Anna in the pub in Wellesbourne where she had met so many thespians of the late 'sixties. But something awoke a *frisson* of awareness in Anna as she stood contemplating this small, plump, elegant, woman of confidence and beauty, with her light brown pixie short hair; a *frisson* of something *familiar*. Something Anna recognized as her own potential. In that second sighting of Judi Dench, Anna saw something of herself-as-she-ought-to-be. She had no known sister, no cousins, no mother, no blood relatives from her maternal inheritance to assess her own appearance as she grew and matured and aged. Her paternal aunts were tall, Junoesque, puritanical in their dress and spinsterhood. In an instant, absorbing the woman in front of her, Anna knew a metamorphosis was called for. Dhotis had to go, and that new charity-shop black, a no-choice, bothered her: *You must become a woman,* whispered Mme Reymond from a place embedded in memory.

Judi and Finty moved away, Anna posted her cards, turned and headed straight for Selfridges. She emerged with a wondrously voluminous light ankle-length terracotta and Schiaparelli pink striped number of softest crinkled cotton, a charm of a dress that fell well, as well as floated, teaching Anna of weight and texture and colour in one fell swoop. A sheer cotton scarf, rainbow washed, wound as a turban round her head transformed her; she folded her dhotis into a drawer and her black fell into shadows. She was forty, a late but enthusiastic beginner in the arts of womanly wonderfulness: *Piece by piece,* echoed Sylvia Plath, *I fed my wardrobe to the night wind...*

Sashaying into Mrs Tweedie's on Monday, dressed in the Tent and the Turban, Anna sat in her usual anonymity slightly toward the corner of the room. It was May, after the bitter winter late Spring blossom still filled the trees. She had been sitting with Mrs Tweedie since January, in silent adoration, completely ignored, something she was comfortable with, used to. She first knew it as a test, but as the months passed she simply forgot about that and enjoyed being there, listening, learning, absorbing, *opening.* Suddenly, on this Monday, she heard a ringing voice demanding her attention:

Sitadevi! called Mrs Tweedie across the heads of those in front of her. Astonished, Anna sprung to attention. *Yes, Mrs Tweedie,* she responded swiftly.

You look most becoming, your dress, it is most becoming! Mrs Tweedie's voice rang with authority, emphasising each word. Everyone turned to look as Anna shrank, more comfortable with anonymity: *Thank you Mrs Tweedie,* she managed to say, and silliness threatened: *it's fun isn't it;* a self-deprecating response.

It is NOT fun, said Mrs Tweedie, with a power that blew through Anna like a hurricane, *it is MOST becoming.*

For months Anna had sat, anonymous; for months she had been ignored. Mrs Tweedie had spoken of cooking souls, of leaving them alone, to *cook.* Suddenly Anna/Sitadevi sat upright, in her most becoming beauty, and watched astonished as her mother's mantra took flight, visible in neon sentences, out through the French doors and into the clear sky: *You are fat, you are ugly, you are stupid* – there they were, banners in the sky, fading, fading into the forever, away from Anna, *forever.*

Anna/Sitadevi sat up straight, smiled, confident, *her*self: *Thank you Mrs Tweedie, yes, it is, most becoming.* And it was, *most* becoming. Mrs Tweedie's ravishing smile embraced her – Anna, *had been cooked.* All those silent months were a process. Anna wasn't quite ugly, she wasn't quite fat and she certainly wasn't stupid. She was on her way to womanly wonderfulness.

Is this relevant for a woman's spiritual journey? Anna remembered the beauty of Indian women, knew their innate spirituality, considered it to be so. Her childhood, and all the years to now, governed by her mother's mantra, was damaging and an insult to the Creatrix who made *all* things beautiful – however they fell from Her or His Design. All created things, beautiful. If she was to search for the Divine then to dress anything less than divinely was offensive to Great Nature who is never discordant. Poverty, she knew, was no excuse; in India women would rise from mud and sacking hovels with the grace and pride of a maharani in a cotton sari as exquisitely pleated as the silk of their wealthier sisters; in England the blessing of charity fills shops on every High Street, every village, town and city up and down the country; in France, Auchan, Monoprix! Poverty, indeed, was never an excuse. Collecting, gathering, is built into women's genes, whether gathering seeds or collecting silk frockettes. That day with Mrs Tweedie had electrified her, and there would come many more such moments as Mrs Tweedie, from then on, drew Anna/Sitadevi into conversations, asked her to clarify dreams for others, gave her confidence in trusting her own store of emerging wisdom, taught her the subtle chasm between divine pride and the pride of the ego.

Mrs Tweedie's unequivocal adherence to Truth would sear many an ego sitting in that room, some, many, would leave never to return. To those who remained Tweedie would say: *And from those whom He wants for Himself, He takes Everything. Everything.* As she spoke, Mrs Tweedie's look would scan the room, touch some, rest on others, and pierce Anna to her core. Mrs Tweedie *knew. The death of your child?* said Tweedie another day, *why mourn – unless you mourn for the death of every child, every child throughout the world.* It was a shocking way to learn universal love, non-attachment, life's truth. Not a Path for the fainthearted this Path to the Beloved, there was no insurance policy. Tweedie had said: *And if He demands all, He will take All.*

After all, is it not All His to do with as He wishes? Anna grew in the presence of such a great and uncompromising teacher-by-example.

She recalled a private and privileged visit she had made before setting out on a long pilgrimage to Turkey, Kurdistan, Samarkand, Uzbekistan, following the ancient route of the Masters of Wisdom of Central Asia. Mrs Tweedie had been officially closed on and off since a small heart attack earlier in the year while on a lecture tour in Switzerland. Anna had written to ask her if she could visit on this last Thursday, before what was to be the first of her journeys to Turkey, as she knew she would not see her for some little while. Mrs Tweedie had not, of course, replied.

Anna parked the car in Teignmouth Road and sat for some minutes plucking up the courage to knock on the door. Normally one didn't knock, but this was an unusual meeting. Anna sat. She *might* be rejected at the door. Rejection had been her greatest pain. It was her only framework of reference when she could even bear to look at her childhood. She needed these few minutes to prepare herself ... just in case.

She was welcomed in by Llewellyn. Just five people were present. Mrs Tweedie thanked Anna, who sat down quietly cross-legged on the settee by the door, for the calligraphy الله *Allah*, she had written and sent her. There was some discussion about a video being made, a collection of private dialogues as it were, for posterity; some talk on healing, a New Zealand healer and her friend were present, and the usual cup of tea.

The curtains of the room were pulled closed, Mrs Tweedie wore darkened glasses, she had recently had surgery to implant valves behind her eyes. They were painful still. The healer's friend, doing a wonderful P.R. job on behalf of her attractive companion the healer, told Mrs Tweedie she should let the healer work on her eyes. Anna blinked, it seemed presumptuous: *Don't these gauche Antipodeans know who they were sitting in front of?* she thought, uncharitably.

175

Mrs Tweedie's reply, so elegantly, so gracious: *Darlingk, my eyes are in the Hands of the Lord. If He wishes me to do His Work He will look after my eyes. Either glaucoma will stop me, or death will stop me. Either way it is His will,* melted Anna's heart. Such surrender, such *charity* ...

In the hush of her room Mrs Tweedie spoke of the States of Union: *After a Night of Love,* she said, so softly it was as though she was alone in her soliloquy, *the mind can never be there, can never know ... the moment of mystical union with the Beloved, when during sleep the soul is released from the mental functioning of waking consciousness, is only recalled as the pain of separation on re-awakening. One cannot even prepare for these states* – the hush of her voice continued so softly, slowly – *they just come. They are a Grace. The pain of Love at times is so overwhelming, and such an exquisite pain, that the heart can barely hold it.*

    At the tea table Anna sat opposite Mrs Tweedie who spoke to Llewellyn about his mother related problems before turning to Anna: *I was very moved to receive your letter those many months ago, of your mother's behaviour toward you, and how she has kept you from your own daughter, used ways to keep Martina from you at every level. I know families, some of them are terrible, and we cannot know why. We choose our parents, we choose our circumstances, and when we are ready we can let all of it go. You have the Tibetan prayer?*

    She paused, asked Anna if she had seen Martina: *She has dismissed me, Mrs Tweedie,* and Anna said it with barely a flutter of pain.

    Hmmmm, said Mrs Tweedie, *yes, things are exactly as they should be. Good. All is His Will. Everything is right just as it is.* Later Llewellyn said: *So now you are really free?* and he put his arm around Anna, spanning the chasm of hurt of more than six months before when he had inflicted his personal criticism of mothers on to her. *Perhaps we have both grown,* thought Anna, surprised. At the door Mrs Tweedie gave her A Look, and a kiss: *Have fun in Turkey darlingk, have fun.*

Anna hadn't fully assimilated the idea of Dressing Divinely for the Divine in those early years; she was still shrouded in renunciate ideas of sack-cloth and groan. But *thoughts* would circle around her head from time to time, the more ugly she saw, and there was a lot of it on the streets of England, the more those thoughts would coalesce into *opinions*.

By denying their myriad forms of God-given beauty women deny their divinity: *Is the dandelion ever dowdy? Does the rose hide its rose exquisiteness? Was the horse ever clothed scarred or dirty except by human ill-treatment?* No, God told Job squarely, *the Horse is clothed in strength, in thunder!*

Separation from Nature, our natural being, and separation from the Creatrix is the saddest, most devastating, alienation from self and Self, and Anna was beginning to see, as through a glass darkly, this great blasphemy, this great separation of spirit and matter. She wanted to take the broken young teenagers she saw all over England with their razor blade earrings and ostentatiously ripped jeans, their tongue studs and body piercings, their spiritually vacant and unoccupied faces and say: *I can't let you do this to yourself, you are beautiful* ... but she knew they needed cooking time before they could slough off their own undermining mutilations.

19

Grey Wolf and Round Rainbows

In Grass Valley and Santa Fe, two places Anna had gone on the strength of a powerful dream in the late nineteen-eighties while she was in London sitting with Mrs Tweedie, she learnt two, no, *three*, profound lessons which informed all the years to come. They were spiritual lessons, though not found in the plethora of spiritual books authored by men. Or, in the main, by women either. Her fare to travel was thrust into her hand in notes stuffed in a plastic bag from Edna, a dear friend with whom she was convalescing after a hysterectomy, surgery encouraged by Mrs Tweedie who watched Anna collapse every three weeks in unconscionable pain lasting more days than was usual for such a natural cycle. *I had a hysterectomy*, she told Anna, *in my thirties, it was the best thing I did. Take homeopathic medicines in with you, insist on being given them and I will pray for you. You will be well.*

And Anna knew she would be – well. But, it was a 'well' that crippled her for months afterwards. A new method of womb removal was being practiced, and its practitioner not quite skilled enough in that practice. She woke the morning following surgery in pain; a woman had been brought in during the night and was crying in her pain in the bed next to hers. It was four o'clock. Outside the ward window the morning showed black. No light was in the ward. Prayers for the pain of the world flowed through Anna's heart silently, all those animals in vivisection universities, none with anaesthetic, terribly, horribly, diabolically mutilated, alive; in forest traps, in *anything* less than their natural human-free world – it was too much to bear. *How can you ever forgive us?* she wept silently to the world of creatures and all beings. Prayers flowed endlessly, silently and the ward filled with golden light. The light grew bright, so bright Anna stopped, registered it. A night nurse came in response to the cries of the woman in the next bed, as she stood at the entrance to the ward she said to sitting up Anna: *Goodness it's bright in here, I hardly need to put the light on.*

In the afternoon Alice visited her, a bunch of early golden daffodils in her hand and a beatific smile on her face: *You know dear,* she said through her smile, *I woke at four o'clock this morning to a wonderful sight – you were in your hospital bed surrounded by Golden Beings, and They were all patting you! I knew you would be well after that.*

Anna had the hysterectomy in March 1987 at St Stephen's, and: *We're sorry we didn't get all the cancer cells,* said her young doctor, cancer a surprise revelation to Anna, *you will need to return every three months for us to monitor them.*

Anna thanked him and knew she would never return. She assured him he had done his best but if she held a sentence of three months for the rest of her days her focus would only be on three months, and the power of that focus would rule her life and grant those cancer cells a reprieve to multiply in accordance with the prophecy; she would be dead in a year. She smiled at his consternation. Given no energy, no focus, no attention those errant cells had no reason to live, and thus, Anna would. She remembered the story of a nun in Australia given a similar sentence, who also refused to return to hospital: *Well,* said the nun, *I'd better hurry on with God's work,* and she asked leave of her Order to go and live in Scone, New South Wales, to open a centre for something or other, Anna couldn't recall the worldly details, and lived for another twenty years.

By July Anna was still unable to move, confined to bed in details unbecoming to print, when Edna received a phone call, from Mrs Tweedie. It was July 21st – the Mahasamadhi of Bhai Sahib, Guruji. *Tell Sitadevi I love her,* said Mrs Tweedie, who didn't have a phone. Edna ran across the huge slate floored kitchen, along the vast hall, up the grand oak staircase and along the carpeted corridor to arrive breathless at Anna's small pretty room. They hugged, shared a few tears, and from that moment Anna began to recover. And to discover a voice inside her. A voice of power without precedent: *How dare they,* this wakened inner voice roared to Self, *how dare they cut down this beautiful body, cut out this wonderful womanness, how dare they* ... ignoring her own wise decision along with Mrs Tweedie's encouragement that 'they' do so. It was a visceral upsurge from the Woundedness of her Mother the Earth that roared and wept and cried inside her. A quiet poem by Mary Lisle that she once knew in Australia where such voices were gainsaid in the time it was written and even now, surfaced:

They have cut down the pines
where they stood;
The wind will miss them -
— the rain,
When its silver blind is down.

They have stripped the bark from the wood —
The needly boughs,
and the brown Knobbly nuts trodden into the ground.

The kind, the friendly trees,
Where all day small winds sound,
And all day long the sun
Plays hide and seek with shadows
Till the multiplying shadows turn to one
And night is here.

They have cut down the trees
and ended now
The gentle colloquy of bough and bough.

They are making the fence by the creek,
And have cut down the pines for the posts.
Wan in the sunlight as ghosts
The naked trunks lie.

A bird nested there – it will seek
In vain:
they have cut down the pines.

They have cut down the pines ... a bird will seek in vain. A *frisson* of anguish accompanied her recall of the words. Anna felt she had been cut through, butchered, like the forest of pines where a single bird wept for its lost brood. Yet her mind told her otherwise. She didn't mourn her sterility, her body jumped for joy at the cessation of its cyclical pain; but the metaphor, ah the metaphor of wounded nature remained and became her Womanroar. It would surface wherever Anna felt injustice, to herself, to the Earth and to those creatures she loved.

Almost up and seeking nourishment Anna ached to return to Mrs Tweedie. But in between times another drama sent her reeling, an almost predictable psychic and psychological occurrence under the circumstances. Anna could only tell of it in the second person; coming so soon after her hysterectomy it poleaxed her:

> *Your daughter had appeared in England exactly as you were recovering (no surprise to you with your psychic history of mothers and daughters) from a hysterectomy with considerable post surgical complications. It had been almost twenty years since your golden and pink baby girl was taken from you as a baby; a story still too labyrinthine to speak of, its Byzantine complexities reduced to purest binary – you and she.*
>
> *You are recuperating in Hambrook in the home of friends and, unable to accommodate her, you had offered your daughter the room in the previous home of your Teacher in London; a room which was being held for you, until your return to health and to London and to Mrs Tweedie. To relinquish such a rare offer didn't add to your healing and the next four weeks necessitated the round trip of two hundred and forty*

181

miles three times a week as you drove from Bristol to London and back again. That's a lot of miles to run with a red light glowering at you for a whole four weeks, but your brain took a back seat and you obeyed the call on your time and presence. After all, seeing a daughter you haven't seen for nineteen years, since she was taken from you at seven months old, is not an experience to be gainsaid.

After four weeks things calm down, your long-lost daughter dismisses you, and your brain re-positions itself front stalls. You see the red light. You really see the red light. Fortunately you are at the London end of your journey and you can go round to the Indian owned garage in Willesden Green where you have become a regular customer. You fill the tank with petrol, then open the bonnet and check for oil. You peer uncomprehendingly at the end of the dipstick. It is oddly dry. You stick it back in the motor and pull it out again. Shrugging your shoulders you walk up to Rahim at the cash desk and hold up your dry dipstick. "Rahim" you say to him, puzzled, "I think I've got a short dipstick, have you got a different one I can try?" Rahim turns a paler shade of brown, walks you back to the car, tries the dipstick and looks at you somewhat horrified when you say the little red light has been on for about the last three thousand miles. He shakes his head and says, as only an Indian would, "Modom, you are definitely in the Hands of God. What you have is not short dipstick but very short oil." He then pours gallons, gallons, of the stuff into your motor, marvelling at God's full time job in having looked after you. Chastened, luminously back in your own body and now very aware, you drive more slowly than usual the one hundred and twenty miles back to Bristol.

Missing the great opportunity of her life, a room in the house once lived in by Mrs Tweedie, was devastating. Looking back as Anna wrote that nutshell chapter she could barely grasp what made her give, and give again and give again to people of her own blood. Still recovering from her hysterectomy she found the 240 mile return journey from Bristol tiring, had asked Martina if she could sleep overnight there from time to time. Mrs Tweedie knew this, one afternoon she asked where she slept in that small room. *On the floor, Mrs Tweedie,* brought a sharp intake of disapproving breath from Mrs Tweedie who expostulated: *The floor! while your daughter sleeps in the bed?* She was angry at such discourtesy, not just to a mother but a mother still suffering from surgery.

Martina had a dream during those few short weeks and Mrs Tweedie invited her into the small room she kept for very private matters. She asked Anna to accompany them, an unusual gesture for dreams were those very private matters. The dream she told was shocking and revelatory, a dream of cutting Mrs Tweedie into pieces, and more besides, so carnal and cruel and told so glibly Mrs Tweedie's toes involuntarily curled in body shock as she listened deeply to the young woman who had no insight into what she was telling, and even less into what it was saying of her own mother-wound. Mrs Tweedie gently said after the telling: *Darlinkg, this is not the place for you, go out into the world and live your life.*

Martina took her at her word and left, relieved. Being with a group of people such as surrounded Mrs Tweedie was a strange and novel thing for her. She needed admiration, not meditation and she also needed a mother, but the blood in her veins flowed from the blood in *her* mother's veins which flowed from the blood in *her* mother's veins – and the blood carried pain. The motherblood in Anna's veins was sauced and sourced with hate from her own mother. Hate. A terrible word. A word that was a sentence, and sentenced Anna's life with solitude and searching. Anna was gene-programmed, she could no more be a mother than her own mother had been. Their differences were in the terrible word. Her own mother carried hate, Anna carried confusion.

Mrs Tweedie came with Anna to the door the following day as people were leaving: *Finish!* she said, crossing her hands in front of her stomach with a rapid thrust, *finish with your family. Some families are terrible and we*

183

cannot know why. Your daughter has her karma with them, not with you, not now. Perhaps in a distant future, she paused, looking far away, *she will come to know who her mother is ... or perhaps she won't.* It would be a very long time, thought Anna wistfully knowing she had to know herself first.

There was a poignant codicil: at the year's end Anna stood in the long queue waiting to say goodbye to Mrs Tweedie who closed for Christmas, and to thank her for, well, everything. Suddenly her heart leapt, Martina was ahead of her in the queue. It was the first time she had seen her daughter since her telling of the dream. She was standing there! Right by Mrs Tweedie, speaking. Anna could barely hold herself up as her knees threatened to buckle under the weight of grief. A second later and Martina had turned, did she see Anna? She walked passed her in that darkened room to the front door. Two more people, and then Anna stood by Mrs Tweedie: *Keep your heart always with God, all is well,* her beloved face illumined with an inner light as she looked up at Anna. Anna thanked her again, turned and walked to the front door, found her shoes amongst the pile, stepped into the darkened frosty street and walked, shuffling the damp leaves, late-fallen, neither happy nor sad, not quite numb, one step in front of the other, further and further into the world that loved her and away from the family, who didn't.

Anna learned that her own mother had known Martina all those desolate years of Anna's loss, had kept them apart, and yet ... and yet, as Anna reflected *now,* could anything have been any other way? She had said *Yes* to this family, to this grief, before her own birthing into this world. Martina had said *Yes* and carried the inarticulate anger and loss of a seven month old taken from her own mother. To a baby it would seem that she was abandoned in *her* mother-loss; her rage in her dream of Tweedie deflected, as dreams do, her wish to kill the mother who refused to nourish her, support her. Her father's mother who had reared her overcompensated that loss by surrounding Martina with *their* love. *Life could be unbearably sad,* sighed Anna, as always, to Self: *unbearable in its mystery, unbearable in its destinies, unbearable in its inexorable demand for Itself.*

Anna had a dream some weeks after this last encounter with her lost-forever daughter. She was in America for healing. Perhaps America represented a new world, a new beginning; dreams told so many truths in archaic ways. It was February and snow needed boots. Edna told Anna she had to go to America on the strength of that dream and one afternoon had thrust a plastic bag of five pound notes at her, a special fare was being offered in a Bristol travel agent for a given period of six weeks.

There was a colourful shop on Glastonbury High Street during the 'eighties that made and sold wildly unattractive boots. Anna would take the Badger Bus from Bristol down to Glastonbury from time to time. This particular shop window was one she studiously ignored until one day a spectacularly ugly pair in the window display demanded her attention. She walked away three times and three times they called her back. They cost £33. An enormous sum for Anna. Besides, they were so ugly, she couldn't imagine giving them house room. But three is a Cosmic Calling and she was sensitive to that. She tried them on. They were even uglier. They held fast to her foot as if owning them and she sighed and passed over, with huge reluctance, the enormous sum of money. Not that she would wear them, even in Glastonbury. But she would be Obedient and fly to America wearing them.

Anna would never, *ever* fly British Airways again. Not in her whole life. The food, English food, made her so ill she vomited over the entire Arctic Circle, over the air hostess and over herself. She was weak and no member of the staff would go near her, her clothes reeked, and *they* were not going to soil their dreary little B.A. uniforms. *God,* Anna mused through the dark miasma of her nausea, *how different the response of these twitty little stewardesses from Sidcup or Penge to the compassion shown by their Indian, Malay or French counterparts,* all of whom she had flown with.

Anna wobbled off the plane at Los Angeles, too ill to think, too exhausted to know where she was going, in fact, she didn't know where she was going, at all. Sleep and to be clean was what she craved. A kinder man at an information desk suggested she book into an airport cubicle to shower and wash her clothes and to sleep the rest of the night. She did just that, fighting against the claustrophobia of being confined in a windowless, airless, shoebox. Washed, and hanging her clothes over the open cupboard door to dry, Anna slept until three o'clock. She didn't know which three o'clock it was, and, still weak and weary, she'd had no food since throwing it all up in the aircraft, ventured out to find an empty airport terminal and assessed it must be three o'clock in the morning. She sat on a bench, watching unfocused as a large Native American Indian swabbed a mop and pushed a bucket closer and closer to her. He sidled right up, and said, sideways: *Love yer boots.*

Surprised, Anna thanked him. Her accent gave her away. He asked where she was headed, she didn't actually know. He smiled and said as if it was the most normal thing in the world: *You should go to Santa Fe.*

Where's that? she asked, and he directed her to Terminal One, told her to just hop on a plane, rather like catching a bus, and get off at Albuquerque: *There'll be a bus waiting,* he said, *it'll take you right on down to Santa Fe.*

Anna's gratitude was her thank you to him and to Obedience. She ate three breakfasts on the short flight, wonderful fresh melon and natural yoghurt and hot croissants. *Oh why can't the English ... Well, they can't, bad food is a way of life in England, they'd serve boiled dog and complain to the RSPCA before they'd complain to the chef and that's that,* she said to Self, falling in love with American cleanness and kindness and the best of organic food.

Sure enough there was a bus outside the airport with *Santa Fe* written clearly above the large front windscreen. She boarded, paid and looked for a seat. Walking past already seated passengers every single one commented, *sotto voce: Love yer boots.* She thanked them all and found an aisle seat. An elderly man on her left across the aisle and one row back commented on her boots, heard her accent, asked where she was staying when she reached Santa Fe. Well, she didn't actually know, and Anna poured out her unpleasant flight story. *We-e-ell,* he said with a very southern drawl, he was up from Texas, *I'm flying to Colorado tomorrow but I'm staying over in my home here tonight, you can stay the night to recover.* And so she did.

The home, an elegant mud brick charm with a collection of Katchina dolls that riveted her attention opened her host to tell her a little of their importance. He showed her a spare room, told her she must sleep until seven in the evening when he would wake her and take her to dinner. A good night's sleep after dinner, he said, and in the morning he would drive her downtown after breakfast and leave her by the library. The kindness of strangers, asking nothing in return, added to Anna's amalgam of memories of America.

In Santa Fe she wandered enchanted at the beauty of the place. Unable to afford the hotels she had gone to a library to seek an ashram, a wat, anything. All had moved away, closed down. All that was left was a Peace group. She dialled the number: *Are you a peace pilgrim?* asked the man who answered the phone. Anna thought she probably was and answered yes. *I'll be down to collect you,* he said, and took her home to share his garage, cosy with a working wood burner – it was February and thick snow covered the low hills, making pillows of the sage brush and the small juniper pines – his home was being let to bring in an income.

Richard introduced her to the life of Peace Pilgrim, the extraordinary woman who had, at the age of sixty, left everything to walk, for the next twenty-six years, tens of thousands of miles criss-crossing America to talk about peace to the man or the woman along the streets and the roads and the highways and the byways. She carried nothing but a comb, a notebook, a pencil, a toothbrush. She slept when she was tired, by roadsides, in fields, on park benches, unless someone offered her a bed. By an astonishing irony, she was killed by a speeding car.

Richard had published her writings; her book, a full size publication, was given free. Anna was smitten.

During the next days Anna explored the town, found herself in a shop of exquisite Katchina dolls, Story-tellers of the Pueblos, her heart resonating with a new knowledge of spirituality – *story-tellers! Words!* This was true magic, healing magic. The man who owned the shop was Native to the land, large and softly spoken, he watched her as she looked in a kind of awe at his Katchinas, seeing them as they should be seen, these were sacred, not tourist, images. He likely guessed she couldn't afford to buy, but he began to engage her in talk, it was immediately obvious from her accent where she was from: *Would you like,* he asked after a little time, *to attend a pow-wow? You will be the only white woman there.*

That evening Anna slipped into a small circle of beautiful men and women and children, feeling only a little out of place, she *felt* she belonged there, other lives, other centuries, another of *those* moments. The people gathered in a circle, standing close to each other, the drums were in the centre of the circle, a circle of men were sitting on the floor around the drums and the drums were large. The drumming began. As they drummed the slow, deep, sounds the vibration came up through her legs, mesmerizing her. A little girl standing next to her held her hand: *You can feel the drumming come through you from Mother Earth*, she said, her small honey-brown face shining, looking up at Anna, *it's Her heartbeat!*

The outer circle moved slowly, slowly, stepping from one foot to the other they moved by inches clockwise round the drummers. Anna learned something about Giveaway too, in her excruciating ignorance she had not brought a gift to give. But she watched as a woman had given a shawl, another woman picked it up and let a corner of the exquisite weaving trail on the ground as she moved around the circle in a slow rhythm to the drumming. The giver, seeing it not perfectly respected, gently reclaimed it. There was no hint of discomfort between the women, only humility. *How brave*, thought Anna, observing this, *and how true*. Would she have that courage, to give and retrieve? It wasn't a question of not 'letting go' of a gift given, that was another thing, but a question of sacredness; trailing the shawl on the ground neither honoured the weaver nor the sacredness of its weaving. *Could it be the sacred genesis of the expression India Giver?* Anna mused, a term used pejoratively in her mother tongue.

The following day was market day in the old square. All along the sidewalk Pueblo Indians sat on colourful blankets with their wares, weavings, baskets, katchinas, jewellery of coral and turquoise and silver, in front of them. As Anna walked slowly past, almost everyone, man and woman, said: *Love yer boots*. Suddenly Anna knew why she had to buy those boots. Those boots opened doors in this town of coral and turquoise. Her boots? Turquoise sides, high over the ankle, rainbow laces, and coral dyed toe caps with palm trees painted on! There was a heel patch of coral too – she knew now that these boots had occasioned the direction she was to take from the airport, and even the appalling flight and overnight in a cubical was part of the story so that the Native American cleaner at three o'clock in the morning would see this lonely figure and her preposterous boots and recognise a kindred spirit in his native turquoise and coral.

More was to unfold because of those boots. Anna found the Ark, a bookstore the like of which England had never seen. It wasn't the size of it – which could only be American or Australian, sprawling as it did across a footprint the size of an English supermarket – it was the subject range, almost all of it esoteric or focused on animal and bird wisdom from shamanic lore, or philosophies from India and Japan, philosophies to live by in a sacred manner. As if that wasn't enough there were armchairs and free freshly brewed coffee, England had seen neither good fresh coffee nor armchairs and *free* coffee in those days either, it was the late eighties, and she was, everyone was, encouraged to sit and read. The generosity added itself to her storehouse of memories. Suspending any critical faculty, she wished, then, she could stay in America forever. However, she couldn't. But she could read the notice board and all the colourful advertisements for this or that healing therapy or enlightenment course, most of which Anna had never heard. One tiny modest card, about postcard sized amongst all the A4 vibrancy, and plainly written, caught her attention: *Grey Wolf, Inuit Shaman, talk on Sunday* and gave an address. This, she knew, was for her. It was Saturday. She hadn't missed it.

Seated in a small room with a handful of other people Anna took stock of the man standing and quietly speaking. Dressed in jeans it was his long long braid under a baseball cap and wide golden brown face with deep set oriental eyes that caught her gaze. His talk centred on a young man with a colossal tumour on his cheek. He was standing there with him. Too close to the brain, doctors refused to operate. In ways she could not remember now the young man had called Grey Wolf who had come down from north of Nome to Santa Fe to remove the tumour with a series of sessions – by his hands alone. *The tumour*, said Grey Wolf, *will be given back to Mother Earth through a tree out there who chose to help in the healing. Trees are strong, they help us.* Anna was riveted.

After the talk she approached Grey Wolf apprehensively, not knowing what to ask, what to say. It was likely, she thought from the ridge of now as she wrote of the memory, that she couldn't have delved into her own pain honestly enough to ask for healing. Instead she fumbled about with pretentiousness, a follow-on from silliness. Grey Wolf agreed to her company, but he was flying to Nevada City on Thursday, she would have to follow him there and he would take her on a five day vision quest over a nine day period and she would need time to process in between.

Anna was so trusting, so naive, so longing – she said *Yes* to everything believing it was good. She also knew the time of her heroically unsuitable boots was over, they had worked their magic, she would leave them in Santa Fe amongst the coral and the turquoise and a Pueblo dweller would find and love those boots. She bought a pair of sandals. She also bought a plane ticket, *just like hiring a taxi,* she said to friends, *America is so organized, life is so easy there, practicalities so functional!* And on Thursday morning the whole of Santa Fe poured out on to the streets to wonder at the phenomenon in the skies over the city. The blue heaven was filled, simply filled with astonishing and perfectly round rainbows. No one of them touched another, but there they were, circular planes of seven colours, red all through to violet with blue sky showing at their centres. It was glorious to behold and Anna had never seen such things. Later that afternoon she boarded that plane warmed by the thought of the myriad small covenants directing her journey.

Mrs Tweedie's book *Daughter of Fire*, the complete edition with all her dreams during the years she was with Bhai Sahib, had been published by a small private publisher in Nevada City. When Grey Wolf had told her where he was going Anna had gasped and asked: *How many Nevada City's are there in America?* Only one that he knew of, he had replied. Anna phoned the publisher, who agreed she could stay with them for the duration. She would be mostly out, and promised to be quiet and unobtrusive, as was her inclination. Richard, the Peace Pilgrim publisher, had phoned ahead to an uncle in San Francisco where Anna could stay overnight before travelling on to Grass Valley. California was another revelation – its Great Seal thrilled her, a Goddess and a Grizzly Bear! *How splendid is that,* she smiled to uncle.

Her days with Grey Wolf held her on tenterhooks, he insisted she hover by her host's phone for his calls, times which were arbitrary. He was true to his word though and she did, under his guidance, a Medicine Wheel of the Four Directions, committing all he said to her notebook, travelling to South Yuba River, (where Grey Wolf sat invisible on the fender of his car as she parked behind him – a friend of his had lent her an old sedan for the duration of her Quest – it was part of a teaching, a 'sending' to her mind to blot out what he didn't want her to see, and although he didn't spell out the way he did it she absorbed it and used it successfully herself on occasion); to wild forest, through urban settlements and then to a higher mountain: East, South, West – that was nerve-wracking – and North.

West was the biggest challenge. West was the place of Bear, of hibernation, a place to digest death before life, and would take place at night. Before entering the forest to carry out Grey Wolf's instructions of visualizing page by page of her life and then 'burning' page by page of her recall of each memory, sending it back to its Native Nothingness in the smoke and ash of her visualization, Grey Wolf had asked if he could place his hands over her belly: *You have warring women in there,* he said. She had indeed, so soon after her hysterectomy a mother, a daughter and herself were all still firmly in psychic situ. He told her to visualize the colour green, a healing colour of all life, he told her, as he held his hands over her and prayed in Inuit. Then he told her to walk deep into the forest – he would wait for her at the edge, she was not to be afraid.

Not to be afraid. She was terrified. Not of the Goddess or the Grizzly Bear or Death but night had long since fallen, it was the only nightwalk of the Quest, and black as pitch – who, human, *male*, might be prowling in there? She stumbled, without much courage coming to her aid it must be said, but she went a little further and felt for somewhere to sit. She began her reflections in an unreflective way, fear stalked her. Finally, finally, she reckoned she had 'burnt' 500 pages telling of the pain and loss of her life and turned back to try to retrace her steps.

Grey Wolf was waiting in his van, he didn't comment on her absence; Anna hoped it had been more than five minutes.

The following week, a long gap, she was told to buy salmon and tobacco, they would be honouring North and Eagle. Anna loved Eagle too – she was such a little mouse and the story of Little Mouse moved her to tears. A potter friend had even made for her a tiny blue ceramic mouse, Anna loved it, it lived on her home altar even now, forty years later; she recognized another sign of herself, along with the Cat Who Walked Alone, though she hadn't the cat's courage, then. Little Mouse, a feather story within the Seven Arrows of Hyemeyohsts Storm, inspired her; would she find the courage within herself to ever Give-Away her eyes that greater Beings than she could see? Perhaps one of the great teachers she already knew in her life was Great Buffalo, under whom Little Mouse ran as she crossed the Prairie where eagles looked down? Mice were their favourite prey. Perhaps another of her great teachers was Great Wolf who showed Little Mouse the Sacred Mountain after she had given him her second eye to re-awaken his memory of Who he really was, just as Little Mouse was hit, to become, by her own courageous journey, Eagle herself. Anna would pray to Eagle of the North, and thank such a Great Being for *being*.

Afterwards Grey Wolf met her back in the town and threw at her his greatest challenge, *I'm going to have a hamburger,* said Grey Wolf, *it'll ground me.*

Anna's head spun, she had been a vegetarian for reasons of compassion for decades, here was a teacher, a wise man in tune with Nature, offering his Path, a path not open to cherry-picking likes and dislikes; the privilege of entering any Path demanded an honour, a respect for its ways: *I'll join you,* she was able to say after a nano-second and before her head got in the way. Grey Wolf permitted the ghost of a smile to light his eyes; she'd passed that test too. Anna thanked the animal who died that she might eat of it and it was good. And it was not McDonalds.

Sitting on the grass in Grass Valley with a group of women, Anna watched Brooke Medicine Eagle, slender and long-braided and dressed in cream buckskin, smudge their circle with sage. She laid down her Eagle's wing to address the group simply: *Women should wear skirts, except during their moon time for practical reasons — you work, you are in the world, you need to keep your menstrual pads secure. But when you wear skirts and you don't wear briefs, knickers, you draw the energy of Mother Earth up through you. She will ground you, connect you to her, we women need this. Covering your crotch with jeans breaks that energy, covering your crotch with anything breaks your connection to the divine feminine who is our Mother Earth.*

193

Anna was the only woman in that circle wearing a skirt – *sans culottes*. She hadn't known why she did it, couldn't articulate a reason, but she did now. A warm smile spread up from the earth she was sitting on to fill her whole body.

When she returned to London and to Mrs Tweedie after forty days and forty nights, that Biblical reckoning, something odd greeted her. Llewellyn had read her unheralded appearance in Grass Valley as more than coincident with some issue he was having with the publishers of *Daughter of Fire* and pounced on Anna with accusations so bizarre she could only stand and let them bounce right off her. Once before he had projected other stupidities on her, from his own store of mother-wounds, reflected by Martina's appearance in the group as Mrs Tweedie had watched from the wings, seen Anna's puzzled expression. She knew Llewellyn, she knew Anna ... later Llewellyn spoke within the group of the Sufi Path of Blame. The words of Mani Swami floated in the air: *You will be misunderstood, blamed for things unknown to you* ... Indeed! Martina's appearance had polarized the whole group, mothers of Distant Daughters and children with Awful Mothers or Absent Fathers. Whatever their age, everyone in that group had an issue with a parent or with a child. Anna took the flak ricocheting around that room; Mrs Tweedie looked on, smiling at the *lila* of elephants being played out around her.

Anna, like Sita who walked through the fire proving her innocence against unjust accusations levelled at *her*, would emerge unscathed by the ricocheting and censorious 'opinions' of the group. She would not recall a single face of the many, many who 'belonged' to that group – except a brief encounter with wild writer Philippa Pullar, and Jeanine who loved her.

Jeanine invited Anna to Feuilla, twice, three times, where she told her of wondrous things, things unwritten anywhere that Anna knew: *Remember always your soul is talking to you through dreams*. Anna was spellbound when

Jeanine then softly told her the very same things that Grey Wolf had told: *In the Beginning of Time,* he said, and now Jeanine continued: *Great Beings had come here to earth and planted knowledge, like seeds, in the oceans, in certain trees, certain mountains and certain parts of the earth. When human consciousness was young, seeds of knowledge were planted in certain places. Bees and wheat and ants were brought, these are especially sacred, they were brought to Earth by the Lords of the Flame at the Dawn of Time.*

The little omelette Jeanine was watching over for their breakfast took on a golden hue as Anna digested this wondrous cosmology. She was *there*, at the dawn of Time, and she had known Jeanine time out of mind. *When you go back to Brisbane,* she said, *visit John, he reads people, is able to see influences and connections.* Anna sought him out and knew his gifts to be authentic when he described intimately her father, her mother, and a scenario from Spain in the seventeenth century. How Spanish her mother's looks, black abundant hair, hooked nose, eyebrows raven black imperiously arched, deep olive skin – a West Country link to the Spanish Armada so local legend has it. Anna listened intently. An arranged marriage brought her Grandee father wealth and her mother, of wealthy merchant stock, a title. *Jeanine was,* said a surprised John, who had known Jeanine well, *your father's Chamberlain in that life, she loved you, knew you as a mystical child, taking after your father whom your mother despised for his mystical and impractical interests.*

Well! That took the wind from Anna's sails and though she held its details as lightly as thistledown she sensed the gist of it had a certain purchase. Her father, a mathematician and a musician, held a spiritual affinity with woods and trees and the language of symbol which marked both his profession and his passion.

Jeanine alerted Anna to another puzzle in her jigsaw life. When Anna had drifted into the orbit of wonderful woman like Judi Dench and Brenda Bruce after losing her daughter, losing her home, losing the very ground of her life after being turned away from her father, after being banished from her motherless past, Brenda had schooled her in the scene Judi so poignantly played that year, 1969. The actress believed in Anna's potential, her voice, and encouraged her to audition for Theatre School. The scene Brenda chose for her to study? Hermione's plea, played by Judi, against unjust accusation:

Since what I am to say must be but that
Which contradicts my accusation and
The testimony on my part no other
But what comes from myself, it shall scarce boot me
To say 'not guilty:' mine integrity
Being counted falsehood, shall, as I express it,
Be so received. But thus: if powers divine
Behold our human actions, as they do,
I doubt not then but innocence shall make
False accusation blush and tyranny
Tremble at patience...

That passage was no coincidence, said Jeanine quietly, *you are being shown how to stand naked before God, with* nothing. *He gave you no comforts to hide you, no wealth that would provide you a place where you could have hidden from the world.*

Anna grinned: *Occupation:* heiress, *would have suited me! Yes,* smiled Jeanine, *you've known such a life before, it shows in your love of beauty, refinement, and definitely,* Jeanine added, *you have known cloisters. But shrinking in a convent is not in His plan for you! Your name, Love in the Mist, is your challenge.*

The omelette was placed before her. Jeanine sat down, called Ron to breakfast with them. Anna's thought span in reverse: *You know,* she finally said to Jeanine, *decades ago I was at a satsang with Satyananda. His eyes began to scan the fifteen hundred people sitting in front of him, and he said to us audience, with utter scorn: Butter, you are like butter. I could see his face clearly. And then, he said: Diamonds! I only want diamonds! His words struck me: You must become like diamonds, with clarity and brilliance. His eyes continued to scan the audience: Butter melts at the slightest heat, just as you people collapse at the slightest discomfort.*

Anna chuckled at the memory: *Most people squirmed! They were discomforted. But I felt him cut through me, how would I become a diamond?* Jeanine reminded Anna that when she visited Nishchalananda in the early days of his ashram in Wales he had told other swamis present to: *Ask Sitadevi, she has a knife-edge clarity*.

Jeanine's gentle presence enfolded Anna in love as she continued to give her a footing of confidence in herself and courage to accept her lot: *It is hard-won. That clarity will frighten most people you meet. It is a lonely path to see too much for comfort, yours or anyone's. Candour, words of rapier thrust, very uncomfortable!*

Jeanine's wry, crooked smile spilled right up and through her eyes. Slightly nodding her head she recalled certain past moments of observing the effect Anna's spontaneous observations had on people. They *squirmed* under that rapier thrust and Anna was unaware of it. That candour was disarming for some, destabilizing for others, she could only say the obvious, pierce self-delusion. Mrs Tweedie referred to Jeanine as her 'spiritual deputy', but Jeanine was too fragile to hold the world; it would be Llewellyn, Mrs Tweedie said, who would become her 'worldly executor'.

Anna would have traded God for a loving human partner whose arms would enfold her and keep the storms of the world at bay any day. But it was not to be. Jeanine looked at her with all the love in the world, she had seen the drama of Anna's daughter, watched as the group polarized according to each person's own mother agenda, knew Mrs Tweedie had dismissed Martina as unsuited to the group at that moment in her young life, and felt Anna's brokenness as she leant against the wall when Mrs Tweedie afterwards seared her with: *Sitadevi! And how are you?* Jeanine, next to her, seeing on Anna's face a look as desolate as the cold cracked fields of winter, put her hand on Anna's shoulder in a gesture of abiding compassion to support her. Anna's reply was muted, sounding words that demanded a range she could no longer manage, as she barely whimpered: *I'm fine Mrs Tweedie, thank you.* Rapier thrusts were *de rigueur* in Mrs Tweedie's company too, in the force of her candour one learnt humility. Attention seekers were told to leave. Tweedie was a *force*.

Anna wasn't fine at all, but she grew from the truth of Mrs Tweedie's thrust. Her own golden and pink baby, unseen for twenty years, had turned up in her life as a result of a cousin who would no longer collude with her aunt's, Anna's mother, continued separation between her own daughter and her daughter. Enough was enough. But it wasn't, too much damage had been done.

Good, said Mrs Tweedie, *things are exactly as they should be.* And Anna picked up the shards that rent her heart and continued walking into Life.

20

Satsang with Satyananda

And in between: Anna's memory was sharp, but her grasp of time scales were mostly, and distinctly, skewed. She had a deep aversion to unpunctuality, saw being late as a profound disrespect to the person, event or commitment and was never later than five minutes early for *anything*. In tune with Cosmic tides and planets with their perfect regularity she wondered how the unpunctual would respond to the sun's decision to remain in bed for a year or three; or the stars to stop their coursing and the tides to still, Spring to go off to another planet and daffodils to stay underground. But, when it came to *years*, now that was another thing altogether.

Since her astonishment at Anne's Five Year Plan, and its failure to last much longer than five months in her own scattered destiny of life, Anna had given up on years. Except for the markers in her life – Satyananda, Bede, Tweedie, Jasper – other edges of time, and the year which brought them, could blur without distinction. Recall, a date on the back of a photo for example, would see her raise a quizzical eyebrow: *So long ago?* or, *only last year? surely not.* Like the apocryphal Indian sage who commented to a western visitor: *You people live in time, we Indians live in Eternity,* her years, travellers of eternity, passed unnoticed. Her father never let a birthday pass without a card, sent to wherever she lived, but there was no one else to mark a birthday, an annual event, it was *days* that she remembered.

In India she studied the great texts of the Vedas and the Tantras. One memorable satsang with Swami Satyananda hinted, before she knew, of her future path embracing the wisdom of the Earth, of Bhoomi Devi who opened to give birth to, and opened again to receive at her death: Sita herself.

I am a Vedantin, said Swami Satyananda in his perfect and slightly sibilant English, *but you,* he said, looking around the fifteen hundred people in front of him, *I teach you Tantra. You in the West live in your heads, too removed from your body and the earth that bears you; we in India are never separated from our connection with the great Shakti. We cannot breathe one breath without Her. It is Shakti, ParaShakti, who vivifies all, and in you too, all of you, as Kundalini ascends through your body to unite with Shakti as she descends. It is a circle. Our in-breath and out-breath create the path of that circle. We Indians may pollute our rivers and our roads and we may cut down our forests but we never forget our Mother.*

Jung warned: *We in the West live in the one-dimensional capsule of the head;* how but with the head could we get out of it? Voltaire suggested the garden, the soil, even English humour gave rise to a truism: *Oi think the answer loies in the soil;* but the truism remains buried until our lightbulb moment embeds and awakens it as a *moksha* moment within the body.

Mind cannot jump over the mind, said Satyananda, at another satsang, *meditation is the key.* Or practices like Kriya, or contemplation, or a car crash. Things, events, that catapult us out of our head and into our body – these are the shocks to the mind that mind cannot assimilate. *The ego,* said Satyananda, *stands between you and the Vision;* a visual image that seared into Anna's Self and would re-appear as the guidepost for the *thealogy* she would soon explore along her own journey.

In 1995 – she knew the year from the Invitation she received, kept as a souvenir to grace the cover of that particular photograph album – Anna returned again to India. She was yet to go to France, but she was now fully aware of the Black Madonna and her paper on Shakti and Pneuma, though lost or left behind or given to the Jesuit priest who loved it, expanded her consciousness in an organic and personal way. She lived with the subtlety of it, in small ways it would inform her with increasing emphasis to champion animals and earth above all else. In Australia for too many years she had rescued countless cats, kittens and possums from the horror of live-bait for greyhound owners; had stood against logging and mining and deforestation and councils destroying street trees growing over four metres (because little Johnny had fallen out of one and broken his arm and his mindless parents had sued the council: *kill that tree, councils can't afford litigation,* went the specious argument. Indeed they can't, so: *kill the litigation and shift responsibility to Johnny and his parents,* fulminated an angered Anna). Volunteer for the Australian Conservation Foundation in the early years of her return to Australia in the 'seventies Anna initiated a week long symposium in Martin Place, Sydney, inviting Vin Serventy, Dr Paul Ralph Ehrlic and numerous agencies concerned with threatened or illegally poached wildlife to come together to awaken the public. She sent a telegram to Prince Philip asking him to intervene and stop Gray's flooding the wild rivers, Franklin and Gordon; Liberal's enthusiastically wanted short term hydro-electricity. The Bill was to be passed on Thursday, Anna, thinking wildly outside the box, sent HRH a telegram the previous Friday. The Bill was overturned. She received a letter from the royal equerry to say HRH had responded at once. Small act, great consequence.

Anna didn't end at the edge of her skin, she contained oceans and mountains and plains and forests and all the creatures and birds who dwelt there. *Pick a flower and shake a star,* say the Sage and the Seer, a connectedness which quantum physicists endorse. She *felt* the suffering of elephants, of ants, of rivers and seas, of forest and plain and all creatures great and small.

Twelve years passed before Anna met Satyananda again. She had left the ashram to follow Father Bede, shed her dhotis after seeing Judi Dench at the Post Office in Charing Cross, sat with Tweedie for years, found and lost her daughter, married and lost her Kurd, pilgrimaged across Turkey and Kurdistan and Uzbekistan and been given a ruby ring in Samarkand – a ring she had dreamt of two years before.

In that dream of 1986 she was travelling with her sheikh, whose face she could not see, from East to West across the Himalayan plateau, pursued by those who wished them ill. Her sheikh had turned to her along the way, thrusting a ruby ring into her hand, a rose pink ruby the colour of the *rosa Louise Odier*, urging her to travel fast, he knew he would meet his death along the caravanserai and he wanted Anna to keep safe his Ring of Syncellus. The rings had two tiny gold chains attached: *They are the Chains that bind you to the Beloved*, said Tweedie when Anna shared her dream. Two years later she was idling by a counter in a tourist emporium in Samarkand and a young and beautiful Uzbeki woman sidled up to say: *Have you seen this ruby ring?* Anna's heart split wide open, in the woman's palm was the very ring of her dream. The ring passed into her hand, it had no chains attached, they were unnecessary now.

1988. By the time she reached Kars Anna was more bound to the memory of Yahia the Kurd than the Beloved, having opportunistically met at the airport in Istanbul at the outset of her six month pilgrimage. Discombobulated by the horrors she had witnessed in her week of Ceausescu's Bucharest, morbidly hungry from the absence of food at the Romanian hotel, absence of cafés in the city and absence of even morsels at the monastery of Sinaia, she had fallen for the Kurd with the soot black fur-ringed amber eyes. Without a second thought she climbed into his waiting taxi to be driven to the home of a delightful family. Anna, unwitting, was Yahia's package deal passport to a Better Life. In Kars she intuited a letter was waiting. Before the wonder of email, intuition was all she could rely on. She took off to the Post Office, struggled with the language only a little, asked to see *poste restante*, and laughed delightedly at seeing: *Sitadevi, Kars.*

The following Tuesday saw her cross the border on the weekly train, swapping the soul-nourishing Turkish food and the *muezzin* for more hunger in Georgia. The

Turks and Kurds had cuisine to die for. Outside a small lokanta in the back alleys of Urfa the chef had placed a plate of exquisitely fragrant patlican kebabs on her table. He stood watching. She began to eat. He shook his head: *No;* that was not the way to do justice to his food. He stepped over to her, implying he would show her. Taking her knife he slipped it under the blistered skin of the aubergine and lifted it clean away with two elegant fingers. *Now*, he said, *you can eat.* The sublime smokey flesh melted in her mouth. She admonished herself, she was, after all, only a barbarian, from England, what *could* she know about the refinement of food when fast-fat'n'sugar was all *they* knew?

Georgia – she would write about that between the Yahia of now and the Yahia who was yet to come to Australia. Written in the months as she waited in the comfortable home of a friend, writing up Candle for Kurdistan as a book, on an old borrowed typewriter, sitting in the garage, waiting, waiting.

Her long journey across Russia back to Doğukapı included Leninakan. By now she was protected by her ruby ring and just as well for before reaching Leninakan the train stopped as the city was swallowed in an earthquake that shocked the world and brought to its aftermath the world's aid. One hundred thousand people died that night, how many unnamed creatures from home, hearth, field and forest disappeared too. Anna carried a book of Gurdjieff in her backpack. He was born in Kars, these were his early stamping grounds and earthquakes hadn't fazed *him* one bit.

Back in Kars she was welcomed by those whom she had met during her week before Russia, she stayed more days, bought a train ticket for Artvin, wending her way slowly back to Yahia in Ankara. Her heart twanged, *twanged* a minor key, as the train left dramatically the golden landscape of Kurdistan and stopped precisely at Rize ili to become wet, forested, green and Bavarian. It was uncanny. She had left behind the mystical quality of the golden steppes of a land and a people she had learnt in a very short time to love. She decided it must be a Far Memory thing.

At Sivas Anna dallied more days, such hospitable people, and kindly. She discovered salep, that delicious and ubiquitous winter drink, thick and sweet and warming made from the boiled tuber roots of orchids. Winter was approaching fast. Leaving the warmth of that café she heard a kitten cry, there, in the gutter, attempting to climb the kerb. No mother was in sight. Anna scooped it up and took it into the café. Muslims love cats, Mohammed's apocryphal stories of his own feline friends warmed their hearts, and the café owner gave it a saucer of warm milk at once. But the floor was icy cold and the cushioned chairs too high to climb. Anna went off in search of a piece of magic carpet.

The carpet seller warmed to her story, she spoke a little more Turkish now, and offered her a costly piece of kilim. Embarrassed, she told him even her love for cats couldn't stretch her purse. *How much do you have in your hand,* he said, seeing her clutching something. She opened her palm, a few coppers, a little silver. The carpet seller laughed and folded the soft kilim piece into a bag, patting her hand. The café owner smiled too, and promised to take the kitten home that evening to his wife as he picked up the now contentedly full mite to place on the kilim. He told her the Eye of Allah watched over her, the Eye of Allah saw the kitten and the Hand of Allah guided its Fate to hers. Misty-eyed Anna, contented kitten, kindly men – a small weave of memories to carry her back to a larger Fate with its complexities yet to come.

Yet – Anna could no more live the way *her* ancestors did than Yahia's grandmother could live in the loneliness of urban Australia; neither could, and neither could change, it was a sound comparison. Anna could not live in a Syrian village. There were sadnesses ahead of her; Ahmer their best man died, tortured in a Turkish gaol after Yahia had left for Australia. Police had raided their flat, Anna had long left, but she had taken contraband back with her from London – cassettes of Kurdish music. The police discovered them; they had been watching the foreign woman come and go. In Turkey the Kurdish language and music and dance is outlawed, a cultural genocide. On a bus in Kars Anna had offered the driver a cassette of Zülfü Livaneli to play. At the opening of the first song the entire bus fell silent. The driver removed the cassette, returning it to Anna and gesturing with his hand a cut throat should the police board at the next stop. She had received it from Hoshyar Zebari whom she had briefly met at a clandestine meeting arranged in a Tube station back in London. He'd grinned and told her: *So you will become a Kurd and Yahia will become a Sufi!* His family had been Naqshbandi for generations; Sufism kept him sane.

Yahia and Anna knew the inevitable, he would return to his homeland, or at least would leave her to find Kurds in Melbourne to begin with. She had done everything she could, even finding a tiny nucleus of Iraqi Kurds and co-writing with them a Constitution, ratified, to give them status, a status 18,000,000 Kurds in their homeland had been deprived of since the Treaty of Sèvres and Lausanne when Britain and France divided Kurdistan into five to be shared amongst opposing cultures. Their motherland was bled by Britain and France for its oil. The Kurds, a proud and handsome race, having had their sovereignty thus gainsaid had consequently lost their legitimate access for complaint to the United Nations. Now they watched as their words and cries blew away with the wind. Anna hardly knew whether she loved a Kurd or Kurdistan but her imminent loss was a bereavement she could barely bear.

Yahia was away for the day. She went out to buy a bottle of Port. For some forgettable reason she had been given a prescription for Prozac – or had it been given to Yahia? He was certainly unhappy in sunny, lonely Queensland but Kurds didn't need pills, Yahia knew that, he needed his tribe. When Anna had introduced him to friends his response touched her to the quick: *We are five brothers,* he would say to their questions of family. Anglo-Saxons from anywhere would posit themselves at the

205

centre of their universe to reply: *I have four brothers.* A telling difference in consciousness.

She swallowed all the valium, drank at least half the port, it didn't taste too bad, she was not a drinker, and remembered nothing until bright lights and a kind face hovered over her. *You were lucky your husband came home unexpectedly,* said the nurse, *what made you want to do what you did? Finding you nearly killed him, he panicked so much every neighbour of every flat called the ambulance and four arrived! You're a very lucky woman.* Anna didn't feel lucky at all.

Yahia left thereafter, insisting the pretty cottage they had been blessed with through the then operative First Home Owner's scheme be put in her name only. The staff couldn't believe this proud and handsome man, with his sobbing wife holding on to the counter saying: *I don't want the house I only want my husband!* was asking to have his name removed from the title deeds that protected their joint ownership. It was a low point in a life of nadirs for Anna.

Now her Kurd had gone, and she could not follow; life in a Syrian village with nothing of her own culture around her, nor the freedom she took for granted, was not a life she would survive. With the loss of Yahia, whom she loved, she wondered what she would do with the rest of her life. Would her heart, even given time and tears, survive? Over her life of losses Anna had rarely considered suicide, she saw no shame, many an Indian yogi had deliberately shed his overcoat, but she only made that one serious attempt.

Decades later Anna looked back at her longing for death with a kind of wonder. She knew in her bones, later, that she could not, would not, live one split second after she had used up all her karma, and by then she had discovered a lot more to be used up. She pondered on the perfect death: she knew of three.

Slowly she picked up the broken shards of life where life had once again deposited her – in Australia, in the pretty Queenslander cottage now hers alone. It was here, though how anyone from the ashram knew where she lived she never discovered, she received the invitation to attend the Sat Chandi Maha Yajna in Rikhia, where the ageing Satyananda would pass to his successor his own Chain of Succession. Anna travelled down to Mangrove Mountain to fly with a group of younger generation swamis to Calcutta. She sensed their silent disapprobation: *Who was this Sitadevi who didn't wear dhotis and kurtas?* And more, she was *Catholic*, and someone had heard she was on the trail of a black Madonna, *whatever that was.*

Two days into the splendour of the ceremony came a day of days Anna would remember and chuckle over for years. The temporary toilet arrangements for two hundred westerners and two thousand Indians had been erected across the lane in another compound. When nature called Anna she had to make a beeline for the nearest convenience. Mostly she managed the ones across the street, but not this time. She ran to the – oh no! forbidden! – toilet of the Guru himself, conveniently behind the western group and ringed with roses and incense. When she came out the giant of a swami guarding his guru's loo wagged a finger at her presumption and very crossly admonished her: *Sitadevi! You are verry verry naughtie,* in that endearing Indian-English manner of speaking, and quick as a whip Anna responded with the widest of smiles: *Oh, I know, Swamiji, but God loves a sinner!*

The swami roared with laughter: *Sitadevi! you are sooooo right,* and shoo'd her back to her seat on the ground. Swami Satyananda, Paramahansaji, looked right at her, sitting there with her butter wouldn't melt expression, in the second row. The drummers had entered; the drummers for the Goddess. A caste of Indians devoted to the task since time immemorial they were small and slight and empowered by Shakti herself. The drumming thundered through their bodies, through Anna's body, and Paramahansaji pointed to her and commanded: *Dance!*

Well, he couldn't have meant her, could he? She had three left feet at the best of times. She turned around to see who he could mean. He looked again and repeated,

Dance! Anna felt a prod in her back: *He means you,* she heard from the Australian behind her, *geddup!*

The drummers were reaching a crescendo of rhythm as Anna climbed over the rope cordon to dance – for the Guru. Her mind dislodged itself from, *Can't,* as the drumming embraced and swallowed her whole. She believed that she danced, she was inside the drumming, heaven knows what those outside her could see, but she was the dance, no matter how ungainly. In time, when others would join her on the flower-strewn forecourt in front of a smiling Satyananda, the power of dance left her and she sat back down. She'd had her moment and whatever darshan was being given she had no doubt that it had been received within her.

The next day was the Day of days. The small Australian contingency had been called for private darshan with Paramahansaji, and they were all to wear dhotis. Anna no longer had one. She begged and borrowed a kurta and dhoti and swiftly bought a shawl from one of the hopeful boys selling tourist things outside the compound to turban her head. Today she would attend with the swamis but knowing she had travelled far, far away from any rightful position in the hierarchy of swamidom she positioned herself at the very back of the darshan tent where remained standing room only.

Paramahansaji sat surrounded by flowers, on a slightly raised dais so he could be seen, his left arm propped up at the elbow by a danda, a familiar stance for a kind of comfort Anna couldn't imagine. She watched him intently, happy to stand at the back and see clearly. *Hari Om,* he greeted everyone once they were settled, and *Hari Om,* everyone greeted him in return, the hum of a hundred soft Om's filling the tent.

There was a suspended silence, the anticipation of wise words pregnant. He spoke: *Welcome,* he said, *I hope your travel here was comfortable, you have come a long way, and today I want to speak to you about the Black Madonna.* And Anna's mind disappeared beyond all possible grasp.

The Black Madonna! How did he *know?* She had been absent from any connection with him for twelve years, a time traditional for Wisdom to make Herself at home in a seeker focused only on God. The two hundred people around her dissolved; Anna's piercing, penetrating look arrowed into Paramahansaji sitting far away. She heard and couldn't recall for the life of her a single word he said. But Niranjananda, the holder of the Succession, sat right next to him and Anna would ask him later.

First though, a small volte-face tremored through the group as swamis came out after Paramahansaji's talk, all wanting to know from Anna what this Black Madonna was, and why would Paramahansaji even bother with Catholicism? They wanted to *know*. What was it they had forgotten in their dismissal of their own roots? Because it was of their roots, Catholic roots of which Paramahansaji spoke then, not the broken trunks that followed the Deformation and destroyed throughout Europe every image of Mary pillagers and plunderers could set their hand too, as if he had been following her peregrinations all through the years.

Perhaps he had.

After tea later that day, when there was a rest period and Niranjananda was sitting outside his mirrored and embroidered tent, Anna asked him to explain for her the majesty of Paramahansaji's morning talk. Others were gathering too as he began:

> *Whether we call it Kali or the Black Virgin, both represent the Cosmic Force which is Unmanifest. The name that we give this Force is according to our cultural, social or religious background. In the Samkhya tradition they speak of the Avyakta Prakriti or the Unmanifest Prakriti, where Prakriti, or the Force, exists but it is contained within itself. The word Avyakta comes from the Sanskrit root vyanj and means to cause, to appear, to manifest. It develops as vyakta, to manifest, become visible and apparent. Avyakta means that which has not yet manifested. It is unmanifest, invisible, and imperceptible to human sensory phenomena. In Samkhya it is the unevolved Evolver of All Things; the primordial element whence all the phenomena of the material world are*

developed. The colour of Avyakta Prakriti is black. Black signifies the merging or the unification of everything that is visible.

With light we can look around and see the different colours, we can see the different objects, we can recognise different people, we can recognise different events, but in darkness colour cannot be perceived. This darkness prior to manifestation is neither chaos nor chaotic. Yellow is not seen as yellow, it is black. Grey is not seen as grey, it is black. People are not seen as people they merge with the black surroundings. Objects, buildings, vegetables, trees, plant life, animal life – they are undefined, we are not able to distinguish or recognize them merged as unmanifest potential. That is the state of Avyakta Prakriti, Unmanifest Nature. It is the dimension of the Eternal Now where things and forms exist, names exist, ideas exist, everything is there, qualities are there, attributes are there, but there is no distinction, there is no separation, there is no identification of this being separate to that. It is a Force which contains everything in individual units but at the same time there is no recognition of it. In Samkhya the Avyakta Prakriti is known as Kali, the Unmanifest Nature. The Tantric tradition calls Kali the Force of Time, the Force of Eternity, the Energy of Time, the Shakti of Time. This is not clock time but Eternal Time.

This Eternal Time or Cosmic Time is responsible for the continuation and the dissolution and the maintenance of the entire Creation, of the entire Universe. In relation to an individual, Cosmic Time is experienced in life as the form of the passage between life and death, the growth of the body, the decay of the body, the birth of a body, over which nobody has any control. One cannot control birth, one cannot control death, whoever comes has to go. One cannot stop the ageing and maturing of the body, no matter how hard we try. Artificial means can be adopted to remove the wrinkles by plastic surgery, but there are certain processes of life and death over which there is no human control, only Cosmic energies guide that process. The Cosmic Energy that guides this process is the energy of

210

Kali. In Vedanta, Maya is generally translated as Illusion, but it is not Illusion, it is the Cosmic Force which maintains and nourishes the Creation. It is a different name. Maya is the Vedantic name for Kali in Tantra, for Prakriti in Samkhya.

Experience of Maya happens on two levels. In the subtle level It is seen as Space, or the Cosmic Womb. At the physical level Maya is experienced in the form of an event which can be identified and measured. We can identify the Universe. We can look at different stars. We can search the mysteries of the Universe and we can try to measure, to identify and understand the mysteries of the Cosmos. That process of knowing is also a process of Maya. But the process of not knowing within knowing is also Maya: the process of not knowing within knowing. The Upanishads imply that ignorance or the absence of knowledge leads to darkness. Tamasic darkness. But knowledge also leads to greater darkness and this greater darkness is the Sattwic darkness; the darkness of Maya, the darkness of not knowing. These qualities are known as the three gunas in Yoga, and represent the three stages of human consciousness: tamas describes the dull, the lazy, the ignorant, the point of inertia. It is, of course, far more than this. The second guna is rajas, a dynamic state which describes action, the world of paradox and duality, and a certain hot-headedness, fire being the element of rajas, in contradiction to the luminous quiescence of the third guna which represents the sattwic mind.

The whole of human existence can be codified by the knowledge of the three gunas; for example every form of food falls into one of the categories, and this knowledge can help balance the fluctuations of one's own nature. Meat is rajasic or tamasic depending on the type and the preparation, however onions and garlic are also highly rajasic, a mango is sattwic.

Anna and those around her sat motionless, each absorbing what they were able to assimilate until Niranjananda stopped speaking. The wind picked up, little eddies of dust spun golden in the lowering sun, the moment Indians call

211

cowdust time, that time of day when Nature recovers her breath and cattle return haloed by the aureole of the day's end.

Anna thanked him, walked off to be alone with her thoughts and to write down, verbatim as best she could, the colloquy of cosmic causation that underpinned her own search for meaning. Now, with this great gift of knowledge, she could go to France and fulfil, as best she could, Father Bede's task. She had learned in that nutshell explanation of the cosmic mysteries of the understanding which had been lost: *Heu prisca fides!* alas, our ancient faith. Anna would keep faith with it.

Catholic mystics had always named this, its original mysticism, this *sattwic* darkness, the Dazzling Darkness, the Cloud of Unknowing, a state of not knowing the Known. Different cultures and civilizations have expressed this feeling and this understanding of Cosmic Energy in their own cultural context. It is the understanding of black, darkness, that which cannot be seen, as an *archetype* of our soul, our essence, which challenges the more superficial overlay of religion. And it is this meaning the West lost with the loss of Mary, Virgin, *Black* in the subsequent Christian accretions of its older tradition which would not gainsay its truth. Darkness, the only Mother from which starlight can be born.

Anna wrote much that night before she slept, remembering the simple description she had read of the different gunas, making sense of it in a simpler way: the darkness of the tamasic mind is like that of the man who downs tools at the end of the day, comes home, asks what's for dinner and then eats it quite unconsciously, automatically. The rajasic mind is very much the mind of modern man who comes home, sits down at the table, and twenty minutes later does not even realize he has eaten his dinner. Overloaded with the imponderables of the day his mind jumps from subject to subject without ever touching home base – which was the body into which his wife's wonderful dinner was going. The sattwic mind is the clear mind of the sage, mystic, seer or saint. S/he downs tools at

212

the end of the day and asks what's for dinner, and is intimately aware of every morsel and sensation of what s/he has eaten.

Anna pondered long the possibility of finding again that which has been buried, asked herself how she could awaken her own lost voice, that Vision in Long Darkness. Changing the patriarchal religious hierarchy bothered her, it was neither practical nor possible, changing the sex of Biblical references was hardly a truthful or fulfilling way of changing what needed changing either. The work of the American Medical Missionary, Sister Marie-Therese Winter, does this well. Her liturgies have a tremendous following, and she has brought to vibrant personal identification the many magnificent and nameless women of the Bible. Yet, Anna felt almost betrayed reading her charming book *Noah and Her Sisters* in which Noah was a woman with her own lineage of a feminine Deity. Anna was deeply offended by Winter's invention of the word Godde. Spoken, the word may not offend ears or hearing, that is its subtle sophistry; but Anna's eyes, and her intelligence, were seriously challenged by such credulity. Most Christians are *afraid* of the word Goddess. The word 'Godde' is both meaningless and fatuous and Anna sizzled with frustration, was left with the sense that Ms. Winter was afraid of saying the obvious. Why use newspeak when language already holds a word of power, replete with meaning? That word is Goddess. It was time to go to France.

21

La Belle France: 1996 and 2016

Anna wrote to every airline in Australia asking each if they had a spare seat in the back of their planes where she might sit: *As quietly as a nun, all the way to Paris and back,* to do her research on the Black Madonna. She wrote twenty-seven letters, each by hand. She only needed one 'yes'. She received eight replies; six were 'regretfully, no'; Air France said yes but they no longer flew out of Australia – could she get to Singapore? And one wrote *Yes*, addressing Anna as Sister in response to her 'nun'. When would she like to go? The offer from Malaysian Airlines was open ended, asking nothing in return, no article, no commitment. Partially brought up as a child in Malaya, Anna imagined their generous offer might have been made in the spirit of interfaith dialogue – but she couldn't be sure. And in March 1996, having inspired a friend to accompany her for some of the journey, the pair landed in Paris, picked up their leased Renault, headed for Dijon and their first Black Virgin, and then to their first monastery, l'Abbaye Sainte-Marie-de-la-Pierre-qui-Vire, a Benedictine foundation in glorious surroundings. Here Anna first tasted red wine, the *vin du Pays*, that charming description proud of its local heritage, its *terroir*, and it was good. So was the food of the monastery, grown by the monks and giving Anna her first taste of reality! French food. And it was very good. It became her yardstick from which to judge how bad English food was.

Anna fell deeply and irrevocably in love with France. It was her spiritual homeland as much as India. On their second day, after being awed by the presence and living prayer of everyone in the chapel of the Black Virgin of Dijon, a Madonna of hieratic calm, she drove quietly through the great forests of Morvan to a small mediaeval village where women guests of the monastery each had a cottage of their own. The village had been abandoned, the Abbaye bought it, the monks restored it. Everything about each cottage was charming, the furnishings were genuine antiques, a round boule and ormolu tea-table in her cottage was surely Louis Quatorze; the beauty surrounding her inclined Anna to remain forever in the magical world of serenity created by the monks. Her first experience of a living western Benedictine tradition enchanted her, its impact would drip-feed her soul for years. It was the beginning of a serpentine path that would deepen and direct her own world, slowly, indelibly. Father Bede had made her a Benedictine Oblate in 1986 and although Benedictine foundations were thin on the ground where she lived in Australia to be *here, now*, was a kind of homecoming for her soul.

Anna stayed in convents and monasteries throughout the two month journey through France, each one more beautiful than the one before. Travelling deeper into the landscape, tracing unmarked lanes from wooded valley to high snowy crags, the air so crisp and pure Anna believed herself the first to breath it as she stood at the doors of the smaller, hidden churches in dense forest or on high, still frozen, escarpments. She was privileged to find, or be guided to, or discover for herself, dozens and dozens of Black Virgins, many in tiny churches high above the snowline, in hamlets barely marked on any map. Keys, huge mediaeval iron castings weighing half a kilo and too large for her hand to comfortably hold, could be collected from the barn of a local farmer, once he'd finished milking, or from the old lady with the flower garden .... It was a time of enchantment. Each discovery shifted Anna's way of perceiving; offering new dimensions of relating to herself as a woman and a Catholic. The 'little tradition' represented in the Black Virgin was a force to reckon with.

The journey welded her to a past she belonged to: a mediaeval past where people knew holy images, and that lexicon of arcane comfort offered by the hands of holy images, lowered or lifted and made holy by prayer. Heartbreak, mourning, sickness, loss and love, all flickered through those hands and on to some listening Infinity. Icons mirror the same sacred language. Angels, Anna knew, were a mode of knowledge quite foreign to the consciousness of modern man, or woman; a single feather from an Archangel's wing would shelter the world if called, its whole wing would span a galaxy, but who called on Angels now? They cross our time and space, unseen and unbidden. The virtue-less putti of the New Age vox populi were incapable of manifesting a cupcake, much less comforting a stricken soul.

Anna knew she had sprung from the thirteenth century, felt an ease and resonance there, both East and West as it happened, unlike her discomfort with the modern world she was born into. She held that perhaps she had once been a rather ordinary French nun of that century, cloistered amongst the wild roses that smothered the ancient ruined walls she frequently passed as she drove deeper into this enchanting landscape of France.

Many of the religious houses in which she stayed on that first momentous journey had small shops attached selling liturgical items, herbal products, small artworks and religious carvings. Anna found postcards depicting an enchanted world – bright fields and prancing ponies, poppies and butterflies, wildflowers of wondrous colours. On the reverse of each was written: *tapisserie,* Dom Robert, *En Calcat.* She bought some, kept them as treasured souvenirs.

Twenty years later, all along the central nave of Notre-Dame de Paris, where she had gone to pray with Parisians after Bataclan, were her 'postcards'; the original vast tapestries of those little postcards which had inspired her. That was a holy moment.

And I'll tell you why, thought Anna to you, her invisible audience, as she turned to address you from 2015: *L'Ode à la Création* was coordinated to coincide with the *Conference on Climate Change, COP21, in Paris. Coordinated by its host Government, French, deeply aware of truth threatening us all and all the creatures we love.*

Anna knew that if even one of the visiting delegates had seen those tapestries the result of yet another costly conference of talking heads may have inspired him, or her, with an inner fire of utter conviction that to save our beautiful world and the last three thousand wild tigers was a fire to die for; or, if not to die for, then at least to court political death and fight with courage in the face of the corporate greed that is destroying our planet piecemeal. But, alas, she knew it was no vote catcher. The world of Dom Robert's tapestries sang with his quiet epiphany. Down there amongst the wild fields and farmlands of the valleys of the Montagnes Noires of Tarn, Nature had revealed to this remarkable Benedictine monk a great truth: *La nature est la vraie réalité. La nature ne trompe jamais. La nature est le visage de Dieu: Nature is the true Reality. Nature never deceives. Nature is the Face of God.*

As she read the words introducing Dom Robert's work suspended along the nave of Notre Dame de Paris Anna trembled with the magnitude of what his tapestries were *actually* saying. She found a pew and sat down, her whole vision filled with *Laudes, Plein Champs, Les Enfants de Lumière.* Thoughts spun at dizzying speed, she couldn't have stood if she'd tried to just then because *this was her epiphany too.* As a child, unloved and unwanted, she *knew* God was the horse chestnut tree whose vast branches held her, the black cat who loved her, the dandelions holding their sunny faces as she smiled at them in return, the wind blowing birdsong to her. Oh, she knew God alright; it was just that around her, no one else did. Least of all the Anglican Sunday School teacher who told her her cat wouldn't go to heaven because God, the teacher's God obviously, wouldn't have animals in heaven – they didn't have *souls.*

Anna was seven, the teacher was grown up. Anna hadn't the language beyond indignation to argue, but she knew her teacher was *so* wrong about God. And God certainly didn't look like the man with a white beard in those Church of England Sunday School books either. Anna left Sunday School right then and there and walked quite out of her knowledge of things into a world where the sedges and grasses would no longer know her and the world's roads would not know her shadow for many years. It was her birth as a pilgrim without portfolio, and in that moment, *that* moment in the Notre-Dame, she knew she had completed a circle, a spiral. A Benedictine monk was telling his truth, and hers, to the whole world. 'The sight of love is mother and child' Anna had read the quote somewhere and dismissed it – *No!* said she with the tapestries above her: *the sight of love is roses in the wild.*

He says that woman speaks with Nature
That she hears voices from under the earth
That the wind blows in her ears
And the trees whisper to her.
That the dead sing through her mouth
And the cries of infant hearts are clear to her.
But for him this dialogue has gone.
He says he is not part of this earth.
That he was set on this world as a stranger.
He sets himself apart from Woman and Nature.
And so it is Goldilocks who goes to the Three Bears,
Little Red Riding Hood who converses with the Wolf,
Dorothy who befriends a Lion,
Snow White who talks to the Birds,
Cinderella with Mice as her allies,
The Little Mermaid who is half Fish
And Thumbelina carried to Paradise on the back of a Swallow.
And he says he cannot hear.
So when we hear in the Navajo chant
That a grown man sits and smokes with Bears
And listens to instructions given to him by Squirrels,
We are surprised.
We had been told
only little girls spoke with animals.
We are the birds, the bird's eggs;
We are flowers and fox,

We are eagle, doe and dingo too.
We are cats and caterpillars.
River flow and tidal ebb
We are the weavers, womb and web.
We are the shining of the stars that sing,
Snakes that glide down mountainside,
Milk that gives you birth
We are of Mother Earth.
We are Women.
And he says he cannot hear us speak.
But we hear, we hear, we hear, we hear,
We are Women.

He heard. The monk whose tapestries Anna had carried with her as postcards for nearly quarter of a century, *heard*.

Anna returned home from her 2015 journey, after Bataclan, longing to share her circlet of truth with a kindred spirit. Who better than her favourite Abbot, Abbot Francis of Prinknash Abbey? She emailed him, he suggested a day and welcomed her in the small parlour of St Peter's Grange where he took the wind fair from her sails with the knowledge that not only was Prinknash *French* Benedictine in its origin, and that its sister Abbey was l'Abbaye Saint-Benoît d'En Calcat, but that En Calcat was the very monastery where Dom Robert had lived and died.

> *And did you know*, he asked gently, his words tricking the astonishment that had settled over her brain, which in its surprise had parted momentarily from its usual sanctuary, *that Dom Robert spent ten years at Buckfast Abbey? Or that one of his great tapestries hangs in Leicester Square, in the Catholic Church?*

> Anna sat, an amalgam of goosebumps, assimilating such vast synchronicities. *Why don't you visit our sister monastery?* Father Francis's quiet commonsense washed over her, leaving in its wake grand possibilities for this, her seventieth, year. *All the French connections*, she thought, *and me, half French; it's a half I must learn, must explore.*

219

Anna held out a copy of *Patrick* for Father Francis; this was Bede's monastery too, the book with his Foreword would be coming home, as it were. Father Francis smiled: *Ah,* he said, *you have already given me a copy of Patrick. When we moved back from the big monastery we could only bring a handful of things, our rooms here at the Grange are very small indeed, I chose your book to bring with me, it is beautiful and I am very fond of it.* Tears prickled Anna's eyes, her day had been filled with lovely things.

So to France again. But before that, a visit to Buckfast while she waited to hear from the guest-master of En Calcat to confirm accommodation for her visit in March, and quick a trip to Leicester Square.

March 2016. The threshold of the Trinity of Dark Rising was imminent and less than three months hence Brexit would plunge England into division and Anna into despair, and a bid for political asylum. Farage, Brexit, Trump. As the first two evils came to pass the third, whether evil or not no one could predict, would follow as sure as Goddess made little apples. The first two evils would change Anna's knowledge of herself irrevocably. Brexit threw her a curved ball.

It was four days before she could venture out of her small home into the divided world of insularity and exclusivism and nationalism that Brexit had spawned overnight. It was not a world she wanted to live in, yet proof of it must have lain close to the surface of the English psyche, a lacuna unsuspected, biding a time of intolerance that would re-birth it in the land of her birth, its people time-trapped in a dying Empire that could never relive its days of a *Great* Britain. No longer great, it was now divided; a psychic split not seen since the Dissolution of the Monasteries brought forth all the carpetbaggers and opportunists to support, for their own ends, a king who didn't want a country but an Excuse. Anna couldn't even find an Excuse to justify the folly of Brexit at her front door.

Beyond that front door, on the fourth day, she refused to engage in any discussion with anyone until she met, with a similarly ashen expression, Petunia, a teacher of French at Millfield and a serious contender for the Best-Dressed laurels of Glastonbury. Petunia was as devastated by Brexit as Anna. The two went back to Anna's bungalow for good French coffee and commiseration, plotted escapes and schemes and agreed that they would book a ferry from Newhaven to Dieppe for July 13th, hop into Poppy, Anna's valiant twenty year old red Micra, and drive to Picardie, to *le village de Vismes*, where Petunia would plead, in her superbly accented French – a Scot, her short 'o's' were Gallic perfection – Anna's case for political asylum in the land of her Parisian born grandmother.

The two women had already made a trip to France in April of that year, pre-Brexit, to trace Anna's de Visme relations through two paintings she owned, painted by a cousin of some repute in her day, Denise de Visme. The cream stone cottages of Linars were enough reason to explore, but to add a certain piquancy to their venture Petunia had contacted the Mairie which had led to an introduction to M and Mme Faucon who knew everyone, past and present:

Tout le monde! wrote Anna filling a facebook page with photographs, *I've been ancestor chasing in Angoulême with Petunia Evergreen – star from Glastonbury who speaks flawless French. Together we met magic in the guise of falcons (M. and Mme. Faucon) who invited us into their nest to share with us all they knew. My de Visme's have long gone, but their house on the edge of the woods is there and owned by a marvellous couple who speak perfect English and told us stories. Denise de Visme became increasingly afflicted with dementia in her dotage, and drove her car dementedly about the village. The Mayor feared for her life as much as for the lives of his people. With acerbic French assertion he visited every gasoline station in a ten mile radius and forbade them to sell petrol to Mme de Visme. His plan worked. Denise fretted and fumed and fulminated to all – but on foot!*

We were accompanied by wonderful women all the way: Isabelle d'Angoulême (and did we know she had been

kidnapped by John Lackland – our ill-favoured King John?
Or that she returned to France after his death and is buried
next to Richard Cœur de Lion, another son of Aliénor
d'Aquitaine – who happened to be born in 1157 on my
birthday? We gazed amazed at their tombs in Fontevraud).
Marguerite d'Angoulême smiled at us as she departed to
reign as Marguerite de Navarre whose country I strode
across on the Camino a couple of years ago.

>*And do ask me about Saint Radégonde – my!*
there was a woman! In Saumur we met Anne d'Anjou
before we had our minds properly blown away by the seventy
x eighty-foot fourteenth century tapestries of the Apocalypse
displayed in Angers. We adored the Whore of Babylon with
her mirror, but all this excitement proved too much for two
middle-aged women on walkabout so we repaired to a
convent for two nights, nourishingly dedicated to the Mother
of the Good Shepherd in which to end our journey.

Picardie, visited après Brexit, was a charm, a surprise, and
not an area Petunia knew. But alas *le Village de Vismes* had
no de Visme's or de Vismes living there now and the
Mayor didn't rise to the opportunity to embrace Anna as a
long lost chatelaine, nor offer her the crumbling castle of
her forebears, despite Theobold de Vismes. Chevalier to
William the Conqueror, he had married a Norwegian
princess by the name of *Radégonde!* After a little exploration
of Picardie it would be back to Blighty for Anna.

In the small cemetery of the village lay the
pristine, still tended, graves of six Lancashire soldiers,
barely out of their teens, each with a blood red poppy at
their searingly white marble headstones. Anna
photographed each grave. Later she wrote articles for local
Lancashire newspapers and France Today.

Picardie: a weekend at Cayeux sur Mer, a day *le
phoque* watching along the sand dunes of Mers-les-Bains
but they stayed in a dreary hotel on the *peripherique* of
Abbeville where the ruined façade of the exquisite 12th
century Cathedral stood sentinel to the horror of World
War One. It was all that remained of the entire bombed
out city. Now it was July 2016. They parked beside a river

to walk across the bridge to enter modern, hastily rebuilt, Abbeville. Only then did they see the name: *la Somme.*

The whole region was the chilling graveyard of the blood and bones of how many million horses, how many million men; the soil so fertile, the poppies so red.

Anna was mostly ill on the day they chose to visit the cathedral of Amiens, they would make the short journey by train. Amiens blew their hearts away. Stepping down from the train to enter the vast railway concourse they paused, the concourse had been transformed by two words, one left and one right, running the entire length of each wall, in letters Gargantua could have held and made small: THANKS along the entire left wall; MERCI flanked the entire right wall.

Each letter was separated by more than life-size sepia photographic images of young soldiers in trenches, starved horses, artillery, guns, scenes of mud and utter desolation galleried along the walls – and – Silence. No one walking on that concourse spoke. Separately, each studied the photos, the meaning, the intention, the reminder – *this was the Somme.*

Anna looked down at her feet: wide strips of applied photographic visuals were laid along the width of the concourse paving: blue sky, white clouds, falling poppies. Its simplicity seared the heart. She wept. Petunia turned, tears had armisticed her too. Absorbing the impact of a living memory of a war that had also decimated English rural life forever was stark and real. A million men and a million horses died in the slaughter of that war fighting for unity and peace and 'they' want Brexit? Brexit – England had broken faith with all those who died, and poppies still grow ... We Will Remember Them:

In Flanders' fields the poppies blow
Between the crosses, row on row,
... and in the sky
The larks, still bravely singing, fly
Scarce heard amid guns below.

We are the Dead. Short days ago

We lived, felt dawn, saw sunset glow,
Loved and were loved, and now we lie
In Flanders' fields.

In Flanders Field – John Macrae

Returning to England was a nadir moment for Anna, her heart dreaded it, sank like dead weight. She rued her life of pilgrim profligacy; if only her childhood had offered choices, she would have trained as an opera singer, a lawyer, a journalist, an illustrator of exquisite stories; money and a proper pension; pilgrims don't have pension plans. If there was a moment in Anna's life that etched its intransigence with proof of worldly failure, it was then.

The inner turmoil shook her. Dreams of France and a Family Fold, all fantasy, evaporated. The truth was stark and unforgiving; she would die in that bothie back in Brexitland.

But life went on, and Anna's natural optimism lifted itself over the parapet of the despair that walled her in. Unexpected gifts came flowing into her days. The article she had written of their pilgrimage to Picardie received a certain acclaim, winning her a nomination for the French Media Travel Award. An appreciated accolade. Her Secret Agent put her up in the Shard for the evening's presentations and it was he who stimulated her application for a Swiss passport.

Anna had her Parisian grandmother's *acte de naissance*, but the French wrote to her in French – why wouldn't they? – and she couldn't fathom the pages of bureaucratic instructions to even begin an application to claim citizenship, and thus a pension to live there. Frustration lent wild alternatives. Wasn't her father born in Geneva? Tentatively she composed an email to the Swiss Embassy, and within twenty-four hours received an astonishing response, in flawless English, to say she was registered in Geneva and to ask: *Are you applying for a passport?* Anna laughed, cried, prayed her thanks to her father. However unfatherlike to her he had been obliged to be through his

224

own marital circumstances he had gifted her with immeasurable wealth: a Swiss passport! Anna telephoned the Embassy to hear it spoken: *And would you like an ID card as well?* the young voice inquired. She would, oh, she would!

Anna made an appointment with the Embassy, it necessitated an overnight stay, Secret Agent booked her into Baker Street's Sherlock Holmes Hotel, just around the corner. He would accompany her the following morning to the Embassy interview. Her photograph and fingerprints were taken digitally and with Swiss precision, a receipt passed over to Anna with assurances that all would be sent to Geneva and she would be called in when the passport was ready. Secret Agent looked at the receipt: *And those numbers*, he said, his quiet droll humour to the fore, *are the code to your new Swiss Numbered Bank Account* ... Lunch at Browns, after a walk through Tiffany's looking at green diamonds, Secret Agent setting the uniformed staff on their toes by saying, *sotto voce*, that his lady friend knew her diamonds, she was from Geneva, suggestive of Sequestered Wealth. The staff would read her, looking like Second-hand Rose, as *eccentric*, while Secret Agent played the charade.

Anna's intransigent homelessness hadn't left her with much in the way of material accumulations but she had clung to two family parchments her aunt Zabeth was clearing from her dungeous basement. Anna was on hand that particular day in 1986 and asked if she could have them. One was an Indenture for Deed of Land, dated 1770 in the Year of Our Lord, between Andrew de Visme and the Bishop of Rochester – a mere half acre in the middle of London. The other was a charming illumination of the *mariage* of her great-grandfather to his second wife, her grandmother's beloved stepmother, Alice Boissonnas. Along with these tokens of family connections came a very large genealogy folded four times, worked in spirals on stiff paper, her own pedigree at the top adjacent to the *paterfamilias*, Fortuné-Barthélemy de Félice. These three treasures were her only link to family, for, once her aunts and her father died, her stepbrothers severed the slender connections the older generation had kept alive. The treasures Anna held had been stored for thirty-five years in an old tin trunk, traversing the oceans of the world and the decades of her life. Anna's new Swiss identity was tinderbox to a memory.

Andrew de Visme. Years earlier Anna had been contacted by a landscape architect from Bristol studying the Portuguese gardens of Sintra and the palace of Montserrat; they had been designed by a de Visme. No more light was shed than that *fillip* of uselessness but now Anna took out her family documents and looked again at Comte de Félice, the man's name in scrolls and curlicues grandly prefacing the document and her name right there at the top of the spiral next to it. She went to her computer, appealed to Arfie, who fetched: *Fortunato Bartolomeo de Felice – born 24 August 1723, died 13 February 1789.* The Italianization of his name would surely be the same *de Félice*. The compiler of the facts had included the paterfamilias as the Second Comte de Panzutti. Alice faced with the White Rabbit could not have been curiouser than Anna. A page of fascination followed, ending with a link to the current holder of the title *Comte*. Anna sat for some while digesting the slender possibility of *relatives, family*. She clicked the link. A page opened. The portrait of a youngish man appeared, described as a CEO of a considerable law company, London and Geneva confirmed her trail as correct. There was an email address.

She sat with the information for some days, turning around in her mind what she could say. On the fifth morning she wrote:

> *Dear Philippe,*
> *I do believe we have an ancestor in common. My great-grandfather married your great-aunt* ... and not a lot more.

Anna didn't really expect a reply and for ten days wasn't disappointed.

It was now December. Anna had known the Secret Agent for some years, meeting as they had in an esoteric bookshop owned by a mutual friend in Glastonbury. He had supported her Twinning by coming to Patmos and from time to time would meet her in the City where they would lunch and talk and share. He lived with his mother in that part of London where Samuel Pickwick had retired: "to a house in one of the most pleasant spots near London". Secret Agent was Anna's open sesame to the City she was born in and was always thrilled to explore. She adored being in his company. He *knew* things; his esoteric interests paralleled equally his wide and varied exoteric travelling and pursuits. He introduced her to cocktails, superb lunches and The Savoy and mangosteens and rambutans for dessert in China Tang at the Dorchester, true flavours of Malaya. She discreetly named him after one of his favourite cocktails to avoid identification when she spoke of him to friends.

Secret Agent was erudite, practically all-knowing, a not-so-old Cantabrian, a man-about-town in the most wonderful ways. One particular day he walked her to Gough Square to meet Hodge, that Very Fine Cat for whom Johnson bought oysters; took her to lunch in Ye Olde Cheshire Cheese; explored Southbank and the Globe; passed by St Andrew by the Wardrobe to one of the great Dragons of London guarding the City at the Bounds. Later they spent ages together tracking down the London Stone – that oolithic limestone block once standing in Candlewick Street opposite the church of St Swithin at London Stone in Catholic times.

They arrived to find a crater in Cannon Street, but sleuth work with two strangers and their iPad, standing next to 8½ Skinners' Hall, led them not to Hogwarts but to the marvellous London Museum, another probe into her past prickling Anna's arms with *déjà vu* goosebumps as she began to discover the history of her own birthplace. There was Sparkie, brave cat of the Great Fire; and further on, Pudding Lane where the horror began, and a splendid tea at Montague on the Gardens. So many wonderful treasures her Secret Agent revealed of a birthplace she loved and wished, truth be known, she could return to. Johnson was right: *tire of London and tire of life.*

In her seventieth year Secret Agent invited her to London: *Bring a small case to stay over,* he said mysteriously and revealed no more. He met her coach at Hammersmith. Tall, suave, tweeded, wearing a cap from Locks? Lairds? and wrapped in a wondrously coloured scarf, his natural composure revealed a quiet humour, though rarely his thoughts. Secret Agent, occupation heir, was heir to freedom. Giving nothing away he suggested they take a cab to the destination he was keeping secret.

Anna leant back, repositioning her thoughts: *Taking cabs and not glancing at the meter, now, that's a way of life;* but she *had* polished her boots and washed her hair and done the best she could; *à la mode* Glastonbury was one thing, in London's inner city and in the company of Secret Agent, quite another.

The cab slowed, soon all traffic stopped. Splendid horses with liveried and helmeted riders came briskly from her right through Wellington Arch, followed by a black and gilded open coach with four red-caped men riding pillion, great bay horses harnessed in four. A dignitary, royal? was sitting inside the handsome coach and wearing a spectacular black bicorn plumed with a forest of white egret feathers held back by a golden barrette. He was speaking to a large gaudily dressed couple from one of the African nations; a tour of such grandeur made Anna wonder with momentary mischief if they'd pawned their nation for the ride. She photographed the spectacle, thrilled it was part of her own day's mystery tour. Then, she recognized the Strand and the cab swung left into: *The Savoy!*

Anna's enchantment with the silver Christmas display all but overwhelmed her, an Alice in Wonderland moment to smile over forever. The charm of the Red Lacquered Lift, the courtesy of the uniformed bellboy who didn't bat an eye at her tiny travel-worn, frankly unappealing, single piece of luggage. Secret Agent, leaving her settled in her marvellous room, returned to his mother. Anna gazed out at the Thames, sacred River!, from the seventh floor, the combination of a perfect sunset and her friend's kindness made her weep, just a little.

In the bathroom Anna found specially created perfumes for body lotions and soaps and shampoos – intoxicated by their sublime fragrance she knew she'd risen to heaven: roses, sandalwood, Grasse! She did as she had been bid and switched on the TV: *Madame de Visme – Welcome to the Savoy*. She sat giggling with delight.

At the thought of Anna's response to his gift for her seventieth year his heart warmed as he travelled home. She may be unused to the attentions, may appear gauche compared with the cool self-entitlement of the legendary hotel's usual guests, but he knew her happiness and natural charm would win her hearts and coronets; she was a natural aristocrat, people responded to her all-embracing smile. It was she who had encouraged him to find his own courage to travel. And travel he had, since then. To the Bushmen of the Kalahari; to ancestral homes in America; to Girona – beloved Girona in the company of a woman whose destiny there as a golden fifteen year old many decades before had carried her into its hidden heart, and off to Hollywood to marry ... well, it was an Adventure he was thrilled to be part of now, included in the golden years of the woman of secrets, and in the intimacies of a story still unfolding. A story he knew would change things, historical things. He sent Anna her books, she had visited Girona with his map of its secrets, wondered if the two women would meet ...

A few days previously Philippe of the Title had replied to Anna with a long email of connections and coincidences, family histories and eccentricities, intrigues and an invitation to meet. Secret Agent's gift, so timely, could not be more appropriate. In the charm of her seventh floor bedroom overlooking the Thames, Anna could now email Philip: *Meet me at the Savoy*, as to the manor born.

Philip had been forced to change *his* surname as she had been forced to change hers when their respective mothers had divorced the better names. He had also, as Anna had, anglicized his first name as more fitting to the ordinary. He was charming and cultured, with *presence!* His pretty, ethereally thin, blonde wife, plump Anna's antithesis. Even had Anna been *so* much younger, as the lovely couple were, she would still have seen herself as she suspected they saw her: wearing a hotch-potch of second-hand clothes, face bare of make-up, dumpy and brown. But she *learned* things, interesting things, things that fed her soul.

Philip was a natural raconteur of family secrets: Fortunatus, Fortuné, Fortunato, had been a Franciscan friar. Such facts resonated with Anna's endless penchant for cloisters; her other world of icons, saints and holy ones, and jolly well explained something in her genes; who was she forever searching for? the monk? the unattainable? Anna listened with her whole *being*, appearances no longer distracting her attention. Fortunato was uncommonly bright. Born in Rome he was educated by Jesuits and secured not one but two Chairs at the University of Naples. That explained another thing too. But then, whence came the progeny?

Philip had brought folders filled with photocopies of family documents and interest to give to Anna, too much to explain, too little time! Their gist was: Fra Fortunato, a Franciscan, was sent to console the spiritual needs of Contessa Agnese di Panzutti, or was it Contessa Agnese de Arcuato? They fell in love and eloped, to Berne in Switzerland, he throwing off his Franciscan habit and loyalties somewhere over the mountains. They arrived penniless, survived by virtue of his learning, but soon enough, *que orrore,* her husband tracked them down and dragged his wife back to a convent where she was silenced for the rest of her poor incarcerated days.

But, there were two stories, the other explained certain anomalies: Fortunatus rescued the Countess not from her husband but from prison. Why? Anna, small brain dazzled, neglected to ask the obvious. The title had been passed by decree, in this version, by the Contessa di Panzutti who held it *suo jure* from the first Count's Will to

Fortunato. Fortunate indeed to earn a title from an irate husband!

Fortuné could never return to Italy. Whether his beloved Agnese was incarcerated in a convent or died the wife of her rescuer, in due time Fortunato married another Countess, canny man, and founded the first printing press in Yverdon, wrote his *Encyclopédie d'Yverdon*. He died there, having married four times, his various wives giving him thirteen children.

"Fortunato de Félice, 2nd count Panzutti, (1723–1789) an Italian nobleman, author, philosopher and scientist" sits one below Jean-Jacques Rousseau in the list of the town's notable people. Such facts barely mattered; the story itself romance enough for Anna.

One final *fillip* of the day: when Anna's email dropped into his inbox, the name *de Visme* stopped Philip in his tracks. For twenty years he had been driving in and out of his home, built on an estate which grand entrance still maintained the pillars of the original gatehouse. Every time he drove through though invisible gates, Philip said, he *registered* the plaque, placed there as a reminder of the estate's former glory, ownership and provenance. The name on the plaque was: *de Visme:* the very de Visme responsible for the gardens and palace of Sintra.

22

Emotional Dilemma – Carrot or Cow

Anna had been a vegetarian for more than thirty years. She couldn't bear the cruelty of being otherwise. She had, it is true, honoured the Medicine Wheel moment with Grey Wolf, but back in London, and then Australia, despite her Kurd who loved lamb and kofta and kebabs, she remained essentially vegetarian. Her Kurd had long since left.

1996. Anna had spent months in France, tripping happily up and down mountains and valleys searching for her Black Virgins; pausing at Saintes-Maries-de-la-Mer in May for the gathering of Gypsies; she had been pushed by the gendarmes holding back the throng of tourists into the procession itself, an unexpected grace. Had walked behind the parade of Lords and the Ladies *l'Arlésienne,* the ladies each carrying a white lace parasol and wearing costumes of *rubans* and tight waisted *fichu; eso* or *plastron,* silk or satin skirts and all had faces of beauty and grace. Then came *les gardiens* on their wild white Camargue horses of the *etangs* and: *Attention!* called a young gypsy walking behind her as a horse stepped back and almost left a hoof print embedded on her foot. Anna was in heaven. She walked with the King of the Gypsies all the way to the sea, where the horses turned in a row in the littoral's foam to welcome the bearers of the bones of the Maries in their reliquary taken from the church that morning to re-enact their arrival after the Crucifixion.

Three Maries: Mary Jacobe, Mary Salome and Mary Magdalene, Lazarus and Maximus with Joseph of Arimathea, uncle of the Virgin, he who prepared the tomb for Jesus, he who went on to Glastonbury. And Sara from Egypt, Sara the Gypsy. The gypsies claim *her.* Anna had placed a red rose in Sara's ribbons that morning in the crypt. She would be carried to the sea too. Two thousand years ago the Gypsy Queen, with her Sight, recognized the holy women, the Maries, as they sailed in to her shores. Put to sea in a coracle, denied oars, they all survived, of course, and had drifted to Râ, the town that changed its name to honour them.

Silkstone, Australia, 1996, Anna was home again with her memories of that and of all that Father Bede had asked of her. She developed toothache, nothing prepared her for anything sinister. Her teeth were good, but the pain grew shocking, and rapidly. She went to a young, too young, dentist nearby. The dentist didn't say much, didn't comment on the fact that her decision to remove the tooth had nothing to do with the tooth. She barely pulled, and the tooth fell out attached to half Anna's jawbone; a whole wedge of honeycomb that should have been bone. But the pretty young Greek dentist said nothing as Anna looked questioningly at the honeycomb. *Is that what bone ought to look like?* she didn't ask. And should have.

Some weeks after the dentist Anna gathered up papers she had written about her time in France as preliminary research into the Black Virgins. She had enrolled in a course on Interpretive Tourism of all things, and with arms full to take to the library for photocopying, she tripped on the bottom stair of the high-set veranda.

She couldn't get up. Her feet sort of *crumbled.* She felt no pain. She crawled up the steps to the old, circa 1910, back door which, its top half being coloured panes of glass, and bottom half a golden hoop pine, allowed her to reach the keyhole without having to stand. She phoned Darren at work, he came soonest. Without pain she wasn't alert to the sinister. Without a dentist's warning that honeycomb was not bone, Anna did nothing for five days until her feet swelled, she hadn't been able to walk, but had crawled from room to room assuming all would return to normal. It didn't.

Time to act. Darren took her to the Ipswich General. She was sent to x-ray. The Chinese radiographer was wiser than the Greek dentist. *I shouldn't be telling you this,*

233

he said, *because the doctor will tell you when I send over the x-rays, but you have such serious osteoporosis I think you should be prepared.*

For what? Anna wondered, but thanked him, and Darren wheeled her across to the waiting room. In due time the doctor called her in. He switched on the light behind the x-ray plates. Anna peered at them. *Shouldn't there be bone in there?* There was no white. The doctor's face itself appeared whiter than the space on the x-rays where bone ought to be. He said, almost apologetically: *I'm afraid you'll never walk again.*

And that was that. There was nothing he could do, the multiple fractures in both feet were the result of osteoporosis so advanced he could offer nothing. It was a big puzzle to Anna, whose thoughts wouldn't compute. Thoughts are used to running along familiar tracks, known ways – *never walk again?* That was under the radar of *anything.*

But it was true. She couldn't walk. For four months she sat, moved about by crawling, not knowing what to do but pray. She didn't pray to *walk;* she knew that not walking was already Known, she prayed for acceptance and for courage. Her whole world, her entire universe, had shrunk to four walls. She would need a miracle to accept it.

One afternoon a neighbour brought in a local newspaper, four months had passed since the x-rays. No doctor ever showed up, no phone from a caring medical professional ever followed her fateful, life-altering visit, she was to all intents and purposes written off by the Australian medical fraternity as a lost cause. Anna and Darren had organized her days to include lunches ready prepared, and books and whatever to be close at hand as her feet wouldn't walk. It was a bleak period. When her neighbour had left Anna glanced idly at the paper, until: *Homer Lam, physiotherapist, open for consultation, Booval.*

Booval – goodness, the suburb of Booval began where her street ended. The address indicated the practitioner shared rooms with a Vietnamese doctor there; could *Lam* be Chinese? Anna had faith: in the Chinese as medical practitioners, in the prickles along her spine when she read the advertisement, in her own fate. She phoned, made an appointment for Darren's next day off – he would wheel her down there in the wheelchair that sat on the front veranda, too large for the doorways of the small house.

Homer welcomed her. He took one look at her right foot, blotched purple, and another at her left foot, blue to the ankle. Moribund. Completely. *Ho!* smiled the handsome young Chinese, *you have Sudeck's Atrophy. Serious. I think I can help. You must come every two days for treatment. It may not be quite too late ...*

Sudeck's Atrophy: *a pathological process of dystrophy and soft tissue and bone atrophy developing after an injury; severe osteoporosis and muscle atrophy from the loss of the use of a foot after multiple fractures.* Now Anna knew what is was, it had a *Name*, she could tune right in to Homer's healing. He was so positive, so confident.

Homer had a clinic in Hong Kong, he specialized in atrophies. Perhaps four hundred years of foot binding had left Chinese women with congenitally fragile foot bones, at least for a few generations since its outlawed practice. Homer had looked at her feet and offered the diagnosis in his stride. Anna had her miracle. And the miracle got bigger.

Homer, at the age of thirty-two, had applied to three universities for his post-graduate work, one in America, one in Canada and one in Australia. St Lucia in Queensland replied first, he took it up, and set up practice with Dr Ng, two minutes away from where Anna lived. However, the real miracle was: St Lucia was forty kilometres from Anna's home; the circumference of choice for Homer to join a practice was two hundred and fifty kilometres. In an area like that are thousands of doctors. Thousands. From the whole of S.E. Queensland to choose to land at the bottom of her street just a few weeks after he arrived, was the miracle.

For the first weeks Homer did masses of massage to both feet. Using hand manipulation, acupuncture and

TENS machines he breathed life into her morbidly blue feet. Homework for her was running those feet under water as hot as she could bear it for ten minutes four times a day. She was not, absolutely *not*, to attempt to stand. Her feet had no pain, no feeling. Nerve endings had sort of died when her feet crumbled under her when she fell, the nerves must have crumbled too. She couldn't feel. Hot water had to be gauged by hand so as not to burn. And: *You must eat root ginger every day, osteoporosis, and arthritis,* Homer added, *are Yin, ginger is Yang. You are too Yin, you need Yang in your diet, always.*

After four months Homer told her to get off his physio bench and stand on the phone directory. Brisbane phone directories were not very thick in 1996. *Now jump,* he said, and she froze, ice-cube solid. *No way,* her body howled silently, *no way was body going to drop that amount of pressure onto two dead feet.* Anna stood, pole-axed, wavering backwards and forwards, unable to make a move to floor from book, a jump of a whole one and a half inches.

No hurry, said Homer, sitting on the physio bench watching her, *take all the time you need.*

It *was* a long time. Perhaps fifteen minutes until her body and mind united in trust to – *jump.*

Good, grinned Homer, *now don't do that again until I tell you to.*

Anna lay back down on the physio bench while Homer worked her feet. Absorbing the past minutes she was struck by a light-bulb moment: *Homer,* she said, lifting her head from her muffling arms so he could hear her clearly: *I know why you did that!*

Why?

Because the shock sent a message from my feet to my brain to say please send me blood, we are not dead!

If only all my patients were as responsive, he thought, and said: *Yes, and we have a long way to go but this message should be the turning point. The body has been withdrawing calcium from the foot bones to fund the rest of the body. Not good. Gangrene comes next, body rejects dead parts. But,* here was the warning and his demand she turn from veg to non-veg: *you* must *eat meat from now on. You produce too much phosphorous, it is your nature,*

236

your make-up, and phosphorous inhibits your body's absorption of calcium in any form except blood. Blood carries calcium from first degree protein. You can swallow a barrow load of tablets and all the calcium will pass straight through. I want you to begin to drink ox blood.

Ox blood! Even if Anna thought she could get the stuff down her gullet she didn't know where to get it. *Abattoirs*, suggested Homer helpfully.

Anna didn't go the whole ox, she couldn't, but slowly slowly she incorporated meat into her diet, slowly slowly her feet strengthened and slowly slowly Homer worked his miracle. She walked. It took four years before her feet walked without her brain thinking for them but she was out of the wheelchair within six months. She, they, her feet, had to re-awaken their cellular memory. Anna would 'think' how they should flex or bend over sand-dunes, hard tussocks of grass, the wrongly weighted camber of a poorly laid pavement.

Nearly twenty years later she contemplated the Camino. Calling Homer from England early one morning, to catch him at work before he went home, she asked, after delighted hullo's and catch ups: *Homer d'you think my feet could walk five hundred miles?*

He asked why. He was Catholic as well as Chinese, pilgrimages were a known part of his culture too: *The Camino*, said Anna, and: *Are you still overweight?* Homer replied. She laughed heartily: *Yep!*

Good, he said, *all that weight-bearing, body and backpack, perfect! Your feet will be stronger than they have ever been!*

And so she walked. Perfectly.

There came another light bulb moment for Anna between the Carrot and the Cow. The transition from veg to non-veg was not easy. It awakened a kind of consciousness to every mouthful of flesh she ate, though she drew the line at piglet *anything*. Fish, fowl, pheasant, cow, lamb, mutton, goat – wherever she was in the world, eating of whatever the culture expected, knowing that a creature had died so she might have bones enough to *walk*, drew a prayer from her in thanksgiving, *every time* without fail. She didn't eat meat, or whatever first degree protein, at every meal, mostly during any week vegetables or cereals won the toss. Taking in a mouthful of carrot one lunchtime Anna stopped the food reaching her mouth. She sat, processing a new thought. Every meal of animal, fish or fowl that she ate was graced with the grace of gratitude – *but she had never thanked the carrot in thirty or more years of being vegetarian.* Shock, Anna's thoughts ran full circle: *God loves cows as much as carrots, why am I not thanking them?* From that moment she understood something so subtle as to humble her heart: *Cows and carrots are equally beloved, differently sentient probably, but equally beloved. From now on I must thank Every Mouthful of Anything I eat.* Thenceforth, she did.

23

Interlude – Beautiful Pauses

Anna had relinquished all aspirations of worldly gain, sighed over the few worldly endeavours she *had* been called to engage in: the 'Instruction' to twin the Holy Isle of Patmos with the ancient Isle of Avalon while she was sitting in the Cave of the Apocalypse after her Greek Tragedy; an invitation from a young Romanian, called in a dream after a long illness to drive to Glastonbury from Bucharest, requesting Anna accompany him back to Romania to release in a sacred ritual the millions of souls of soldiers, civilian victims, women and children, and horses, always the horses, caught in the landlocked Dacia as marauding millions passed through over millennia. It proved a profound experience for them both.

Anna realized nothing she had done had ever provided any foothold on the ladder of success. At sixty, officially retired from decades of gainful unemployment, her legitimate retirement bequeathed a warp taut with loss and woven with relief. What she gained was a surcease of struggle to prove herself *anything*, and a bus pass. Her life as a pilgrim without portfolio, and most certainly without a pension plan, had proved a multi-coloured mosaic of many hues, paved with the tesserae of memories. The tapestry of blended patterns she had always seen as disparate, disconnected one to the other, seen from the ridge of *now*, appeared woven seamlessly into a whole.

Ten years later Anna reached the three score years and ten of biblical span. A plump little thing of very slender means, her survival seemed rather miraculous. She thought she *could* have died a hundred times...

Death was an interesting thing to reflect on. Each time she went on a Big Journey, such as walking the whole 700 kilometres of the Spanish Camino at an age when most people were contemplating comfortable retirement to potter in their garden and dandle grandchildren, Anna convinced herself she would not return. At sixty-eight and thus living in the shadow of God, Anna contemplated death's *how* and prepared for it by leaving her Requiem Mass and choice of music with the priest of St Mary, Our Lady of Glastonbury. The young priest blessed her boots and staff and *mochila* preparatory to her Camino at Mass on the Sunday before she left (she chose the anniversary of Father Bede's death to begin her pilgrimage) and when she returned six weeks later she was surprised that he wasn't surprised that she survived: *I knew you'd make it,* he grinned.

It was not in her remit to know the *how* death would take her, but she held dear three perfect deaths known to her, one close and personal, two others renowned. Each moved her greatly and she hoped hers would be as benign.

She was on comfortable terms with death; at her birth the position of the Sun and Mercury sat in the Eighth House, Scorpio's house, and, being a pragmatic little Virgo by birth-date, such influence was wholly wise and beneficent. From those Scorpio depths she could apply a sense of proportion to the Meaning of Life – and Death. Anna had not needed to seek God, she came in to life Knowing; frequent re-arrangement of her perceptions along the Way were necessary until Goddess, naturally, revealed Herself. God and Death were Big Question-Marks for most people but she blithely applied William of Ockham's Razor with regular finesse to the sillier notions and bigotries of the *vox populi*. Death interested her. Beautiful deaths: she saw them as beautiful pauses between lives. She prayed she would make a beautiful death.

Penelope Chetwode's lifelong passion for India, and her love of horses great and small, her two accounts of travelling in equine company and the courage with which she ventured, in her increasing dotage, on adventures most women would quail at, stimulated Anna's imagination and in some very small way, encouraged her own decision to travel to India in her own dotage. Chatwin's account of his friend's death led Anna, reading it, to suspend her breath momentarily before releasing a sigh of awe at its telling.

In her late sixties Penelope had been prevailed upon by a prestigious travel firm to embark on a career as guide to her beloved India for wealthy American widows. She insisted on selecting her own itinerary, giving her the chance to re-visit the small and often out of the way temples she had discovered and so admired during her many years there; she had been born in India long before its Independence. The women tourists agreed to anything of course, they were travelling with a Lady, and by osmosis the title extended their pleasure and prestige. At a point on her final tour, undertaken when she was now well into her seventies, Penelope had paused, hesitant as to which path her far-remembered temple could be reached, and asked her group to wait while she went ahead.

Time passed. More than the pause Penelope had hinted at. The women grew concerned. Her local guide grew concerned. The decision was made to follow the direction she had walked and there, quite quite some distance, they saw her, sitting on the temple steps. They thought she was asleep, but she had died, right there, her soul shaken loose by the presiding temple deity, to travel on the wind. Anna's initial apprehension as she read Chatwin's account – she just *knew* it was leading to something – changed to a slow release of suspended breath as she looked up from her book and sighed in awe of such synchronicity. Such was a death she would dream of for herself: alone, quiet, in a place that held her, body and soul. Penelope had included the richness of her Catholicism in whatever she wrote, and her embrace of all that was great in the multi-faceted religion of her adopted land resonated hugely with Anna. She would often retell the story of Penelope's death to her own friends; watch their responses of wonder and awe and goosebumps. It was a perfect death.

Pierre Teilhard de Chardin had a perfect death too. The manner of it Anna didn't know, but its *timing*, now that was a source of wonder. He had written in his notebooks: *Death may catch me in my wanderings but better that than to sink at my moorings... I wish to end my life in the gesture, or providential circumstance, which best bears witness to the Vision for which I have lived.*

He had died on Easter Sunday. Thus he travelled with his beloved Christ to his own Resurrection. As synchronicities went it took some beating for a priestly death.

The last of her trinity of perfect deaths was personal. During the nineteen-eighties when she had been granted the unheralded privilege of being chaperone to Father Bede she had, at his request, taken him to Mangrove Mountain, to the Satyananda Ashram there. It had not occurred to either of them to call ahead, mobile phones didn't exist and besides people came and went and if their visit coincided with lunch they could join the queue. But Father Bede, even then, was not young, and furthermore was a guru to a considerable following in his own right. Many of the Satyananda swamis of the time had read his books, many indeed were lapsed Catholics. His tall, white haired appearance, of commanding gentleness, could not go unnoticed. Word flew like wind around the ashram and swamis appeared from everywhere to ask his blessing.

Bhaktimurti was Anna's friend. She was also the mother of the ashram mother figure, the latter a strong young woman who had become the female figurehead alongside Akhandananda, the young man sent by Satyananda from India to Australia in the nineteen-seventies to found an ashram from which would spread the message of Yoga from 'door to door and shore to shore'. What Anna, Sitadevi then, was unaware of were the rumblings of discontent in the very fabric of the ashram administration. Its unfortunate result was spoken of for years afterwards for on that day Swami Akhandananda had not shown to his guest the respect due to an equal, more than an equal, an Elder Equal.

Father Bede did not bat an eyelid, regardless of what he may have thought. But sitting on the floor to eat lunch with the common lot, no matter how adoring, while Akhandananda and Shishyananda ate separately elsewhere, aloof and from an especially created menu, made Anna wince. It made Bhaktimurti wince too, regardless of her daughter's status, for she and her husband had sold up their Sydney home and each left their professional practices to fund the ashram's foundation, relinquishing their Australian identity to be given swami names. Their daughter and their son became part of that foundation. Bhaktimurti's husband, Karmamurti, was sent to America to establish the message of Yoga. Such was the spirit of renunciation then, taken seriously and in great humility, giving everything, not knowing there would be anything in return. *Blank cheque,* Mrs Tweedie would say, *He wants a blank cheque, no insurance policy accepted. She* had given her entire fortune, vast properties in Argentina and Australia, to Bhai Sahib to use as he wished.

Later in the day Akhandananda deigned to give Father Bede an audience.

Later still, as she was driving the miles back to Sydney to where Father Bede was staying, he invited Anna to Shantivanam: *Come back with me,* he said, *soon,* but Anna was held by her beloved aging Jasper and she knew she couldn't, then. She had asked him as she drove the long highway back to Sydney, which, of all the books he had written, was his own favourite. He had replied and ... abandoning the steering wheel to one hand while reaching with the other down into her handbag, laughing, pulled up his favourite: *Return to the Centre.*

Mine too, she grinned, revealing her own copy, a complicit moment. She gave Father Bede her copy of *Chasm of Fire* for light reading, it had recently arrived at the Theosophical Bookshop in Sydney and Anna had sat on the floor devouring it right there in the bookshop until closing time, mesmerized by the revelations and by the magisterial face of the old woman on the back cover of that first edition. Anna had bought the book, little knowing the profound impact it would hold for Bede and for herself.

Within months the ashram at Mangrove Mountain rumbled to an almighty explosion: politics and apparent corruption and worse besides – Anna never could decide which side to fall on the judgement of Akhandananda: *Did he? Didn't he?* She knew too well the many-layered truths that govern any accusation, even one as sinister as this was reported to be. Media loves sensation. Akhandananda was later to commit suicide and Anna felt great sorrow for the young man, a young country Indian obedient to the dictates of his guru to come to Australia, out of his depths in a highly materialistic society, a man who had 'seen' her and her Path and who had given her, on that hot hot day so long ago, her name: *Sitadevi*. Twelve years would pass before her brief re-connection with Satyananda, who had astonished her with his knowing of her 'journey to the Black Madonna'.

As Anna was leaving for Shantivanam, so Bhaktimurti had left the ashram. Her daughter had relinquished her title rôle after the explosion and she took with her a substantial amount of money to build a glorious home in the Nerang Hinterland with views of blue hills and great lakes, wildlife in abundance. For her parents, now approaching their seventies, Shishyananda built a small one bed-roomed cottage on the land. Karmamurti returned from wherever he had been and he and Bhaktimurti were together again after decades of separate and devoted service to Yoga.

There had been no contact between Bhaktimurti and Anna once she had left for Shantivanam, from where she had continued on to London at Bede's suggestion to find Tweedie: *Her book, it is most impressive, you must find her*, he had said to Anna, and so she had. Anna finally returned to Queensland four years later with her Kurd, for Mrs Thatcher would permit John Bull to bring any wife in from anywhere, but Mary Rose held a different status and Yahia was refused entry. Reluctant to leave Mrs Tweedie, but called by love, and her marriage in Ankara, Anna headed back to Australia to wait for Yahia there.

How Bhaktimurti found her Anna never knew, but one day she opened the door of her cottage to find her there. A young swami accompanied her and the three women met with mutual affection and a shared love of the sacred texts of India. Yahia had gone, but: *Alas the Kurd;* Anna was able to smile now, and the friendship between the two older women grew apace. Anna was to move again, first into the wheelchair, and then to North Queensland and more years passed. A desultory kind of correspondence linked her with Bhaktimurti until their letters ceased altogether.

Sharman sold her prestigious property, including the one bedroom cottage, for a considerable profit in due time; the amount a dizzying fiscal fantasy to a renunciate such as Anna. Using sleuth work to track down Bhaktimurti she learnt she and Karmamurti had gone to the New Zealand ashram, to their son who was its head. Anna phoned, and: *Bhaktimurti died, you know* ... but Anna didn't know, and, shocked, wanted to hear every last detail.

She and Karmamurti were very happy to be together again. They were out walking and Bhaktimurti said: can we stop a minute, I feel a bit tired. *They sat down, on a handy bench close by; she rested her head on Karmamurti's shoulder — and died. Right then. Right there.*

Anna melted; it was a perfect death.

Anna prayed, often, to Life: *Make me worthy, Life, make me food for the moon, You are the Mystery, may I be worthy of a good death, a quiet death, and ready, when You call me Home.*

24

Two Middle-Aged Women on Walkabout

Caroline and Anna first met in 1986, after Anna's Stratford year. Anna had puffed her way up Park Street in Bristol and walked into a slimming centre where Caroline was then working. They clicked, ignored the slimming, and went to lunch together. During their meal Caroline confided, prompted by Anna's accent, that she had wanted to visit Australia since she was ten years old. A decade later, with emails new magic, Caroline wrote that she was coming in October, 2001, in celebration of her 60th birthday. She wanted to visit sacred sites, to meet an Aboriginal Elder. *I am not coming,* she emphasized, *to visit white Australia.*

Caroline arrived at the tiny tropical airport of Townsville wearing dark blue woollen trousers and a huge pink angora polo neck jumper in the hottest October for years. She and her luggage were among the first off the little plane which brought her down from the international airport at Cairns.

It was thrilling to welcome Caroline, who marvelled at the fact that she simply got off the plane, walked across the tarmac, and found her friend just inside the door. They walked out of the door on the opposite side of the airport building to Anna's old Alfasud. Townsville then had the most pleasant airport in Australia.

Caroline was melting like a raspberry sundae in her winter clothing, but Anna insisted on stopping along the airport drive to show her a Bowerbird nest in the bush beside the road. Its arching bowers were lined with the bits of blue anythings that so fascinate this bird: plastic, paper, bottles, pieces of glass; even an old blue hairbrush. Mr

Bowerbird used this bower every nesting season, adding to the blue decor to attract Mrs. B.

Caroline responded with delight at the scenic route along the recently created Strand, its palms and sea and art work and play areas and shaded sails; the colourful, chattering Lorikeets and elegant high stepping Sacred Ibis enchanting her. Magnetic Island was a hand length beyond the stretch of sea. For first impressions, this was pretty impressive.

Once home Caroline peeled off her woolly winter persona, showered, put on the cool turquoise sarong Anna had laid out on her bed, ate some fruit and yoghurt, and had a comforting cup of good strong English tea. Anna could be cruel: jetlag is best dealt with by tuning in to local time, distraction was the key to survival, after a little sustenance she took Caroline straight into town for some suitable tropical retail therapy.

Caroline bought three delicious dresses. Two were flavour and favour to an Aboriginal Spirit Journey, the other a frivolous filmy layered turquoise and sunshine yellow French number which naturally needed shoes to match. Anna owned variations on the same themes. Off then to Papoucci to buy the most enchanting pair of sunshine yellow sandals with clusters of tiny yellow flowers across the toes for Caroline's tropical transformation. Hat next. Back to Townsville Hatters for a wickedly wonderful hat, signature to their pilgrimage: *When one is searching for the Divine*, said this new Anna whom Caroline hadn't known before, *my maxim for any pilgrimage is to dress divinely.*

Days drifted by in an idle manner while they discussed and re-discussed their route north. Everyone told the Caroline she was mad to try and pack in what she intended to see in the short days she had scheduled. The closest town north of Townsville was 110 kilometres, and the women were planning twenty times that distance. Convinced, Caroline extended her stay, altered her flight ticket, prepared herself for flexible possibilities.

On Saturday the two went to the House of Prayer. The priest that day was a sensitive man whose homily of the

Australian government's ghastly attitude to the refugees dying on a ship off their shores, refused asylum, made Caroline weep. She had never been to a Catholic Mass, or imagined such a priest. Sitting in a circle of comfortable chairs Dave, the priest, sat with them. He wore his usual weekend T-shirt and shorts. Most, including Dave, kicked off their sandals at the door. Caroline saw Dave bathed in light, a lilac light, as he spoke and it moved her greatly.

Later in the afternoon they visited World Vision. Oddly, Caroline felt compelled to buy an olive wood carving from Palestine of Our Lady.

They left for their pilgrimage on Tuesday before dawn, choosing to hire a car as Anna's antediluvian Alfasud pre-dated air-conditioning. October days were steaming up and tropical rain would make driving a sauna with the windows closed. The rental car company generously offered them the car on Monday afternoon; they could load the night before, ready for departure.

After tea and fruit, their day began. The most beautiful terrain of tropical North Queensland begins beyond Ingham and Anna always made a habit of stopping in to see Tony, from Sicily, at the Olive Tree for a cappuccino and Australia's best bruschetta, made with Tony's home grown basil and garlic, after the first long leg of the journey north. Caroline took the Italian opportunity to load up with Italian cheeses and imported olive oil and balsamic vinegar and artichoke heads and delicious Italian breads and olives, as well as other tempting titbits, for the picnic Anna had planned in the licuala forest of Tam O'Shanter National Park near Mission Beach many hours further on.

The day went well. Tony's bruschetta was excellent; the Hinchinbrook inlet was awesome; the Cardwell National Park Habitat Centre the best Caroline had seen. Another couple of hundred kilometres and they swung into Tam O'Shanter to picnic under the licuala canopy. Anna sent out songlines for a Cassowary as they parked the car.

248

The picnic area was secured within a corral of stout timber half log fencing; cassowaries are huge and hungry and two middle-aged women on walkabout with *food* – very attractive. Rustles in the thick undergrowth, a low boom almost beyond range of human hearing, and suddenly, in the forest clearing – a cassowary! Caroline and Anna had goosebumps! The huge bird stayed watching them a long time, bowing its horn-crowned head and its long blue neck, before silently stepping back into its own world, leaving the ladies to lunch.

The coast road wound round Bingil Bay to arrive at El Arish back on the highway north, and they turned left at Silkwood to climb the Tablelands to Paronella Park. Silkwood is known for its 3 saintly relics from Italy, for this was the heart of sugarcane country where Italian immigrants came and suffered greatly in the early years of settlement. Anna took over the wheel then, and Caroline absorbed the extraordinary panorama of green rolling hills, forested or pastured, ringed with range on range of mountains in silhouetted shades of deepening blues and mauves as they drove higher and higher.

They reached Paronella by 3 o'clock, in time for Mark, the owner, to attach them to the last guided tour of the day around this magical place. Paronella was the vision of José Paronella who arrived from Catalonia in 1913. José eventually died of cancer brought on by a broken heart after insensitive neighbours had refused to clear backlogs of fallen timber banked up river. The great floods of 1946 created a colossal tidal wave which swept down with thousands of tons of logs and water, devastating his life's work. His vision lives on in the astonishing beauty of the parks and grand avenue of kauri trees he first planted, now a towering thirty metres, but the lichen covered crumbling ruins of the castle he and his wife laboured over for decades, and built by hand, whispers something haunting and sad. They dreamed of castles for their children, they dreamed of grand staircases and chandeliered ballrooms for their community, a quixotic blend of a miniature world. José and his wife mixed and processed every ounce of concrete themselves, their handprints plainly visible in the ruined façade.

On they drove to Atherton to stay the night at an orphanage for spectacled fruit bats. A photo of Jenny's tiny orphans was the London Times Magazine photo of the week a few weeks before Caroline's arrival, for her it was a must-see.

The road between Paronella Park and Pteropus House runs through many miles of high rolling grazing land, partly forested, with very little evidence of human habitation and virtually no traffic. Suddenly, on a high range with spectacular views, two cars seemed to appear from nowhere to close in behind the women. They turned a bend and met with two cars coming in the opposite direction. The impatient cars behind could not overtake; and just as well, for there in the centre of the road was a tiny, terrified, *black* kitten.

Anna braked, leapt out of the car, ran down the middle of the road frantically flailing her arms to halt the oncoming cars, letting the kitten negotiate his getaway. Instead, the tiny creature turned, took one look at her, and ran full pelt to leap into her flailing arms, which closed about him. What now? She could hardly turn the kitten back onto the road, and there were no houses until the next township, twenty kilometres away, a tiny one like this could not have wandered so far. Back in the safety of the car, s/he, (too small to tell), had flopped into Caroline's lap. Cuddling him she saw his torn paws and split claws and scuffed raw skin over its eyes, as if in a tumble.

Anna turned the car, backtracked to the sugar mill but no one there wanted to know about a kitten. One man offered to take it to the animal pound but neither Caroline nor Anna would hear of such a thing. After such a big adventure for such a small kitten it deserved to live. One of the men told her that yesterday he had rounded up a batch to take to the pound when a sack filled with a litter of kittens was hurled from a passing car. It was likely that this kitten got away.

It was now curled up exhausted, and very dehydrated, on Caroline's neck. The women drove on to Pteropus House, two hours away.

Having The Birl, they didn't know if it was a Boy or Girl so settled on The Birl, rather better than The Goy, completely altered their plans. Inland at Split Rock the daytime temperature was so fierce they could not leave anything in the car while sightseeing. The immediate challenge ahead was finding somewhere to stay with a kitten. Would they find a B & B to welcome the three of them? Australians were not known as the world's greatest cat lovers.

Grey Wolf had taught Anna that no spirit journey can commence without a power animal, without a test by Mother Nature, and without humility on the part of the seeker. *A power animal is not something you choose,* he warned, *everyone wants elks or mountain lions, kestrels or eagles. If you need grounding Spirit will give you a carrot vision.*

Caroline had said emphatically she had come to Australia for *black* Australia. Both women knew there was no such thing as happenstance when one began a journey with sacred intent. This kitten was black, coal black. This weak black kitten must be, then, the power animal for at least one of the two middle-aged women on walkabout.

They arrived late to Pteropus House, shopping on the way for kitten food, cat litter and a tray. Jenny was away collecting her nightly quota of orphan pteropi, spectacled fruit bats. Claire who greeted them was a guest resident and English. She knew Jenny would not want cats on the premises – but it was so-o-o late and the kitten was so-o-o tiny, so-o-o tired … and so Claire said, her English compassion coming to the fore: *Just stay and rest. Tomorrow is another day.*

The Birl ate without break. Introduce the litter tray. No way! Yet s/he was obviously distressed and needed to piddle. *Brainwave* – Anna brought in a scoop of good earth and sprinkled it on top of the litter perfumed to appeal to humans and voila! The Birl jumped in, scratched a wee hole and emptied a bladder so full the two women

251

turned their heads away, trying not to laugh and embarrass one so well-mannered kitten with its back to them. All sorted, they showered and went to bed, though barely to sleep – The Birl purred the whole night, loud, joyous and at lion-sized volume.

The following morning Jenny accepted the night-time stowaway with good grace, *fait accompli*, and took Caroline and Anna to meet her orphans. The trembling baby fruit bats, Flying Foxes, were adorable, Caroline helped her dropper feed them as they trembled in their flannel swaddlings. Adult fruit bats, huge creatures whose wings can span a metre or more, are very gentle, and feed on fruit and nectar. The orphans are a nightly collection as parents suffer electrocution on the huge overhead wires.

Their itinerary included lunch with Rose, a German artist, who was horrified at the thought of a feline on *her* property! She refused to allow The Birl out of the car, fed the women rapidly, and equally rapidly gave them the phone number of a group of apartments in Port Douglas, on the sea's edge between reef and rainforest. The rate was attractive since the collapse of Ansett Airlines, the tourist economy temporarily collapsed.

Anna confessed: *Kitten*. The answer, a regretful: *No*.

She asked the voice to please give her six other phone numbers from her local phonebook of apartments in Port Douglas. A man came to the phone. He was English.

I am so sorry you can't take us and our kitten, Anna explained, *your apartments have been recommended, please can you help us with other local phone numbers? We are from Townsville and don't have your local directory*. There was a longish silence, then: *Oh, you can come here*.

Relief. The manager didn't mind cats in the slightest, and Ansett's collapse meant most of his apartments were empty so they were given a superb cottage all to themselves, with its own garden, separate from the other accommodations which were attached to each other. They settled in, confident The Birl would thrive in the safety of an air-conditioned cottage with food, water, milk, biscuits and kitty litter while they went on Walkabout round Port Douglas.

St Mary's by the Sea, its huge picture window behind the altar, framed a view of the sea as pristine as on the day of Creation, the little white timber building ringed by foxtail palms, the prettiest of all palms, which stood like prayers around it. Along the bay the shops were magnets for two middle-aged women seduced by must-haves for a walkabout ... but first, food.

Immigrant Italians had long since left the cane fields and were now creating gastronomic history with restaurants of quality and menus of imagination: penne and gorgonzola, spinach and cream sauce served with rocket salad brought forth paeans of praise and in turn, very full tums. They waddled home to fall into their respective bedrooms and beds and sleep the sleep of the just. The Birl chose Caroline to sing to, all night.

Split Rock, a marvellous gallery of Aboriginal rock art as old as any in France, called them. Interim days were spent exploring the cool mossy gorges of Mossman Gorge, the spectacular rainforest escarpments lined with massive trees, epiphytes and vines; colossal boulders like Narguns ensconced in and along the chilly streams created shallow pools to refresh from the steamy humidity. Electric blue Ulysses butterflies as huge as a hand darted everywhere. The women found a pool of their own, pulled on their togs, removed and rolled up their dresses to place on a rock and laid down their hats. The chill water brought gasps every body-inch of their slow descent. Caroline could bear it no more and sank in to her neck. *That* gasp reverberated over the rocks. The water's chilling effect exhilarated them, they felt cleansed in and out, a baptism for the following day.

The rather lush shops in the small, elegant main street of Port Douglas lured them downtown for retail therapy later. No sign of any Aboriginal elder for Caroline, but a very grand off road vehicle was hired for the devilish drive up country *and* she fell for an opera length rope of pearls from

Wicked Willies: *Oh!* She gasped accepting his lure: *I must, I must – I've never seen pearls like these in England!* Caroline was elegant, always perfectly bejewelled *à plomb*, carried herself with poise and grace, caused heads to turn wherever she walked.

Vivified by water and pearls and an excellent lunch, stopping by The Birl for top up cuddles and his fourth meal of the morning they considered, with many daylight hours left, going on to Daintree River. Pulling in to the Kuku Yalandji office at the entrance to the Gorge the two women parked the car and walked up to the door.

The office was a smallish room with a few pieces of indigenous art, some posters, and a glass counter behind which stood one of the most beautiful young women Anna had ever seen. She was so beautiful Anna did a double take as she walked through the doorway. The young woman was busy fiddling with the till, a computerized piece with a mind of its own. Exasperated sounds were forthcoming at closely spaced intervals. In the opposite corner a small slim Aboriginal man wearing a baseball cap was showing a couple of tourists a didgeridoo. Caroline and Anna wandered around for a minute or two until the young woman asked if she could help. Anna asked her vaguely about leaflets for the Gorge, Cape Tribulation or Daintree. Caroline was just as vague, though she focussed on buying a booklet about the Kuku Yalandji. The Aboriginal man left.

Another Aboriginal man walked in. He was, Caroline said afterwards, a most beautiful man. Small, slightly built, wearing an Akubra style hat over thick grey hair, grey bearded, very softly spoken, an aura of arcane calm surrounding him. The beautiful young Aboriginal woman behind the counter referred the vague questions of the two women to him. They turned, to give him their full attention. Anna told him they were going to Split Rock on the morrow, asked if there was anything they could do, or could take as a gift to Spirit that would guide them into walking there in a sacred manner?

The man looked quietly at the two white women looking at him, introduced himself as CJ, and gave his

Aboriginal name. He said they did not need to take anything, but stepping back lightly he swiftly placed each hand in turn under his armpits and just as swiftly withdrew them to draw them down from Caroline's head to her toes, as if stroking her aura. He repeated the process with Anna. *Now*, he said, *Spirit will welcome you, you carry our scent.*

Caroline, through tears, said: *I have been waiting to come to Australia since I was ten years old. I am now sixty.*

CJ replied softly: *That's a long time to wait to come home.*

He began to explain that he was not from that country, Split Rock country, that was Quinkan country, and at that moment Caroline gave a shocking cry, clasped her hands to her head and almost collapsed on to the glass counter. CJ was unperturbed. Anna sent love to her stricken friend whose pain was apparent, watched CJ, trusting. Sonja, the beautiful young woman, brought a chair. Caroline sat heavily into it, by now she was sobbing and crying out with the searing pain bounding from side to side of her head as she clutched it. CJ placed his hands over it: *I cannot heal her, she is not in my country*, and Sonja said she would call Harold, the young man who had been showing tourists the didgeridoos as Caroline and Anna came in to the shop. He belonged to this country here.

Harold came in, his eyes flooded with compassion when he saw Caroline's state. CJ repeated what had passed between them. Harold said he was a healer, a shaman in training with his father, who was trained by his father to be a healer for his people. He had not quite completed his long apprenticeship, but if Caroline would give him permission he would offer his healing power. He was so humble, almost reticent, and his eyes were deep pools of compassion.

Caroline could barely whimper. *Yes, please, I understand about healing because I am a healer myself.*

Harold placed his hands on her head and Anna witnessed an astonishing phenomenon. As she watched, Caroline's face its familiar features underwent a dramatic change, her nose widened, her mouth changed – Anna took an involuntary intake of breath. There in front of her eyes was the face of an old Aboriginal woman. It was still Caroline, but it was as if a face from long long ago had been revealed, had come home.

All the years she had known Caroline, Anna always described her to other friends as having Aboriginal eyes. Her eyes were the colour of honey, of amber, (which Aboriginal eyes aren't necessarily); but more, Anna always remembered them as having no pupils, (which Aboriginal eyes don't necessarily lack). In fact Caroline's eyes aren't really Aboriginal eyes at all – *but they were now as they looked out of that ancient face carved out of time.* Caroline's eyes do have pupils, and sometimes they reflect light from the *inside*, rather than from the outside. Anna knew the phenomena, had seen it in the eyes of an Afghan, a Kurd, and an exquisite Indian girl, a beggar rag picker whose radiant smile lit up the railway station at Jaipur.

Harold moved to stand in front of her, his eyes focussed directly to her head, his hands held above. Long long minutes passed. At length Caroline relaxed and managed a weak smile. Her face resumed its more familiar aspects. Harold asked if he could look at her aura, he found it in good order, grey, red and blue, quite a different sequence of colours to those popularly seen by western healers. He acknowledged the difference before he told her what he was seeing. Anna quietly told them how she had seen Caroline's face become that of an old, old Aboriginal woman. *Yes*, said Harold in his gentle way, *you see my grandmother, she come in to heal Caroline.* He said the pull of Spirit back to Australia was too powerful for Caroline's body to cope with, which was why she felt such pain. In due time Harold left as quietly as he had come.

Caroline and CJ continued to speak, CJ said she should go to his country for healing: *You have waited such a long time to come home, my spirit tells me it waits for you in my country. My country is a healing place, many hours from here. Terrible things had happened up there in that place, my country. Massacres. A hundred years ago. My father was a tiny boy and his own father was shot under him. He was running with him on his shoulders to escape the 'whitefella bully men'; they came out at weekends to shoot us Aborigines. It is a healing place up there now, my country.*

He looked at Caroline intently, said softly: *And my country is called Woman's Dreaming. It is Woman's Country.*

The words hung suspended in a cocoon of magic and power, the horror of CJ's story woven in the interface.

CJ turned to Sonja, asked that she give them leaflets about this place. It was named Yindili. On the simple leaflet were the words: *Healing Sanctuary, Welcome to Buru, Be Part of the Dreamtime Healing.* Caroline started to clasp her head again, crying: *Oh no, not more.* CJ said again: *You must go to my land, my country Yindili.*

Caroline was weeping quietly. CJ looked intently at her: *Fifty years is a long time for Spirit to wait to come home.*

This was Caroline's vision quest, not Anna's. Anna asked CJ mundane questions: *Roads? Four-wheel drive vehicle? Bedding? Food?* Things she might be able to offer practical help for Caroline to access the wilderness leading to Wujul Wujul, his country. Caroline was quintessentially English, Anna felt responsible, a little, for enlightening her to the differences between the country lanes of Cornwall and the slithery unsigned tropical rainforest tracks, *sans* mudmap, of Far North Queensland. CJ gave the vaguest wave of his hand in reply, told Anna to take Caroline home and let her sleep. As they left he touched her arm: *Come to my healing place another time.*

Caroline collapsed exhausted on her bed, The Birl bounced all over her. Anna left her to rest and went down town to look for something sweet to bring her for when she awoke, it would replenish the energy drained by pain. A couple of hours passed before she returned with a chocolate mousse from the Coffee Club. Caroline was awake, drained still, but rested. She floored Anna by quietly saying: *I looked into CJ's eyes, they had no pupils.*

Anna made a salad, they ate it quietly, showered and called it a day. Laura and Split Rock was one helluva drive tomorrow.

It was indeed one helluva drive; the infernal fires could not be hotter. Later they learnt temperatures had touched 34C in Townsville, 39C in southern Queensland and 43C Out West. Laura was Out West. They drove through the doors of hell. Even with air-conditioning on the coolest possible setting the radiant heat and dryness outside the vehicle parched their throats.

The first part of the journey was very pleasant, up over the ranges through Julatten to Mount Molloy for tea and toast, yoghurt and bananas. The tin shed café's owner commented on their dress and hats: *Never seen the like up 'ere in these parts, youse look like proper laidies!* Caroline's thanks for the compliment, spoken in cut-glass Queen's, proved his perspicacity.

The mountains looked so cool and green from where they sat but once back in the car the road led them into parchment country very quickly. Hundreds of kilometres from Port Douglas they turned left off the last bitumen at Lakeland Downs to enter the dust bowls. At least, in answer to Anna's most fervent prayers at dawn, the road was not a stinking charnel house of dead, maimed or dying cattle, kangaroos, wallabies, pademelons, possums, emus, smaller birds, or even tiny rodents. Night drivers must have been on holiday. Miraculously they passed only two road kills the whole day — a dingo and a wallaby, both too obviously dead to stop and check.

On and on and on they drove, the occasional passing or oncoming car enveloping them in blinding dust storms. Straying cattle caused them to slow right down to allow their unpredictable nature time to decide whether the brown grass might be a greener shade of burnt on the other side of the road, though Caroline's lead left foot gave Anna cause for mild panic.

Eagles soared on thermals above, swooped low to catch an unsuspecting snake to wheel upwards with it in their talons. The country was vast, dry, and every shade of brown from palest fawn to deepest umber. Patches of blood red flowering *abel moschus*, a ground hugging plant with flowers like hibiscus, added occasional colour to the palette of infinite browns.

They drove on and on, the distant escarpments began to close in as they passed the campsite of the Laura Festival when the road became bitumen to the rock art galleries. The short bitumen stretch had been built to protect the ancient sacred art from the contemporary corrosion of swirling traffic dust. Although the art had been re-touched over its 30,000-year existence, its preservation was crucial.

The few trees in the car park were tall, with slender scorched limbs, twig-like, reaching upwards; sickle-drop leaves in diminishing clusters cast no separation between white-hot sun and searing light. The women opened the car doors to each brake into a sweat. Jamming hats on their heads and filling bilums with water bottles and fruit the two women began the long ascent to the galleries.

Caroline's face grew pinker and pinker under her recent Spanish tan. Concerned, the pair stopped, drank water, and continued in this manner all the way up to the colossal boulders making up the first gallery. The split in the rock for which the galleries were named showed startlingly apparent as they rounded the last mammoth boulder and reached the lee. Gratefully they sat on the wooden seats thoughtfully provided by some funding agency or other, and silently drank more water, relishing the shadows and the breeze caused by the height and the funnelling of the air under the rocky overhang. Silence, punctuated by the odd comment about the paintings as their identity clarified: yellow women with grand breasts drawn at right angles to their bodies, echidnas belly revealed, red dingoes, two men carrying a lung fish, huge turtles, short mischievous Quinkans and very tall good Quinkans. Handprints spray-outlined with different ochres faintly seen, and the folds and crevices of the boulders themselves lent more than mysterious faces with lopsided grins and winking devilry to the scenes in front of them.

Modestly refreshed, the two dripping dames gathered up all their remaining energy and staggered up to the next two galleries to peer at full length good Quinkans and other animal drawings. There were no seats and they staggered back down with decisively mutual swiftness. On the higher escarpments were many more galleries but the suffocating heat had done for them.

After an hour or more of just being there Anna stood and walked to a large stone bowl under the main overhang. It was filled with sand and ash. Prepared, she lit incense and turned to face East to pray for many things, for Caroline's sacred journey, for Afghanistan, for the refugees Australians were so churlish about allowing in (in this country everyone has come from somewhere else, some with far less claim to sanctuary or asylum than the poor wretches currently out at sea). For many things she prayed, included one for herself, that her search for *That* would be realized , *Somewhere*.

There was really only one dress option for this special day – their almost matching *Java Bazaar* loose flowing numbers with deep ochre Wandjina style Aboriginal figures, on a black background for Caroline and a navy background for Anna; their only difference. The friends had no hesitation about wearing similar clothing, and with their splendid hats they cut a dash. Such mundane considerations, they knew, were not the purpose of the pilgrimage; the purpose was to honour the tradition they were entering, and to blend, as much as it was possible for two whitefella middle aged matrons, with the environment.

Now they stood quietly, preparing to leave, whispering: *Yalana*, thank you, as Harold had taught, to the Ancestors for granting this blessed and uninterrupted interlude. Voices came up from the gully; a tour group was about to appear. As the two middle-aged women on walkabout rounded the first boulder they were met by a breathless group headed by a woman their own age wearing stiff white shorts, a tucked in shirt, socks and trainers. Her face was the colour of pomegranate and she was awash with sweat. Her jaw dropped when she beheld the two, now cool and elegant, in sandals, flowing appropriateness and Ascot hats, in front of her. She held them in inconsequential conversation, eyeing them all the while. Anna laughed. The woman found words: *You look marvellous! And so cool!*

Caroline and Anna agreed. They both knew the woman's clothes would not allow her to cool down, belted and buckled around her middle, they would hold the heat. Anna said impishly: *We women should leave that sort of gear to the men!* exactly as the tour guide appeared, dripping with sweat from his regulation trousers, long sleeved shirt, belt, socks, boots, and stifling felt Akubra: *Youse look cool,* he said in good local vernacular as the cool pair sashayed past him, smiling, back to the boiling car. It's true, no clothing really combats such temperatures, but Anna reckoned that Arabs knew a thing or two about cool, loose, dressing in the desert where many a mad dog and Englishmen...

It was dark when they reached The Birl, contentedly curled up in a basket of artificial palms which now bore serious signs of collateral damage. The women had clocked up almost six hundred kilometres. Caroline was wising up about distances in the Big Country.

That night Anna had a dream. It wasn't actually a dream because the shock of it woke her and she could see the same vision with wide-awake eyes. A long Quinkan-thin ancient Aboriginal man was hovering above her. She knew he was searching her soul.

When Caroline woke she told her of her experience. Caroline had not dreamed, but: *Yesterday from the time we left the bitumen at Lakelands I saw men bounding alongside our car, they were unnaturally tall and thin Aboriginal men, carrying spears and keeping up with us all the way to the car park at Split Rock. Then they left us. They weren't with us on the return journey.*

Were they ancestral spirits of humans, or Quinkans? The day that unfolded ahead remained a complete blank for both of them, so immersed in yesterday were they.

Sunday was decision time for Caroline. The hired car from Townsville needed to be returned by Tuesday, which meant leaving on Monday. If she was to get to Wujul Wujul she would need to hire another off road vehicle and contact the 'old fella' to let him know she was coming. After breakfast she phoned the number CJ had given her. CJ was not there, but she explained her story to the voice on the phone who said, in turn, he was leaving that place and would be in Mossman that evening. He introduced himself as Sunny, and: *Would you like to meet up?* He named a café and a time was agreed and Caroline replaced the phone.

Suddenly she gasped, and clamped her hands to her head, crying: *Oh no, not again!* Speaking to Sunny had precipitated a recurrence of the shocking pain in her head. She went to lay down and Anna spent the next hour wetting and freezing tea towels and applying them to Caroline's forehead. Eventually she said: *I have to go, I simply have to go, tomorrow*, and having said it, her headache ceased. Later she went to book the four-wheel drive, and the pair spent the afternoon packing their belongings and planning for all contingencies. Anna would take everything back with her to leave Caroline with one tiny bag for toiletries, a change of clothes, a torch, her journal. Buses left Port Douglas for Cairns regularly and she could get a coach to Townsville from there, it would take around six hours. Caroline phoned Darren, whom she had re-named Darwin, to tell him Anna was returning the following day with Black Australia. *Oh no*, he said, without a *frisson* of discouragement, *not another cat…*

Sunny met them that evening as arranged in Temptations. Much of the conversation was desultory, quasi political, speaking again of the terrible massacres that had taken place, filling in details that history will never own. Details like the 'bully men' who slaughtered half-caste children because white men denied any liaison (a euphemism for rape) with Aboriginal girls and women. After some hours skirting around the real issue burning Caroline so much, Sunny said that if she wanted to make the journey north she should go back to the office of Kuku Yalandji and ask CJ's sister to arrange for someone to accompany her. He made a couple of lengthy phone calls to someone, gave the women a dire warning that The Wet was imminent, told them Wujul Wujul would then be inaccessible. His next words turned Anna into an amalgam of goosebumps. *That country,* he said, *that country is Woman's Dreaming. Only a woman can heal that place.* Caroline heard it too.

That night eleven inches of rain fell. Looking out of the windows the following morning revealed the roads had turned to rivers. Unperturbed, Caroline planned. The women said their goodbyes to each other. Nothing would stop Caroline now, and, despite every possible obstacle placed before her, she would get right to CJ's father.

Anna drove south in rain so blinding the car could only crawl, even with full beam headlights on, all she could see was a wall of water. No traffic passed her, or came from the opposite direction. The Birl was curled up in the big round Burkina Faso basket she had placed on the passenger seat, calm and trusting.

Days passed. Anna heard nothing from Caroline. Then she phoned, the Wet had threatened them all and CJ's father had told her to leave for her own safety. She had made it back to Port Douglas and would be home the following afternoon.

Meanwhile The Birl proved to be a boy and to complement Darren's Arthurian contingency of felines was duly named Merlin.

Caroline's Story:

When we parted, she said, *I drove on to the Kuku Yalandji office to find it closed. I went round the back to where I could hear voices and introduced myself. The woman smiled a welcome, said she was CJ's sister and told me to make a cup of tea for everyone.*

Gail heard Caroline's story, but no, there was no one to go with her or guide her through the rainforest. However a mudmap was quickly scribbled, the directions were, essentially, cross the Daintree on the ferry and keep driving north until the Black Stump (a proverbial bush icon) and turn left. Keep driving. That was it. *Easy,* thought Caroline.

She set off. The rain was a blinding wall, driving through it was to challenge all her expertise. Some time passed and Caroline reached the Daintree ferry. She was the first on. She sat in the car thankful for the protection it afforded against the liquid carnage outside. Musing on the many moments that had led to this moment she was dimly aware of an agitated male voice calling over the loud speaker system for passengers to come and get their tickets, the ferry was shortly due to depart. More and more insistent came the voice. Suddenly a good British penny dropped: *Good heavens,* registered Caroline, *he means me! He wants me to climb out of this car, drown in the deluge to reach him in his dry little space, and buy a ticket!*

She battled with this upside down process for a minute, realized she was Downunder anyway, and with her usual aplomb, battled her way through a wall of rain to purchase a ticket from a smugly dry man. A certain lack of gallantry registered, she had travelled on many such ferries in her time around this planet and not once had any ferryman ever expected her to step down from her car to come to *him.* She took the ticket, scorching him with A Look she hoped would penetrate *something.*

Across the other side Caroline had more pressing concerns. The rain continued like a blinding silver sheet to diffuse her visibility to a matter of feet ahead of her. Dimly she was aware of slithering escarpments on either side from time to time, and of waterfalls threatening to career the car over the track at every turn. Hours past. Periodically the rain eased and Caroline was able to thrill to the sheer beauty of the glistening forest around her.

Then the bitumen ran out. She was on mud. A new dimension was added to *slippery.* The rain increased, driving on the track took every ounce of concentration, waterfalls were now flooding the road which was still ascending, trees were being blown down, huge vines weighed down by water draped across the track: *I've never been so challenged.*

Eventually she saw the equivalent of the proverbial black stump, and turned left. The road didn't look much like a road, just a river of slithering red mud spewing onto the Wujul track. Water gushed down, creeks either side of it were rising in front of her eyes, threatening to engulf any suggestion of passable track.

On and on Caroline struggled to keep the car to the tracks which she was not even sure were under her. As she told the story Anna did not think she knew of many people who would attempt such a perilous undertaking alone, without a mobile phone, not even telling the rangers.

Caroline drove on this frightful terrain for nearly an hour. She held the slithering vehicle as straight as she could, and saw all around her the creeks rising and fallen trees building up to roadblocks. Through a second gate she went, and finally admitted she could go no further. There was no indication she was even on the right road, though she knew the directions of drive north towards Cape York and turn left were about as accurate as she could expect – there was, after all, only one road from which to turn.

Gathering all her strength Caroline managed to turn her vehicle around without canyoning into outer space on either side of the track and reluctantly set to return the way she had come. *I prayed, how I prayed*, she said to Anna, *if I am meant to do this I need help, I need a guide.*

A long half-hour further on and the rain eased again. She knew she was nearly at the original turnoff. Suddenly, to her left, she saw an Aboriginal sitting in a clearing with his swag and esky. Stopping, she called out to him and asked him where was PJ's place?

You just come from his place, he said, *bit further on.*

Oh please, Caroline pleaded, *can you come back with me?*

Well it just so happened he was waiting for his mates to come down from near that place to pick him up. He had driven his girlfriend's car down this far as she was too frightened to drive alone, she had gone on and he was waiting to go back up. Caroline hadn't seen him sitting there when she turned left onto the Wujul track. If she didn't mind his muddy boots then he'd come with her. They would pass his mates on the way. And they did. The sight made Caroline chuckle; driving an open top Jeep both men wore swimming goggles against the sheeting rain, and one had a woolly snood tucking all his hair back. Snoopy and the Red Baron riding in tandem.

The men took it in turns to get out and drag fallen trees from the track, open and close gates, warn her when they were approaching the treacherous red mud, a mud so viscous it drew her four-wheel off-road vehicle down into its sticky substrata and threatened its progress. As they climbed higher the rain eased again, and quite suddenly the men halted, told Caroline the place she was looking for was over the next ridge, and said goodbye. She cruised into China Camp and pulled up next to a man painting a corrugated iron construction sky blue. It was a new shower room, CJ's father wanted to bring the sky in.

Caroline was given a bed, her pillowcase was a clean T-shirt. All had been prepared as the men sensed someone was coming, they sensed it was a woman, but in such intimidating weather they did not for a moment think that the English lady Sunny phoned them about would make it.

Once she had made the connection with CJ he did not accompany her or guide her, he only told her to go to his country to meet his 84 year old father, Chala. That first night a grand stew of vegetables, chilli and fish was prepared, washed down with copious amounts of black smokey 'billy' tea, followed by doorstops of white bread and thick butter.

CJ's father told Caroline a story: *I was young, strong, used to cut sugar cane all the way from Daintree down to Ingham. One time I was so exhausted I collapsed and died. Whitefella came and declared me dead. But during my death Jesus came and told me my time wasn't up, I had to go back. I didn't want to go back, I ask Jesus can I stay. Before he sent me back Jesus ask the Angels to show me a Spirit place, and the beauty of that place was beyond compare.*

266

Chala did not want to return to earth, but such was the force which he sprung back to into his body, he lived on, and: *The man holding me had a coronary! But that's another story!*

I've been wanting to get back to that place these last years, it was Paradise, but he knew it was still not his time. There was something he sensed was unfinished.

Caroline excused herself from the campfire: *I could barely see through my tears,* she said, *but I knew why I'd bought that little olive-wood carving of Our Lady from World Vision.*

She came back and handed the tissue wrapped gift to Chala. Chala's eyes filled with tears. It was his turn to cry. *Many people come to this place and they cry,* he said, *I never cried.* But now, he must: *You are a woman, you come to this place from the Queen, from whitefella's country. You come to sit with me and hear my story, you understand. You bring me Jesus's mother. She knows our suffering. You walk on this land, my Country, you walk on painful memories, you walk on Woman's Dreaming.*

Answering a call of half a century, of how many lifetimes, completed a spiral for Caroline. A healing.

> *Yundu Ngulkurr Baja Ku – Yundu nguli jawan ngulkurr bajaku*
>
> *Yundu binil bajaku*
> *Yundu kuku manu baja*
> *Ngali wawu jiday jundu!*
> *Wawu Baja, Jinkalmu.*
> *We love you very much for coming to see us.*

Jinkalmu wrote the farewell words in Caroline's journal, he thanked her Aboriginal guide for bringing her to them. Caroline cried. Chala cried. Jinkalmu cried.

24½

The Dot

Shortly after Caroline had returned to Cornwall in 2001 Anna left Australia to return to the West Country. It was not an easy decision. This time she really was going on a one-way ticket and her treasures would remain with Darwin.

Months beforehand, Anna had contracted Ross River fever, a local non-recurring malaria. Before moving to Railway Estate she had lived right there in O'Reilly Street, a step away from the mighty River itself. Walking was painful and slow, her joints inflamed and inflexible. There was no cure but time.

On her last Saturday Anna attended the liturgy at the House of Prayer, smiled at the plaque she had bequeathed them from her garden to theirs:

The kiss of the sun for pardon,
The song of the birds for mirth,
One is nearer God's Heart in a garden
Than anywhere else on Earth.

It was a popular garden commentary penned by long forgotten Dorothy Gurney in the nineteenth century; her father and husband had been Anglican priests. Mrs Gurney, in a garden epiphany, became a Catholic; her husband had too.

On Sunday Anna went alone to Magnetic Island for the last time. She took the bus to Arcadia, it seemed appropriate, its very name a promise of paradise. The great granite boulders no longer discombobulated her focus, as they had for two whole days on her first visit – Captain Cook's compasses were similarly charmed and discombobulated, causing him to name the granite island Magnetic.

Anna walked slowly to a rock she knew, sat on its warmth, dangling her hand in the clear water. The ripples drew sunlight, something glimmered. She reached down. Her fingers followed the refraction of lightshaft to contact something non-marine. Closing two fingers about its tiny form Anna lifted her hand to find – a golden cross, a ruby set in its centre. Amazed, she looked closely. It wasn't actually *gold* and the ruby not exactly a *ruby* but as a gift from the sea she loved it and as a protection against the tsunami's of an unknown future, she held it dear. Had it been carated in its goldness would she have taken it to the local store? The police station? Academic really, the little cross in her palm was a metallic imitation; and who knows how long it had sat there, that rock wasn't exactly a waystop for tourists.

The final morning dawned, Anna woke early. A last walk called. Later Darren would drive her to Cairns to overnight in the home of a shakuhachi player before her early morning flight. She walked through the dawn as far as Oonoomba, to the end of the village suburb before turning back. She passed no one and no one passed her, the world of humans still asleep.

Light rimmed the horizon, ribbons of pink and apricot silhouetted the low trees. Sadness and birdsong filled her heart. It wasn't easy to explain what called her to leave, even more difficult to explain why she couldn't remain. The birds, always the birds, and the warmth of tropical air on her skin, like silk, and the sea, unswimmable for much of the year – sharks, Townsville's old abattoirs drew them and they stayed; and Portuguese men-of-war warned everyone off. These were formidable preventions to the simple pleasure of salt water bathing for humans yet she loved the Tropics deeply. Its many shades of green and walls of introduced bougainvillea now hybridized to extraordinary colours of peach and rose, of harlequin shades of purple and white; vines of yellow allamanda and blood orange trumpet vines smothering fences and timber outhouses, relics of the past; Anna loved the Townsville palette. And Hervey's Range, out of walking range, but a cooler resting place accessible by car.

Idling along, walking was not easy, her limbs throbbed with inflammation, she was suddenly alert as a man on a bicycle whizzed past her and into one of the lowset timber houses ahead of her. Something in Anna sprang to attention. The bedrock reason for her leaving at all was cruelty to animals. It seemed endemic to the mindset. At least, to the mindset she was continually reminded of in the daily media, in her almost daily experience. Young men do not go cycling at dawn – *with a hessian-covered cage hanging from the handle-bars.*

She couldn't speed up no matter how hard she tried, but she kept the driveway the man had disappeared into in her sights and walked achingly, determinedly, towards it. Turning in she went straight to the front door, which happened to be open. She knocked. An old couple, hard-faced, glint-eyed, appeared: *Whadda youse want?*

Assuming she knew, well she did, actually, Anna said: *A man cycled in here with a possum in a cage, why?* She had a nerve to ask. She had nerve, too.

What's it to you?

Possums are used as greyhound bait and they're used alive, simmered Anna, *have you got greyhounds here? Why else would a young man bring a possum to your door?* Anna had hit the nail. She knew from the few cat-lovers of Australia that pet cats in Oonoomba were going missing at an alarming rate in recent months. She may be limping but she was in fine fettle and when Anna was in fine fettle no one argued. Shakti Herself powered her.

The couple admitted their 'boy' had greyhounds, they invited her out the back to see how well looked after they were. They just didn't *get it.* As if Anna's word *possum* had bypassed their infinitesimally little grey cells.

She declined, walked as quickly as pain would allow her, back to Robertson Street and straight to the phone, leaving the answering machine voice of the RSPCA and the police with the address and the conversation.

The energy supporting her drained away, leaving in its wake a numbing sadness. All this beauty, this Paradise – it was the human cruelty she had to leave.

An hour or so later came a knock on her door as she and Darren were clearing up breakfast. A young woman and an older man stood there, police officers. *We confiscated the cage, issued a warrant charging the man with keeping greyhounds in a residential zone, but we couldn't save the possum. He'd got rid of it. We're so sorry, and thanks for calling us.*

As a farewell to forty years Downunder Anna acknowledged the aptness of her final discharge to the world she loved; and to the alacrity with which the police answered her call. She left later that day, having barely said goodbye to friends she had loved throughout her Townsville years.

Anna's permanent return to England in 2001 brought her back to Glastonbury, friends lived there. Once again she had to gather together an assemblage of garments suitable for seasons. Constrained in her choice by the ever-present penury, but not by her innate taste, her older appearance often caused comment. She could say this, it happened so often and not only on the harlequin High Street of Glastonbury where boundaries blurred. It was frequently observed that the *he* of many a given couple would wear the dress, the lipstick and the carmine toenail polish, while the *she* remained colourless. But when in elegant Bath, or well-to-do Wells five miles and a world away, women and occasionally men would smile or, removing their native reserve, would comment favourably, she believed it might be true. In the Dulwich Art Gallery, a doyenne of good taste had stopped Anna to admire her finely quilted sleeveless full length coat, something Anna had been given with sleeves so badly set she cut them off and appliquéd a blend of similar fabric around the raw armhole. Much that she wore was uniquely adapted and she was tapped, equally often, on her shoulder by a passer-by and complimented. In Manhattan a young man ascending the escalator she was descending called out: *Love your outfit!* In France a woman had gone so far as to lean out of her window in Sorèze, calling for Anna's attention, to express her admiration for *la couleur, l'ensemble.* No obvious beauty herself, she felt herself bounce along in a cloud of renunciation, a cloistered remembrance. There was a time her upright walk echoed a grace elevating poverty to poetry. Her clothes were charity collected, collated and colour-coordinated, and never louder than her landscape. Her passage through this world, said a friend who had known Anna through transitional incarnations as she cut life's cloth to its selvedge, was a minor work of art. *A far cry from dhoti to dotage,* Anna laughed.

Born out of a profound respect for her environment, Anna chose colours of the landscape: ancient stones, copper beech, night, all the ochres of Mungo, faded parchment; knew instinctively the colours blue or white deadened her skin's light. Wearing an ankle-length stone-coloured skirt – she had doggedly searched for and discovered the marvellous Macabi, sent for one from Salt Lake City – she drew praise even as she walked the seven hundred kilometre Camino across northern Spain. *So spirituelle,* smiled many a male French or Italian or Catalonian pilgrim in passing, and everyone did pass her, she walked in shorter increments than most. Her abiding fashion dictum? *Never cross-dress, ever. Leave pants, jeans, collars and cuffs to the boys,* she laughed, *we women don't need to diminish our wardrobe to one-dimensional. Youth has a lovely face; with age comes grace.* A memory of her early mentor, Anne, and her third son made Anna giggle at every remembrance of the scene. Refusing the one-dimension convention, wearing a cream, flower-ribboned panama at a jaunty angle on his head and a flowing ecru kimono, leaning gracefully against the mantelpiece while telling Anne of his work as a kindergarten assistant prompted his mother's question: *And what do the little ones call you?*

Well, mostly, he said, with mild disdain that he was alone in his stylish bravado, *they call me Miss.*

It was now 2013. Twelve years since leaving Australia. Anna longed to return there, not a permanent longing, a visiting moment would be enough. An unfinished chord called her from the past. F.N.Q.? Karnak? to honour Diane? Thérèse and the magic of Townsville? Friends she hadn't properly said goodbye to when she left in 2001? She couldn't define it even to herself. 2001 had awakened in her the land's sacredness; something needed completion.

The country had consumed more than half her life and she missed much, and didn't miss much. A week in Thérèse's company on Gozo, guests of Caroline who now lived there, reaffirmed her lingering loss. Thérèse was *special*, erudite, informed by a natural wellspring of spirituality and human kindness. She lived in Townsville, had attended Anna's Master's exhibition held in the park of huge camphor laurels off O'Reilly Street.

Anna plucked up courage to ask Thérèse if she might stay with her should she manage to save the fare; she felt she had finalities to finalize. Squirreling away every spare penny, filling her tiny French chocolate pot with £ coins each time she emptied her purse, banking the proceeds. Anna didn't smoke or drink; rarely went to the cinema, never to the theatre (too far) didn't own a horse (too costly, though she dreamed of it) and still had a suitcase of tropicals under her bed that were in dire need of airing and wearing. Eight months later she had money enough. She booked the flight to Cairns, internal flights to friends down south and arranged her homeward journey to leave from Brisbane. All she needed now was a day stay in Cairns before her evening domestic flight to Townsville.

Anna fell to researching a Benedictine convent within coo-ee of Cairns airport. There wasn't one, but she happened upon a retreat centre run by two women who were exactly as Anna wished she was, but knew she wasn't. Christine emailed back to Anna: *Our centre is a few minutes drive from the airport, you are welcome to stay the day to rest, I'll collect you and take you back. I may be a little late as I am taking my partner to the eye hospital for morning surgery and will collect her again after I have brought you here.*

Christine's kindness, offered on a day already full, touched Anna. The retreat website gave simple biographies of the two women; L. was a practising spiritual director and counsellor who used the centre for certain clients on certain days; Christine lived on the premises, had once been a nun, offered retreats and quiet time as well as wise counsel. After her long flight, it would be perfection.

Anna planned her wardrobe with less than her usual attention, intending to travel through three temperature zones meant mega-layering, colour coordination in neutral was all she could stretch to in one suitcase, it would have to do. And do it did, in the oddest ways.

On the morning of her departure for Australia Anna returned from the Abbey where she had walked an early morning prayer for safe-journeying to find the sunny wall of her bungalow alive with butterflies, an enchanting sight. Only two days prior to her departure she had found a small French ecru lace butterfly she had kept in tissue for decades, and had sewn it on the very dress she intended wearing to fly all the way to Cairns. The dress was peahen brown, she would team it with a long black crinkle silk skirt, she reckoned crinkle was the order of any long flight. The rest of the wardrobe would be variations of a similar dull. Sandals, one pair, black Ecco, would do for everything and her ancient black cashmere would keep off the southern chill.

However – butterflies were the symbol of Psyche, the soul. Was their prolific appearance a Sign her soul would fly to its maker? Would she die along the way? Would her plane crash? Ever prepared to go Home, Anna thanked the butterflies, went inside, asked the Presences to protect her dollshouse, collected her cases and walked to the bus stop to catch the local bus to Bristol and the midday coach to Heathrow.

The flight to Hong Kong was uneventful but once there she was delayed many many hours – there was a cyclone raging out to sea beyond the Philippines which had so disrupted the weather patterns the pilot of her Cathay Pacific flight had refused to take off. Eventually, *eventually*, passengers were called for the Cairns flight, the pilot navigated through the remaining turbulence, hadn't crashed. *Maybe,* Anna thought of the butterflies, *there was safety in numbers.*

Many flights had been cancelled from Hong Kong, passengers too had cancelled, apparently panicking about the cyclone, cautious about taking chances. Anna's flight was almost empty and she spread supine along three seats to rest through what remained of the night.

Cairns. At eight o'clock she was outside the airport filling her lungs with the tropical air she had missed so much. Like Jenny-any-dots she sat neatly on the bench outside the airport happily anticipating Christine. A car drew up opposite, from it stepped a woman a little younger than Anna, but similar in size, wearing – was it possible? peahen brown and black! In all of the tropics, where women and men dressed wild and Hawaiian, the two women had chosen identical colours: *peahen brown and black.* Kindred spirits, thought Anna, loving Christine on sight.

Christine was unsure whether to like or dislike Anna, her enthusiasms from the airport to the centre were a mite overblown. But she smiled at the peahen brown and black; she chose to wear unobtrusive colours a lot, was comfortable with quiet. This woman, Anna, seemed almost too loud for her clothes. Something jarred, a little, perhaps she was simply tired, some people babble when they were overtired, faced with new experiences. Christine would offer her guest a shower and breakfast and drop her in town while she organized her morning around L.

Refreshed, clean, breakfast over, Cat introductions completed, impulse photos taken of pretty Christine with Cat on lap, and a photo of the two women reflected in the long mirror confirming their quotidian colour coordination, and Anna was almost ready for the sea, the boardwalks, the air of Cairns. But oh my! where Christine left her took Anna ten minutes to readjust to – the *cost,* of *everything.* Her chocolate pot hadn't accounted for such astronomical gastronomy. *Coffee,* she noted, *$4.85.* In the cafés of Glastonbury coffee was £1.50, £1.80. And food!

My goodness, avocadoes $4! They *grew* here; in Tesco Anna bought the tropical fruit for less than half the price. As for houses – well, a million or two might buy a besser block two-bed; modern Cairns had sold out to the Japanese; the Chinese had been there for generations, arriving with the Palmer River gold rush of 1870. Anna's budget ought to stretch to a Chinese take-away for lunch over at the Food Mall. It did, but the Mall was grim, noisy, filled with obesity – her rosy remembrances exponentially sidelining reality in her twelve year absence. A sun-raddled scrawny older woman of Anna's age, dressed in a vibrant orange floaty ankle-length sundress, clawed a tray of food and sat at the table opposite. The woman smiled, her luminous orange lipstick had strayed way beyond her God-given lips when she applied *le maquillage* that morning and Anna smiled warmly in response, warmed by memories of dotty old dears, *dear* to her! The *essence* of all that she loved remained.

Christine, a jewel, collected Anna after lunch, brought her back to her quiet suburban centre, showed her to a room to rest in for a couple of hours. Later, Anna woke, abuzz with anticipation: Townsville! She'd lived there as a child long before returning as an adult.

Memories: Blueboots, the Strand lifer, giving pony rides, up and down, up and down for twenty years, the old saddle cutting deep sores into his back, his withers. Anna had begged to buy him, and she did. Her father had sent her £10, an enormous sum then, and Blueboots was saved. Twenty years of plodding had atrophied any ability of his legs or his intentions to do anything other, but she loved him. Pat sold him behind Anna's back while she was at school one day – back to the man or to the abattoir Anna never knew, a cruel memory.

With her £10 she bought a wild black badly broken skinny bush mare and loved her passionately, kept her out on a farm beyond Kelso belonging to a St Anne's girl, after whose family that suburb was named. Unridden during the term, the wild black beauty threw Anna and herself over a stockyard fence in wild abandon, rose and planted her dainty hoof fare square on Anna's jaw as she lay, shocked.

For the rest of her life Anna ate accompanied by gristle grinding an organ fugue in her ear. Yawning reached a crescendo of gristle on gristle, heard outside her ear, people looked startled, commented, but had to put up with it. *You should be on the inside*, laughed Anna, used to it. Worse was her broken coccyx. Fourteen years later in Bristol, Edna, seeing Anna bend over, observed a lump, a lump that wasn't part of any normal anatomy. *What's that?* she asked, and when she heard, took Anna to a young osteopath in White Ladies Road. Martin took weeks to unlock the body's compensatory cushioning to the injury Pat had neglected to take her daughter to a doctor to examine, but in time Anna left smiling and walking and pain free. Mostly, and for much of the time.

A posting south for Brian meant Anna lost Sickle Moon – to a lovely artist who took her Out West, where her family had a station. Lynn Martel, an older St Anne's pupil, sensitive to Anna's loss, painted an oil of Sickle Moon, named for the perfect white sickle on her black forehead, to give her before the mare was horse-boxed to a home to remain wild and loved.

Moving back to Townsville thirty-six years later was a watershed year and Anna fell in love with Australia's best-kept-secret. Southerners flew right over its charms to Cairns, the tourist tart. Here in Townsville Anna had come to put her life into a book, a *thesis*. *Who*, Anna mused quite to herself on that plane, *would ever imagine such a thing from such an unschooled* flâneuse!

She had met wonderful women who had imagined for her, and set her path to JCU. Stephanie Cowie, met by that synchronicity of the gods when Anna took a wrong turn in her car to Brisbane one day, her first drive after the endless months of work by Homer to get her on her feet again. Where Anna stopped to reorient herself she saw a notice on a tree telling of a dinner on Saturday. She went to that dinner, a very big deal dinner, and sat next to...: *Oh*, read Anna on her table neighbour's name tag, *I once knew an Edward Cowie but he was married to a Judy.* Her beautiful dinner table neighbour laughed: *Yes, he was, she was ex-wife number two and I am ex-wife number three; he's now living in Devon with wife number four!*

Ice didn't exist at that memorable dinner, and when Stephanie, ex-wife number three, inquired as to Anna's presence at such a private dinner for the Siddha Yoga company of friends, and learned of her wheelchair year and her search for the Black Madonna, she told her to get herself to Townsville, to JCU where Edward had gone after Wollongong to set up an Arts Fusion department, and find the marvellous artist named Anneke who was a supervisor there. Anna knew then that Magic was Afoot when both her feet had crumbled – she hadn't driven into Brisbane for a whole year, had lost her way that day and seen the Tree.

She was *so* excited sitting there on that plane.

An hour later Anna stepped down onto the tarmac, thrilled to see TOWNSVILLE in colossal neon lights across the runway high on the airport building. She took a souvenir photo. A hefty weight on her shoulder made her turn in alarm: *No photos. Security breach. This is a military zone.*

Good grief, thought Anna, *same old paranoia! It's a neon sign fer heavens' sake!* She smiled an all-embracing smile up at the giant looming over her to ask innocently if he would like her to delete the offending image: *I haven't been here for twelve years, it's my favouritist city in the whole of Australia!* Giant mellowed.

She walked directly into the lounge to see Thérèse and Peter and Denise all waiting, each dressed in royal blue. A Royal Blue welcome! Quick photo! Then, a Japanese meal on the Strand: *How could she have ever left this paradise,* thought Anna savouring every unfamiliar morsel.

Thérèse showed Anna into her room, Anna's favourite room in the world, its French doors opening on to the wide and gracious timber veranda, with a view through the trees to the sea and Magnetic Island on the horizon. A vast vase of tropical orchids sat on a small table, a large hand-woven Tibetan rug on the floor, clue to her friends' support of Tibetan refugees in Dharamsala.

Their century old highset Queenslander nestled unnoticed from the road below against the red rock of Castle Hill, *Cudtheringa;* the ascent of the Hill by goat track or road led up and up to a view to remember forever. In her absence a remarkable water mist invention had been installed at the summit to greet puffing out-of-practice walkers like Anna. She stood under it in wonder and gratitude. Once up was enough in her lack of condition, it did her in for half the day.

Thérèse took Anna to favourite haunts, surprised her with day trips to places she didn't know, bought gourmet lunches to take to mutual friends, cooked wonderful meals, took her to Magnetic Island for a weekend to the family's holiday apartment in Arcadia, the well-named prettiest of bays with its sandy walks to the headlands and calm sheltered sea, safe from any unfriendly denizens. Thérèse took her to a meal at Peppers too, inviting a charming nun holidaying on the island to accompany them. Their meals were haute cuisine of such flavour and visual exquisiteness all the courses warranted photographs: a pansy, whose blue was born before the colour of sky, flown up from the temperate South, sat on a tropical mango mouse, sugar dusted violets, a strawberry too, poised against hand crafted dark chocolate curls added as edible decoration to the dessert of hand-made sorbet, mousse and tropical fruit. The main meals were just as sublime. Anna acknowledged a *frisson* of discomfort at her friend's largesse, how could she ever repay such gifts, such kindnesses? Her own gift-giving was governed by what remained after big expenditures, like flights, and fear of utter destitution, frequent bedfellow of the past, which left her feeling small and mean. Something she was aware of, and too paralyzed yet to address honestly. Worldly things, so difficult to accept.

Christine arranged for Anna to speak to a group of meditators, on the Tablelands, supporters of the Centre. Inspired by the courteous country friends of Christine now gathered around a large table weighed down with food, it was the Australia she remembered from childhood, an Australia where generosity and neighbourliness were the values of every small town and many a sprawling outer city suburb. Isolation meant good neighbours in those days. The simplicity of honest lives well lived touched Anna who sensed her hosts were too straightforward for the knotted ways of the world. What could she say that would have any meaning to these good people? She spoke of synchronicities, without using the term, the butterflies, the peahen brown and black, the *timing* of things, the necessity of inner listening. *God,* she remembered saying, *writes straight in crooked lines, gives us signs, we must develop a dual listening, eavesdrop on the Heart of hearts.*

It was late when the women left. Christine took the usual route home, a long and lonely road stretching dark far beyond their high beam. A car came up behind, too close, its headlights silhouetting their heads, identifying them as women. Suddenly it roared past them, swung in front of them and slowed. Christine and Anna, of one accord, pushed the locks down on their doors. Christine hoofed it to overtake and speed ahead, the far more powerful car tail-gated them, overtook, swung in front, slowed, sped up. Both women's hearts pounded, the driver was tracking them, unnerving them, it took a lot to unnerve Anna, probably Christine too, but neither knew how many men were in that car, young or old, and menace was menace.

I know a side turn just before that crest, said Christine, *once he goes into the dip I'll turn right and drive without lights a while, with any luck he won't be local and won't know it. If he comes looking he won't see us without our lights on.* The women fell silent, each praying as she saw fit. The minutes were tense and the energy from the car ahead, sinister. Christine commented on how she felt threatened by it. Anna's nose prickled.

Her memory was true, the car ahead dropped into the dip and momentarily disappeared exactly as the little known track appeared on the periphery of their sight; Christine switched off the lights and swung expertly right, on cue. There were no street lights on the Tablelands, only in the sparsely distanced towns, the moon was quarter, shedding little light but stars and knowing the terrain like a local meant she could give him the slip. Very nervously she continued, ears keened for revving motor, eyes peeled for moving lights. She made it to a bitumen road. They'd lost their follower, could drive fast and straight to Cairns whose lights were glowing orange on the horizon ahead. Those moments fused friendship.

The following day Christine had a surprise: *Hop in,* she said, *we're going down memory lane.* Karnak Playhouse! Despite a sign saying PRIVATE, KEEP OUT, Anna went in, she needed to find someone to share her small story of Diane with, wanted to set her own prayer in the landscape for Diane. A very, *very* angry woman, shouted at her, shook Anna from her exploratory wanderings, had already bitten Christine waiting in the car at the gate. Anna bounced over to her, all smiles, the woman was having none of it. Anna prattled on, she knew what she was doing, and the edges of the woman frayed just enough for Anna to weave her way in. She misheard the woman's name, *Deirdre? Desiree? Despina?* No matter, having dressed Anna down to microscopic (*fat chance,* thought Anna, *I might be small but I am a miniaturist dwelling in epic visions*) the woman reluctantly calmed down and took Anna to Diane's memorial, allowed her one minute, before walking her briskly back to the gate. Mission was accomplished, a prayer for Diane.

Christine was not so sure she agreed with Anna's cavalier disregard to Keep Out notices; it was *wanton* behaviour she indulged in. Time for another memory, back to Mossman, coffee called.

Oh Christine, this is where I came with Caroline on our middle-aged women walkabout twelve years ago! It's still called Temptations! Oh, and look, there's the same seat! The same mirror, oh, we have to sit here! The same table, it's free, no Sunny though, Anna cast a swift glance about the large premises, which slotted perfectly into her memory. *Well, maybe the counter had changed, and perhaps the actual table ...* but otherwise. *And* she knew where the loo was. Anna was prattling again.

It must be excitement that does it, thought Christine, getting used to Anna's enthusiasms.

With second sight Anna had worn her twelve year old Wandjina dress, she didn't know what Christine had planned for that day, but *Aborigine* felt right. Her golden hare-jumping-over-the-silver-Tree-of-Life earrings of Hannah Willow echoed the leitmotif for her life: *I will run and run forever where the wild fields are mine.* The words comforted her, felt *known.* She sat at the table under the same mirror, the same vase behind her. Everything in her stilled, she was blessed to be here: Christine, the butterflies, the peahen brown and black, all coalesced — awe was not too strong a word for *now.*

An old Aborigine paused on the street beyond the huge wall of window Anna was sitting behind. He was weaving just a little, a grog bottle in his left hand. She gazed in his direction, unfocussed, somewhere else, vaguely aware of him peripherally. Suddenly *something* happened, something indefinable, inexplicable. The man stopped still, stood upright, very much in charge of himself, lifted his right hand and pointed his index finger at Anna through the glass window. The effect was shocking, a bolt had shot from his finger to her heart and she sat bolt upright, singularly focussed. His mouth moved but she couldn't hear his words. He held her gaze. His finger — arcs of energy burst into her heart, loss on loss gushed forth. The old man laughed, lowered his hand, resumed his public charade, wove on.

Tears from *years* bathed her face. A new knowing woke. A demand she take responsibility for the good in her that she had denied for so long, had *given away*, given away her power, given away her-self-as-Anna. Christine was still at the counter buying coffees, waiting for their snacks to be prepared. Anna had to access what had just happened, quickly, before it slipped back into its secret genesis. What *had* happened? Images surfaced before words, and then: Caroline couldn't have made her journey to Wujul Wujul without her. Without her, without Anna, magic couldn't connect the dots: *Anna was the dot.*

The realization overwhelmed her. She had denied it for decades. It was necessary to own it. The old Aborigine wasn't Sunny, though she was sitting in the same moment and the same seat as *then,* but time kaleidoscopes, non-linear, spatial, *now.* Anna didn't need to know the outcomes of *being there,* wherever *there* happened to be on the planet, but she had to own her Obedience that had brought her there, wherever it was. It was *her* Obedience that set in motion possibilities and eventualities: Caroline's spirit journey; reading that note about Grey Wolf; icons for St Mary's; ritual for Romania; Twinning; Tigers and Taxi Drivers; and her own *being here now* to be awakened by an old Aboriginal man, the *essence* of that country, Woman's Dreaming.

Christine set the cappuccino in front of Anna. *Bliss,* mused Anna from her topside mind, *real coffee, Australian baristas trained by Italian immigrants for a century could teach the English a thing or two about how to make coffee in a consciousness of tea drinkers;* she drank her coffee silently as if the act alone would hold the world in place.

Christine watched without words, allowing Anna's tears until they stopped their riverine cascade. She waited. Anna shared what she could. How could she speak? What came out wasn't what she *knew* but it would have to do. Christine understood. They took each other's photo under the stress-washed light-blue and ochre-shuttered mirror painting; the scene interchangeable with Anna's walkabout moment with Caroline and Sunny, *here* twelve years earlier. That was a dot, and Anna claimed it. It was an epiphany moment.

Anna's return to north and Far North Queensland was a time of re-enchantment, being among friends, wandering the Strand entranced by the annual exhibition of Ephemera she had arrived in time to see; a surprise birthday party on the 8th amongst women she admired: Marie, Helen; women she loved: Anneke, Denise, Claire and most of all Thérèse and Peter who arranged it all: Thérèse the dearest of friends, Peter, the best of men.

Leaving the House of Prayer after Saturday Liturgy on her birthday morning, Thérèse had specially taken a Madonna to place on the small table that served as an altar, it being Her birthday too, Anna looked down at the garden path and called in astonishment. The Liturgy had, after all, been about Mary; Anna's Townsville was bound up with Mary, the *Black* Madonna. Dropping to her knees on that meltingly hot morning Anna tenderly picked up a soft, black, sort of flattened in the heat, image of a chubby black goddess: *Look, look!* she drew everyone's attention to the marvel. The women cackled with laughter: *You've been away too long! That's a squashed black jelly baby you're holding!* Mnemosyne was an unreliable Muse.

24¾

Letter to a Lost Loved One

Anna flew South to Anne and Alan, blessed days in their company after decades of absence; stayed in a paradise further south than Sydney with a tale of hell to tell; missed the Parer's by inches, or a few hundred miles, but, *Who'da Thought It,* would soon meet Mandy and Family under Penniless Porch far away in Wells. Down even further South she learned of the Drover's Boy – an episode of unknown Black Australia that appalled her:

> *In the Camooweal Pub they talked about*
> *The death of the drover's boy*
> *They drank their rum with the stranger who'd come*
> *From the Kimberley run, Fitzroy*
> *And he told of the massacre in the west*
> *Barest details – guess the rest*
> *Shoot the bucks, grab a gin*
> *Cut her hair, break her in*
> *And call her a boy – the drover's boy,*
> *And call her a boy – the drover's boy.*

The boy, the girl; bucks, boys; gins, girls – *how could anyone?* ... but they did. And there *is* a Stockman's Hall of Shame though it is spelt Fame. Ted Egan sings his song on YouTube, *listening* reveals the horror, he cracks open the great Outback myth of mateship and macho. Anna met Bob Marchant, his paintings of the Drover's Boy giving birth to a half white half black baby, more harrowing than the poem.

Brisbane, then, to the hospitality of Hilary and Alan. Anna walked South Bank; ate muddies in the Mall, in the open, to be seen and to see – would her daughter walk by *now?* This was, in one sense, the *raison d'être* of her trip. Would shared blood give them eyes to recognize? She took the City Hopper up and down the River, got off at Storey Bridge, shades hung suspended there: *Fern, Pavel Forman, Dagma*; got on again and off again at New Farm. Was it possible? In a canyon of towering brick and concrete a tiny gap –15 Llewellyn Street – untouched, overshadowed by mini-skyscrapers, the same tatty home she'd shared with Fern half a century before was still standing.

Anna took a trip up to Caloundra to overnight with her oldest friend. Fern's smile still overwhelmed her tiny frame, her courage, her heart, her *kindness*. Anna felt small, humbled by qualities Fern highlighted by Anna's own lack of them. The two, ultimately, had little in common but love and a shared story of past marriages on shaky grounds to reluctant foreign imports; one, Yahia, her Kurd, the other, Vijay, Fern's Indian from Fiji. Both men were, in a sense, citizens without state, living under foreign sovereignty. The friends' re-connection one of those golden threads thrown down from the songlines of stars.

They reminisced: Anna was at the counter of the ANZ bank, Chalk Street, Lutwyche that day, the odds of their re-encounter, a million to one. There was a kerfuffle at the door, someone unsuccessfully trying to open it to enter, a man rose to help. Hobbled by pain in walked a smile that lit up the room, and: *Fern! Nigelle!* What Threads wove those stories? Anna had been living a world away for *years*, Fern, in Fiji. This Timing of the Gods set the entire bank applauding their reunion. With no email and flâneurial lives, the friends had no contact for twenty-two years.

Heidi came in from out of town, the pair met at the Art Gallery, Heidi in love and beyond beautiful that precious day in the sunshine, slender, dark-haired, radiant, gentle. Basking in the slender beauty of her friend Anna was aware of a *frisson* of discomfort upwelling, more subtle than the word implies, but definitely on the fringes: *fat*. Rarely had Anna been as tiny as her underlying bone structure, and food, that *bête noir* of her life, would make sure she never did. Sometimes, like now sitting in Heidi's glow, her bones wanted to be shed of the weight, wanted to be blown through with the wind, the wind of Spirit, Anna supposed.

It was Heidi who had given Anna the exquisite white lace of the Madonna from her family's private chapel in Austria. The incomparable gift was the perfect transition from Black Virgin to White Virgin for the art display of her thesis. Anna made a banner with it, lightly stitched on palest blue tie-dyed silk, shimmering blue-hued to white, stitched the double layer to a larger background of heavy deepest indigo damask silk for her collaborative exhibition of Vision in Long Darkness to accompany her Master's, her *task*, set her by Father Bede.

The women were reminiscing, sitting on the sun warmed seat in front of the Gallery window in which was hung, huge: MY COUNTRY – ART FROM BLACK AUSTRALIA. Anna would see the exhibition three times. The star-poles of the Aboriginal women pierced her heart. During the day and into the night a star is hidden by an old woman in a special feathered string bag. Just before dawn she releases the star on a long string. It ascends to the very top of the tallest pandanus tree, surveys all the places it has to visit, and flies to Arnhem Land to herald the Dawn. As the sun appears the old woman reels in Banumbirr, the Morning Star, by its feathered string, to be hidden again until the next evening. The star poles had *sung* to Anna. Called her there three times on a songline she almost couldn't hear. On the third visit, she heard.

The exhibition, and that of Aboriginal art, including Clifford Possum's eye-watering dot journeys, took up three floors. On this day, just hours before she was to fly home at dawn on the following morning, unresolved in her dream to find, to meet, her daughter, Anna was willed to walk to the topmost floor. It appeared empty. A closer look revealed that a section of the Gallery had become an installation resembling a very large room. Pine slats, about an inch deep, were paralleled on two sides, running the length of each wall, maybe eight inches apart, running from low on each wall to an imagined ceiling. A desk and a table were at the far end of the U shaped space. Curious, Anna read the small typed title at the edge in front of her: *Letter to a Lost Loved One*. Her heart lurched from its moorings.

An artist, with an Asian name, perhaps a woman, had written an explanation underneath those words of fire: *Please feel free to write a letter to someone you have loved and lost; if your loved one is alive but lost to you, the Gallery will post the letter for you if you include the address. Envelopes and pens and paper are supplied, on the desk ahead of you. If your loved one is dead and you wish to leave your letter in the slats provided, in or out of an envelope, the artist will take it for you and using ancient ritual return it to its Origin. It will not be read or unfolded, but will be taken in a sacred manner.*

Anna's heart pounded, tomorrow she was leaving, she would leave with all she had hoped for and more besides, but her *daughter*, Martina ... Anna was alone in that space; she sat for an eternity, was it an hour? writing a love letter for her daughter, a letter to her lost loved one, telling her she had come, asking forgiveness for all she hadn't been to Martina, leaving the faintest of tracks ... here in this letter. Which she then folded with prayer and care to place *exactly so* in one of the slim pine ribbons along the wall for the artist to take. She stepped out of the holy space. *Cleansed.*

The following dawn Anna flew back to England, and home to Glastonbury where she was called by Holy Mary (*oh She knew what it was to lose a child*) to Mass. Father James was speaking of Assisi. The word burned into the wound of her still raw heart. Assisi was where she must go, for Christmas.

St Francis had her well in hand. As Anna descended the steps to the little museum in Santa Chiara a force stopped her in her tracks: the robe of Santa Chiara hung behind glass: *she knew it*. Anna's choice of clothing, in some form or another, resembled this long, flowing, garment. Anna wasn't the saint who wore it, no matter that she lived in Glastonbury where such incarnations proliferated, but she knew the *essence* of the thing. St Francis would tell her to walk the Camino the following May, but he kept secret from her his own journey of 1214. That she would discover along the Way. Then, she would walk in the footsteps of the Saint, their imprint embedded 800 years before, she would also learn that the Benedictines of O Cebreiro had welcomed St Francis – *and* held the two cruets of Joseph of Arimathea's Grail.

25

Spectre Begins With S

Camino de Santiago. Anna returned after forty days and forty nights, another of those biblical reckonings. The walk, a thing she couldn't imagine herself capable of doing, shifted her power base to *confidence*.

Three years after that Walk she received a letter. It contained the briefest of sentences but the name that signed it enshrined more than half a century of anguish, loss, abandonment, rejection; just about everything that would break a heart. Out of the heart that had broken so many times gushed a tsunami. It cleansed the clarity of the: *No!* to which she responded to that unheralded letter. *Half a century!* Longer than half most people on the planet had lived. The letter was signed: *Stephanie.*

Anna sat holding the small folded A5 token of information. Fifty two *years* and not one word, *not one word,* from her sibling. *Why now!* The tsunami in Anna threatened to burst long shored up dykes; she *thought* she was safe from drowning; *thought* she had resolved her life of loss, but here it was, vast and as clear as the nonchalant words she held in her hand.

I thought I should let you know our mother had died...

Our mother? I never had a mother, cried Anna to the world. *You had the mother,* she wrote to Stephanie, *I didn't know a mother, ever. Why now? Why contact me now?*

Anna's reaction stunned her. Hadn't she resolved *anything.* Had her life just been a fantasia, a baseless fabrication? All that so-called inner work she thought she had done: *All are melted into air, into thin air,* dissolved, an insubstantial pageant. No revel this, merely a little life such as dreams are made on, not yet rounded with that final sleep.

The letter Anna wrote back carried a storm of pain, yet she included her email address. She didn't expect a response however much she hoped for the explanation: *Why now?*

She'd had two dreams of her mother exactly four years before when her father had died. Her counsellor, working on Anna to attend his funeral, had said: *Well she's dead then, wouldn't you think? Those dreams of yours are pretty conclusive.*

Anna agreed. She had been woken at two o'clock one morning by thunderous banging on her front door. She was well asleep, her mother appeared as a spectre through the knocking: *Go away,* Anna said into her pillow, refusing to get up to open the door, *it's too late for you to apologise; it's now between yourself and God.*

The following evening, in her second dream, she had seen her mother in the driver's seat of Poppy. A friend, unknown to Anna, was in the passenger seat. Anna was furious: *Give me my car keys at once,* she demanded, *and both of you get out of my car!* As she held those keys, in the dream, Anna knew she was in charge of her own life, she was firmly in the driver's seat, her mother had gone: *at last.*

Mostly likely dead, she and her counsellor agreed again. Anna would never know if it was true, there was no one to tell her. By one of those odd quirks of fate that coloured the weave of Anna's life, her counsellor's name was Stephanie.

And here, four years later, was her sister, a spectre from beyond how many tears? telling her after half a century of silence, *her* mother, not Anna's mother, had died. Those earlier dreams – could they have been a transference from her father who *had* died, four years before, still loving the woman bent on destroying him, and their daughter, Anna?

A terrible memory surfaced. Anna was nine years old. The family was in Changi. Her mother was carrying on an affair or three with a variety of young English officers down at the Mess pool, Nick, Brian, Squire ... Her father, helpless in the face of his wife's alley cat morals, would disappear for endless hours walking the island working out binary sequences, walking out his pain, working out how to keep his wife from military censorship and the ignominy of being packed off home.

It was the Mess Ball: Carriages at Three. Guy would not attend, would not be humiliated and hurt – the death of his own mother had left a hole in his heart that could not carry broken. Pat wanted to go to the Ball with Brian. Guy would do the right thing for appearances, take her there, collect her at three.

The following day, who knows what happened that night, Pat was again at the pool, up in the bar, drinking with Brian, Nick and Squire. Anna arrived from school with her father. She waited at the bottom step, it was a highset Mess, the Officers, perhaps fifteen, maybe twenty, stone tiled steps, back-breaking – if one was to fall. In the rain, cloths were laid to prevent slipping. It was not raining now.

The group in the bar had seen the arrival of Guy and his daughter, it was a cue for Pat to leave if only for appearances. Guy climbed the steps. Anna heard loud words. Pat positioned herself behind Brian, slug white in his swimming trunks, pudgy. Anna knew he didn't like her. Or her father.

Guy climbed higher, Pat peeked provocatively around Brian's shoulder. Squire, drunk with last night's tipples threatening to topple him at any minute, shouted at Guy to go home. Guy reached the third step from the top, Pat smirked – all these young men, protecting her, on *her* side, attracted to *her*, heady stuff. Suddenly Squire lunged. Anna, appalled and mute, watched her father fall, cracking his back on every second step. It was 1955.

In 1995, forty years later, after Anna had reconnected with her father over those annual cups of tea in Stately Homes or Grand Gardens, Guy made a momentous visit to her in Silkstone, the other side of the world. On one of the days he had asked how to get to Brisbane. He wanted to go alone. Hours later he staggered up the steps of her modest Queenslander cottage, the pain

292

on his stoic expression all too apparent. He spent the next three weeks in bed, unable to move. Her near neighbour, a handsome Prussian, came in to play chess with him but it was a difficult time, Anna had to be nurse, caregiver, wash and dress her father – rôles nothing in her life had prepared for. Guy left Brisbane in a wheelchair, helped into the plane, had cried as they parted. Anna cried as she said goodbye. She cried inconsolably when he said he loved her.

Guy's enforced immobility had gifted father and daughter time to tentatively speak the unspeakable. Guy had gone into Brisbane to seek Pat after forty years, Stephanie, whom he'd never known. He was distracted by the cliffs along the river, attracted by the abseiling. Allowing the distraction, he approached the guide who agreed to let him have a go, harnessed, at climbing the cliff. He fell. Never made it to his destination: *My back,* he said, *is crumbling, my surgeon says operate, but gives no guarantee. The vertebrae have fused ... Coming here was a risk I had to make; attempting to abseil a risk I was foolish to take ...*

Anna's childhood-long dormant memory surfaced. *I know why your back is crumbling,* she said with Sibylline clarity as she described what she had seen four decades before; *that* moment, her horror, his fall, her mother's collusion with the laughing young bullet-proof men.

Guy lowered his head, his voice, when it came, low: *I don't remember...*

Waves of compassion engulfed Anna. *He couldn't remember.* Buried so deep was his memory of it, too deep for access. She waited, and then asked the question that had burned all her life: *Why did my mother hate me?* Guy looked up out of eyes still wet: *I don't know sweetie, she ... hated ... me too,* his words muffled, puzzled, seared in their honesty.

Later Anna would smile, shaking her head at the *rightness* of wrong things: her father being here at all, their time together. He wanted to find Pat – but the best laid plans of mice and men are God's silver tears. Abseiling! Only her father would be tempted by something so alarming. Alice had once told her how he had said cheerio to Angela one afternoon and not returned for a week, he'd gone for a long walk. Now here was Stephanie on the edge of Anna's life. Well, she didn't want to meet a sister who hadn't shown a skerrick of interest in her health or well-being in over half a century – but she would move heaven and earth to meet a tiger. Seventy-two was a good age to make light of a weighty subject. It was time to go to India. India *solved* things, *quickened* her soul.